Building the Village

A History of Bendigo Bank

Alan Mayne holds a ResearchSA Chair at the University of South Australia, where he is Professor of Social History and Social Policy in the Hawke Research Institute for Sustainable Societies. He received a Ph.D. from the Australian National University in 1980, and worked until 2005 at the University of Melbourne. He is also a Visiting Professorial Fellow in the Centre for the Study of Law and Governance at Jawaharlal Nehru University in Delhi. His core interests revolve around sustainable communities in urban and rural society.

By the same author

Fever, Squalor & Vice (University of Queensland Press, 1982)
Reluctant Italians? (Dante Alighieri Society, Melbourne, 1997)
The Imagined Slum (Leicester University Press, 1993)
The Archaeology of Urban Landscapes (with Tim Murray, Cambridge University Press, 2001)
Hill End: An Historic Australian Goldfields Landscape (Melbourne University Press, 2003)
Eureka: Reappraising an Australian Legend (Network Books, 2006)
Beyond the Black Stump: Histories of Outback Australia (Wakefield Press, 2008)

Building the Village

A History of Bendigo Bank

Alan Mayne

Wakefield Press

Wakefield Press
1 The Parade West
Kent Town
South Australia 5067
www.wakefieldpress.com.au

First published 2008

Designed by Liz Nicholson, designBITE
Typeset by Wakefield Press
Printed and bound by Hyde Park Press, Adelaide

National Library of Australia Cataloguing-in-Publication entry

Author:	Mayne, Alan.
Title:	Building the village: a history of Bendigo Bank/Alan Mayne.
ISBN:	978 1 86254 832 9 (pbk.).
Notes:	Includes index.
	Bibliography.
Subjects:	Bendigo Bank—History.
	Community banks—Victoria—History.
Dewey Number:	332.109945

This is the first book in the Hawke Intersections series of books that aim to foster the social sustainability and social justice goals of the Hawke Research Institute for Sustainable Societies.

This book is dedicated to my sons Tristan and Justin: two young Victorians, whose father is a Queenslander, grandfather a Western Australian, and great-grandparents South Australian.

Contents

Regional bank: Bendigo Bank's Charing Cross headquarters, 2008.

Acknowledgements

This book was made possible by the collaboration and unstinted support of Bendigo Bank. I was given unrestricted access to the bank's archives, and open-ended question time with its staff. Although the book has been published to mark the bank's sesquicentenary, I was left free to write as I chose and to draw my own conclusions.

I especially thank Robert Johanson and Rob Hunt for their vision in initiating this project late in 2002 and for backing it throughout. Many people associated with the bank's development generously shared with me their memories of people and happenings in Bendigo since the early twentieth century. I acknowledge in particular John Balsillie, Bill Beischer, Ken Cumming, Owen Davies, Allen Guy, Richard Guy, Russell Jenkins, Edith Lunn, Ian Mansbridge, and Bruce Reid. Others told me how the bank's broadening activities overlapped with other places, events and developments, and I thank especially Malcolm Anderson, Tim Fisher, Greg Hadlow, Jim Kennan, Clem Kerp, David Matthews, John Millington, Max Ormsby, Stewart Petering, Marion Riley, and Max Trenorden.

On a still broader canvas, I thank Peter McPhee, Barbie Cornell and the Mildura and District Historical Society, and especially Charles Fahey. If I have not responded adequately to all of Charles' suggestions, there is a limit to what can be achieved in one book, and I encourage others to build on it. When I began this project I hoped to exhaust all the possibilities offered by the bank's archives, but I have only touched the surface.

The logistics of working my way through the bank's records were daunting, and many staff members of Bendigo Bank went out of their way to help me. I give special thanks to Jean Wright and Owen Davies. Owen was a sounding board throughout, and carefully read the book in manuscript. I also owe much to Emma McKenzie, Jamie Eckett, Kylie Draper, and Julie Scullie. The bank further supported the project by hosting two well attended regional history seminars in Bendigo in 2004 and 2005, and by assisting two of my University of Melbourne 'History in the Field' students, Melissa Brien and Barbara Lemon, to collect oral histories. I drew usefully upon the work of three earlier historians of the bank: Michele Matthews, who undertook a series of taped interviews during 1995, Tim Hewat (*Banking on the Bendigo*, 1992) and Frank Cusack (*The Sandhurst Building Society*, 1981).

I thank the staff in the pictorial collections of the State Library of Victoria, the State Library of South Australia, the National Library of Australia, Public Record Office Victoria, the National Archives of Australia, *The Age*, *The Herald Sun*, and AAP. Illustrations are courtesy of Bendigo Bank unless otherwise credited.

I am grateful to Paul Wallace for meticulously editing and indexing my work, and to Wakefield Press for producing such a handsome volume. This book is the first in a series of publications undertaken jointly by Wakefield Press and the Hawke Research Institute for Sustainable Societies at the University of South Australia, where I now work. I acknowledge the hard work of Gerry Bloustien in making this series possible. There are many overlaps between the themes of this book and the Hawke Research Institute's focus upon social inclusion and sustainability. I am proud to have been director of the Institute.

I joked many times over the years as I prepared this book that my wife Judy King kept me chained to the desk in order to ensure that I completed it. She has been my fiercest critic, my greatest helper, and my dearest companion along the way.

Foreword

This year, 2008, marks the 150th year since the founding of the first Bendigo Building Society. This marvellous history by Alan Mayne is an important part of our commemoration of those events.

Our purpose in celebrating this sesquicentenary is to help us position the company now known as Bendigo and Adelaide Bank Limited for the next generation. It is to test ourselves, as the current directors and managers, against the record of those who preceded us, and to recount some of the events and experiences of which we have been a part in the hope they will be useful to those who succeed us.

Sometimes the day-to-day tasks of dealing in the perennially uncertain and volatile financial markets can seem overwhelming. We do believe that, as we back our way into the future, we will make better decisions if we make them informed by the history of those who had to deal with similar issues in different times.

There are clear, consistent principles which have prevailed through the history of this organisation. The reasons James Sullivan and Joseph Abbott joined with 150 others to establish the first society on the tented goldfield of Bendigo in 1858 are fundamentally the same reasons David Mathews and Rob Hunt teamed up to establish the first community bank in Rupanyup and Minyip in 1998—there were communities which were being shut out of the financial system but which needed institutions to marshal their savings so they could build their balance sheets. The reasons the society survived and continued to report profits each year through the bank smash of the 1890s (according to Geoffrey Blainey, the worst banking crisis ever) are the same reasons it survived the Pyramid crisis in 1990—managers invested conservatively; they did not just mimic the fashionable practices of the competition; the society supported its borrowers, including those who were in difficulty; and, most importantly, it retained the trust of its depositors.

What is now Bendigo and Adelaide Bank is the result of many different companies and building societies joining together over many years into one company and, in turn, joining with others through community banks, joint ventures and partnerships. While the story recounted here principally follows the history of one entity, many of the same kinds of experiences are to be found in the separate histories of those other entities.

This company matters a great deal to many people and to many communities, and without them it would not exist. If our customers prosper then so will their communities. And if the Bank has contributed to their prosperity, then it too will succeed. Because we care deeply about the future of the Bank, we know it is important to reflect on its past and the lessons to be learned from its history. As Theodore Dalrymple has written: 'Those who care nothing for the past care nothing for the future, for what is our future if not our successors' past?'

Robert Johanson, Chairman of Bendigo Bank

Introduction

Building the Village

Australia's Bendigo Bank began in a village. It started 150 years ago as a local building society on the Australian goldfields, in the heartland of what would become a new nation. In July 1858, residents of Bendigo, then a newly settled gold-rush community in the centre of the infant British colony of Victoria, banded together to pool their resources to build permanent homes and businesses. In the following year, and in another village, transformed by the gold rushes into Australia's largest settlement, a boy was born to English immigrant parents who would in adult life be a builder of a different sort. The place was Melbourne, Victoria's capital, and the boy's name was Alfred Deakin. He became a visionary liberal-progressive politician, a leader of the movement for Australian nationhood and, in September 1903, prime minister of the new Commonwealth of Australia.

A little over a century later, in May 2005, Rob Hunt, Managing Director of Bendigo Bank—that former goldfields building society now transformed into the nation's largest regional business—spoke in the Alfred Deakin Innovation Lectures. In Hunt's address, Deakin's historic vision of social democratic nation-building was reformulated into a breathtakingly alternative banker's strategy to 'build stronger, more sustainable communities' in present-day Australia.[1] In doing so, Hunt referred explicitly to history.

Banking, said Hunt, had originated in early modern Europe to build prosperity at the village level. In early villages, he explained, some inhabitants had more money than they were able to spend, and others had great ideas and aspirations, but little capital with which to implement them. Banks originated to bring those parties together. And in doing this they necessarily became more than handlers of money; they were also brokers of social capital, whose transactions were grounded in reciprocity and trust. Those principles, translated centuries later to the European settler society established in Australia, were expressed at its grassroots by the first generation of house builders and pioneer businessmen who founded a Bendigo building society in 1858. They would continue to characterise the Bendigo initiative as it expanded across Victoria, and then the new Australian nation, over the following 150 years.

Bendigo claims to be 'the home of building societies in Australia'.[2] The development of that first building society over the course of one and a half centuries, from a proto-bank into Australia's largest regional bank, is a history that deserves to be told in a different style from that found in conventional biographical histories of grand institutions and of the great men who founded them. The story of Bendigo Bank is more than an economic history of a financial institution. It is more than the life stories of its managers, directors, and principal shareholders. It is also, and equally, the history of men and women building Bendigo from a village into a city, and building many villages into a nation.

The sustaining mission of Bendigo Bank and its antecedents has been to help build robust, self-reliant and resilient communities. That has been consistently good for business: local capacity building has fed and been sustained by the emergent bank. But capacity building has also energised and transformed the nature of that business, as the plans for building a village were adjusted pragmatically on multiple fronts (sometimes to maximise opportunities for growth, sometimes as local disappointments led to amalgamations and realignments of business practices so that the bank could survive) in order to work in communities and regions across the nation. In building a major national enterprise whose affinities nonetheless continue to resonate with regional Australians, Bendigo Bank reasserted the ethical and self-sustaining village dynamics of banking at a time when the banking industry as a whole sought to disengage from the village and its social responsibilities in order to maximise profits. Bendigo Bank's national Community Bank network, begun in 1998, made explicit its vision to build partnerships with communities in cities, suburbs and the countryside that would deliver strong business growth to the bank and to its community partners, and simultaneously generate substantial social benefits for local communities.

Ethical and sustainable banking, as Bendigo Bank has shown, is grounded as much in the continuing village accountabilities of services offered and social benefits derived, as in the socially disengaged stock market volatility of global capitalism. The history of Bendigo Bank demonstrates that 'building the village' is not a footnote to Australian regional history, nor the preserve of present-day micro-credit providers such as the Grameen Bank in the developing world; it is a core principle for sustained and socially responsible community banking in the twenty-first century global economy.

In this broader sense there is an important further dimension to this history of Bendigo Bank and its theme of building the village. This book traces that theme through building the bank, the town, the city, the region, and the nation. However, it also describes the creation in the bank itself of a sense of the village, of community, and of its shared opportunities, responsibilities and rewards. It is not going too far to suggest, following the Nobel Prize winning economist Joseph Stiglitz in his prescriptions for global social sustainability, that as business social responsibility strengthens, companies will not only be seen to be working with communities, but will themselves 'be thought of as communities, [as] people working together in a common purpose . . . And as they work together, they care about each other, the communities in which they work, and the broader community, the world, in which we all live'.[3]

Chapter one, *Bankers*, examines the establishment of Bendigo Bank (formerly Bendigo Building Society) in 1995 within the turbulent setting of late twentieth-century Australian banking. These tumultuous years were shaped firstly by the upheavals in the banking sector after the 1981 Campbell Report into the Australian financial system, and secondly by the shock waves in Victoria following the collapse of the high-profile Pyramid Building Society in 1990. The chapter describes how the new bank weathered these storms and transformed itself from a Victorian building society into a national bank for all Australians.

Chapter two, *Neighbours*, delves backwards in time to trace the modern bank's origins and development during the nineteenth and twentieth centuries. It moves from the founding of the first building society in Bendigo during 1858 to the last of the mergers with other Bendigo financial institutions in 1991 that completed the genesis of the Bendigo Building Society. This story of institutional change is a base from which to explore how Bendigo's building societies delivered social benefits to their neighbours. These societies originated and endured as mutual benefit associations that supported local communities in Bendigo, and later Melbourne and Geelong, to build homes and livelihoods.

Chapter three, *Settlers*, shifts focus from city communities to the countryside, and describes the widening engagement by Bendigo's building societies, since the 1860s, with rural communities in Victoria and southern New South Wales. It explains how these long-standing relationships with country townspeople and farmers were translated from 1998 into Bendigo Bank's partnership with Elders Australia Limited to launch a rural bank for farming communities across Australia.

Chapter four, *Communities*, takes the story of Bendigo Bank full circle by showing how its history, and its awareness of that history, continue to condition and inform the bank's partnerships with Australian communities. Community Banks were launched by Bendigo Bank in 1998 as a network of community-run banks parallel to its existing branch network. In 2008 there were more than 360 Community Banks and Bendigo Bank branches throughout Australia. Community Bank encapsulates the historical essence of Bendigo Bank and the community-tested legitimacy of the banking style and services that it offers Australians for the twenty-first century.

chapter

1

Bankers

Bendigo Bank has a short but eventful history. Although its progenitors' histories stretch back to 1858 (*see* chapter two), the bank itself was established only in 1995. This chapter gives a snapshot of Bendigo Bank in 2008, its sesquicentenary year. However, its main purpose is to explain the metamorphosis of Bendigo Building Society into Bendigo Bank during the 1980s and early 1990s, and to begin to account for the new bank's consolidation and growth from the mid 1990s to the present day (which are further explained in chapters three and four). In looking across these years, from 1982 to 2008, it becomes evident that Bendigo Bank was born in uncertainty, but drew strength from those unsettled times. As Richard Guy, Bendigo's chairman from 1986 until 2006, said with a chuckle shortly before his retirement, those were 'heady days'.[1]

Bendigo Building Society's turbulent last years as a proto-bank, following the release of the Campbell Report into the Australian financial system in late 1981, coincided with a period of volatility and restructuring across the sector that was unprecedented since the Great Depression. Between the early 1980s and the mid 1990s, Australia's banking sector was deregulated and entirely transformed, and much of the building society industry went into decline. During these years Bendigo Building Society became the largest building society in Victoria, and the third largest in Australia. However the collapse of the high-profile but chronically over-extended Pyramid Building Society in 1990 unsettled the entire sector. Even Bendigo Building Society endured a nail-biting period as nervous depositors queued to withdraw their savings, but because the society had sound foundations, investor confidence soon returned. Bendigo Building Society (with assistance from the state government) effectively reshaped and consolidated the Victorian building society sector, taking over the ailing Capital and Compass building societies, and leading the sector's negotiations with government regulators about the future of the industry. Having weathered these storms, Bendigo Building Society looked back over its long history since 1858 and noted with pride that it had returned a profit in every year of its existence, including during the depressions of the 1890s and 1930s and the Pyramid crisis of 1990–1992. But in 1995 this proto-bank became a full bank. Deregulation of banking, and the instability and decreasing competitiveness of building societies within the changing Australian financial sector, had forced its hand.

At first glance there is little in common between the Bendigo Bank of 1995 and that of 2008. It is now a national, not a Victorian, institution. Its size and products are very different today from 1995. However, its character today accords with the strategies, targets and underlying principles that its senior managers set during the uncertain years when the bank was established in 1995. Their thinking then was shaped by the history of their institution since 1858, as well as by their assessments of the difficulties and opportunities presented by the changing nature of Australia's economy and society. Rather than paying lip service to the tradition of local engagement that had been established since 1858 in neighbourhoods and farming communities across Victoria, the new Bendigo Bank harnessed this tradition to modern-day banking practices as it built up a presence across Australia. Its commitment to building communities became stronger and more socially responsive as the bank's community engagement broadened in scale, scope and social mix. Bendigo Bank's managing director, Rob Hunt, is impatient with the 'stuff' that some bankers mouth about 'the triple bottom line' in their newly discovered corporate social responsibility plans. Genuine social responsibility, he says, goes deeper than 'a bolt-on . . . corporate social responsibility unit', although he welcomes any improvements in business social responsibility.

Rob Hunt, managing director of Bendigo Building Society and Bendigo Bank, 1988–2009.

Hunt has long maintained that by developing a different banking model that broadens the links between a bank and the communities in which it works, 'the natural outcome will be a triple bottom line'. Hunt, who became chief executive officer in 1988 and managing director in 1990 when the company was still a building society, has overseen the implementation of that different banking model at Bendigo Bank from its establishment in 1995 up until 2008.[2]

The transition from a successful Victorian building society into a distinctive Australian bank is well expressed in the replacement of the former Bendigo Building Society's headquarters (which had been opened with fanfare by Prime Minister Bob Hawke in 1988) with a new office complex in 2008. Bendigo Bank's headquarters, a bold and stylish architectural complement to the bank's sesquicentenary celebrations, is one of the largest commercial developments, and the first such complex with a 5 star Green Star energy rating, in regional Australia. It is an appropriate centrepiece for the largest business based in regional Australia. Bendigo Bank's base remains Bendigo, Victoria's largest inland city. Greater Bendigo's population increased from 84,000 people in 1995 to 100,000 in 2008. However Bendigo, which for most of the bank's 150-year history occupied almost the entire horizon of its early managers, is today only one element in a nation-wide organisation. Since 2004, over half the bank's branches have been located in other states and territories of Australia. Bendigo Bank's evolution into a national banking force was highlighted by the expansion of its Community Bank network into every state and territory between 1998 and 2006 (*see* chapter four), the launch in 2000 of Elders Rural Bank in partnership with Adelaide-based Elders Australia Limited (*see* chapter three), and its merger with First Australian Building Society in the same year and subsequent integration of First Australian's large Queensland branch network and shareholder base into its national network. This remarkable transition from a Victorian building society into a national bank was capped late in 2007 by Bendigo Bank's merger with Adelaide Bank.

The Bendigo and Adelaide Bank Group is, in 2008, Australia's seventh largest bank out of the 25 banks operating in Australia. It employs over 5000 staff and operates 400 branches. The Group declared a half yearly profit of $73 million

Bendigo and Adelaide Bank's new headquarters, The Bendigo Centre, will be completed during the year of the company's 150th birthday celebrations. The building is in the heart of Bendigo's CBD, literally a stone's throw from the original office established in Charing Cross in 1858.

Regional Australia's first 5 star Green Star commercial building, The Bendigo Centre's distinctive coloured external blinds prevent much of the sun's heat from reaching the working environment, sharply reducing air conditioning energy use.

Bendigo Bank

The Bendigo Centre introduces 21st-century 'green' building design into Bendigo's renowned Victorian-era streetscape.

after tax in February 2008. Bendigo Bank's profit after tax for the full financial year to June 2007 was $122 million, and Adelaide Bank's was over $104 million. Their combined assets at June 2007 totalled some $43 billion, and reached over $50 billion during 2008. These are big numbers, but the Group is a minnow in comparison with the largest Australian-based banks. Its combined profits for the 2007 financial year were roughly one twenty-fifth that of the largest Australian bank, the National Australia Bank (NAB), which posted an after-tax profit of $5.5 billion in 2007 and had assets valued at $484.5 billion. The Commonwealth Bank held assets to the value of $425 billion and declared a profit of $4.5 billion. The ANZ bank came third in 2007 with assets of $393 billion and a profit of $4.2 billion. Westpac came a close fourth, with assets of $375 billion and a profit after tax of $3.5 billion. The St George Bank, like Bendigo a former building society and today Australia's fifth largest bank, declared an after-tax profit for the 2007 financial year of $1.2 billion, resting on an assets base of $125.6 billion.[3] The insurance and finance group Suncorp-Metway is the sixth largest bank in Australia, declaring a 2007

The Bendigo Centre will accommodate 1000 staff with excellent amenities in air-conditioned comfort – a long way from chopping the wood to keep the society's six staff warm in 1930.

after-tax profit of $1 billion and having $61.2 billion in total assets. St George, the bank closest in character to Bendigo Bank, has over double the staff of the Bendigo and Adelaide Bank Group (though only slightly more branches), and the Commonwealth Bank, which supports the largest banking network in Australia, has 1000 branches and 35,000 staff.

Bendigo and Adelaide Bank is a small but distinctive player in the Australian banking sector. The merger brought together two historic companies that had both begun as building societies. Adelaide Bank was formed in 1994 from the Co-Operative Building Society of South Australia, which was established in 1900. It later absorbed the Hindmarsh Adelaide Building Society, whose history dates back to 1877. The Bendigo and Adelaide partners bring together different but complementary operating strategies. Adelaide Bank specialises in wholesale banking, providing wholesale mortgages, funds management products, portfolio funding, and the expertise that comes from being one of Australia's largest margin lenders for investors in equity markets. Adelaide Bank also has a retail presence in

South Australia, where Bendigo Bank clearly was under-weight. Bendigo Bank is a retail bank that deals directly with depositors, investors, and borrowers from both the business and consumer sectors. Whereas Adelaide Bank's wholesale activities bring with it exposure to the global tightening in credit and increased pricing for wholesale funding since 2007 as a consequence of the sub-prime borrowing crisis in the United States, Bendigo Bank has been substantially insulated from the direct effects of rising wholesale funding costs because some 80 per cent (and in some years over 90 per cent) of its loans are financed by retail deposits. The strength of the merged entity is that it now has the capacity to cater for changed conditions in either the wholesale or retail financial environments.

The bulk of Bendigo Bank's lending is also retail, which is split between residential-based and commercial loans. Almost three quarters of the bank's lending is made up of loans that are supported by high quality mortgages over residential homes, with business loans forming between a quarter and a third of its lending. Often business loans are also secured against residential security, as such security provides the most economic cost of capital for the business. This proportion of home-based to business loans reflects in part the historical orientation of Bendigo Bank as a former building society, but it also reflects the enormous income that has been generated since 1998 by Bendigo Bank's new Community Bank network. Bendigo Bank Chairman Robert Johanson acknowledges with a smile that the continuing strength of home-based lending has persisted 'despite our best efforts'.[4] The bank's 2001 annual report declared that 'One of our primary aims in converting to a bank was to develop the capacity to service the business sector in our communities'.[5] This was pursued in part by expanding and modernising the trustee and wealth management services that had long been offered through Sandhurst Trustees, and in addition a specialised business banking division was established in 2002 to provide commercial loans, overdrafts, leasing, trade services, superannuation, insurance, and financial planning. Funding for these activities are provided through retail, wholesale, and securitisation markets. During the financial year to June 2007, these activities contributed $27.5 million to the bank's pre-tax profit, but Community Bank contributed another $26.6 million. If Community Bank's profits are added to those generated by the bank's proprietary branch network and agencies, it is clear that Bendigo Bank's profitability and identity remain grounded in the everyday banking needs of Australian communities. The bank's distinctiveness and its resilience lie not so much in its business services, nor even in its home-based lending, but rather in its role as what Johanson calls a 'transactional bank', a bank that develops deep and wide-ranging relationships with its customers.[6]

Bendigo Bank is a distinctively regional bank. In both its history and its present-day business orientation, the bank's relationships are anchored in rural and regional Australia. It is Australia's largest regionally based company. It has an extensive local branch network relative to those of the larger banks. It also maintains a substantial network of agencies in smaller communities, and uses them as 'stepping stones' for communities that seek to join the bank's branch network.[7] It has established banking facilities in remote Aboriginal communities, such as the Cape York community of Aurukun which had previously been without banking services for almost 20 years. But Bendigo Bank's transactional relationships today are not limited to remote and regional communities. As its Community Bank programme highlights, the bank's community-building partnerships have in recent years become as much a feature of city and suburban neighbourhoods as they are of the bush. Community banking embodies the '"Bendigo way" of banking'.[8]

Deregulation and Adjustment

That 'Bendigo way' had been trialled and rigorously tested between 1982 and 1995, a watershed period in the company's development into a fully-fledged bank. The year 1982 was especially portentous. In that year Bendigo Building Society became the first building society in Australia to join VISA International and issue VISA cards to its customers. In doing so, the society explicitly engaged with national and global innovations that would revolutionise Australia's finance sector over the next decade. Building societies led the banking sector during the early 1980s in harnessing new technologies so as to facilitate financial transactions by their customers. They introduced automatic telling machines (ATMs) and, in 1983, launched a shared national electronic funds transfer system using a standard debit

Proto-bank: Bendigo Building Society's Bull Street office, early 1980s.

Building a branch network: Bendigo Sandhurst Building Society, Mildura, early 1980s. The 'Society Sam' mascot was retired when the society became a bank in 1995.

card, Cashcard. Bendigo Building Society's managing director, Brian Thomas, selected his most computer-savvy senior executive, Rob Hunt, to oversee the introduction of the society's VISA and ATM programme, sending him to the United States to develop expertise in electronic banking. Thomas went head to head with the banks in other ways, rapidly building up a branch network across much of Victoria, and introducing new products in competition with the banks. Thus Bendigo Building Society entered the secondary mortgage market in 1985 and joined superannuation funding late in the decade. However, in one key aspect Thomas did not imitate the banks. He decided against converting the society into a bank. Although since the early 1980s he had maintained a file on banking options, and astutely assessed the costs and benefits of becoming a bank, Thomas was confident when he retired in 1988 and handed over his position to Hunt that the society's best option was not to become a bank.[9]

Thomas' decision was influenced by the massive changes to the Australian banking industry that had taken place since the Campbell Report began to be implemented in 1982. These developments occurred during the early 1980s against a troubled backdrop of declining rural and manufacturing exports, drought, rising inflation and unemployment. Federal Treasurer John Howard established a committee of inquiry into the Australian financial system in January 1979, and appointed Keith Campbell, the head of property developer, Hooker Corporation, to chair it. Forty years had passed since the last major inquiry into the Australian financial system, the 1937 Royal Commission on Money and Banking. The Campbell committee was widely regarded as 'Mr Howard's baby', and was expected to

Brian Thomas, secretary of the Bendigo and Eaglehawk Star Permanent Building Society, 1964–1978, and manager and managing director of Bendigo Building Society, 1979–1988. A great believer in branch banking, Thomas not only greatly expanded Bendigo's reach, but also had the prescience to promote a young Rob Hunt.

echo Howard's views and adopt 'a doctrinaire market-oriented approach' in its recommendations.[10] Australia's building societies, which had grown strongly during the 1960s and 1970s and hoped to replace savings banks as the major source of home finance, held their breath. Lightly regulated by state governments, they had enjoyed a competitive advantage over the banks, which were stringently controlled by federal regulations.

The Campbell Report, which was handed down in November 1981, delivered what Howard expected and the building societies feared: a set of powerful recommendations for the deregulation of Australian banking. The old distinctions between trading and savings banks were swept away. So too were government restrictions on the amount of bank lending that could be advanced to home borrowers, and the housing loan interest rates that could be charged. Housing loans had been the niche market for building societies, but now 'their competitive position [was] being cut away'.[11] The banking reforms had an immediate impact on the building society industry, whose lending declined sharply. Successive annual reports by Bendigo Building Society listed the 'many challenges' that the Campbell Report and its implementation were creating as building societies repositioned themselves in response to the deregulation of banking and the 'accelerating' pace of financial change.[12] The defeat of the Fraser Coalition Government in 1983 by a Labor reform team headed by Bob Hawke, and Howard's replacement as treasurer by Paul Keating, only accelerated the pace of market-driven fiscal reform and the full implementation of Campbell's recommendations (the Martin Committee of Review, which Keating appointed to assess the Campbell Report, endorsed it in 1984). Keating removed government control of the Australian dollar's

Richard Guy, chairman of Bendigo Building Society and Bendigo Bank, 1986–2006

exchange rate in 1983, and in 1985 lifted restrictions on the entry of foreign banks into Australia. He warned in 1986 that without fundamental marketplace reform Australia could become a banana republic. Bendigo Chairman Richard Guy reported glumly to shareholders at the society's annual meeting later in the year that 'the financial industry has become extremely volatile with deregulation continuing and the licensing of 16 new banks', the upshot of which had been to place building societies at a 'distinct trading disadvantage' relative to banks.[13]

The banks felt the heat as well as the advantages of these loosening controls. A number of highly publicised bank failures attested to the pitfalls of overindulging in a market without safety nets. The once iconic state savings banks were brought unstuck by the new operating environment. The State Bank of Victoria—undermined by the speculative excesses of its merchant bank arm Tricontinental, which racked up a 'staggering' debt of $2.7 billion[14]—was sold to the Commonwealth Bank in 1991. The State Bank of New South Wales was taken over by the Colonial Mutual Life Association in 1994, and the State Bank of South Australia was sold to Advance Bank in 1995. Other long established banks transmuted into new corporate entities. For example the National Bank of Australasia merged with the Commercial Banking Company to form the NAB in 1981, and the Bank of New South Wales combined with the Commercial Bank of Australia in 1982 to form Westpac. The Commonwealth Bank was privatised in stages between 1991 and 1996.

However, it was the building society sector that experienced most of the pain of deregulation. Their position in the market for housing finance was challenged not only by the banks, but also by new players. For example, in 1992 John Symond founded Aussie Home Loans, and in the same year the mortgage broker Mortgage Choice was established by Rod and Peter Higgins. In 1996 the new Bendigo Bank conceded that 'Increased competition in the financial services sector by the entry of non-bank institutions into the housing finance market, together with increased competition from other funds management and deposit taking entities such as superannuation funds, has resulted in both margin and loan establishment fee income coming under pressure'.[15] The number of building societies in Australia had peaked during the early 1970s at almost 180 societies, but declined in the post-Campbell years to about 70 by 1985, and to 29 by 1995. The decline was a result in part of mergers, as building society managers sought to adjust to the new playing field of Australian home financing. In 1979, for example, Bendigo Building Society was created when the Bendigo Mutual Permanent Land and Building Society merged with the Bendigo and Eaglehawk Star Permanent Society, and in 1983 it amalgamated with its other local rival, the Sandhurst Building Society. Two years later it absorbed the Mildura-based Sunraysia Permanent Building Society. In South Australia, the Hindmarsh and Adelaide Permanent building societies combined in 1985 to form the Hindmarsh Adelaide Building Society, which in 1992 was absorbed into the Co-Operative Building Society of South Australia to become Australia's largest building society. It became Adelaide Bank in 1994, one year before the Bendigo converted to bank status. Meanwhile, in Queensland, the Toowoomba Permanent Building Society (established in 1875) and the Darling Downs Building Society (established in 1897) combined in 1981 to form the Heritage Building Society, which became Australia's largest building society in the mid 1990s as its larger competitors converted to banks.

As these South Australian and Queensland examples demonstrate, the declining number of building societies was also a result of the conversion of the largest building societies into banks. The first Australian building society to do so was the New South Wales Permanent Building Society, which in 1985 became Advance Bank. In February 1986 the National Mutual Building Society, the fourth-largest building society in Victoria, became the savings bank subsidiary of the National Mutual Royal Bank (which was absorbed by the ANZ Bank in 1990). Victoria's two largest building societies, RESI Permanent Building Society and Statewide Building Society, merged later in the same month to become RESI-Statewide Building Society, the second largest in Australia after the St George Building Society in New South Wales. The new society was four times bigger than Hotham Permanent Building Society, the next largest Victorian society. However, Hotham merged with Perth Building Society in 1987 (after a failed proposal in 1981 by Perth to merge with Bendigo Building Society) to become Challenge Bank (which was absorbed by Westpac in 1995). When RESI-Statewide became the Bank of Melbourne in 1989 (it was taken over by Westpac in 1997), Bendigo Building Society by default became the largest building society in Victoria. In Queensland, the Metropolitan Permanent Building Society became Metway Bank in 1988. Australia's largest building society, St George, became a bank in 1992, leaving the Co-Operative Building Society of South Australia as the nation's largest society until it too became a bank in 1994. St George Bank, meanwhile, merged with BankSA in 1995 and with Advance Bank in 1997, becoming Australia's fifth largest bank.

Bendigo Building Society weathered these events in part through insularity and a retreat into conservatism. Bendigo Bank's current chairman, Robert Johanson, who joined the building society's board in 1988 (around the time that Hunt took over as chief executive officer), recalls that it was then 'still very much a classically run building society', persisting with quaintly anachronistic rituals such as fortnightly board meetings that began with a long lunch and then moved on to protracted afternoon discussions at which strategic planning was put on hold while the directors would 'get down into considering individual loans'.[16] For, as the older directors pointed out, that was the society's reason for being. In 1982 its then chairman, Eric Cohen, insisted that notwithstanding the Campbell Report and the subsequent transformation of Australia's financial sector, 'the Society's principal objective must [continue to] be the provision of shelter finance'.[17] As late as 1991, the Bendigo board characterised as a positive outcome the small proportion of loans that had been directed to commercial rather than residential borrowers, and restated its long-held view that the society provided 'an alternative to the major trading banks for the personal banking requirements of many Victorians. We remain committed to providing home finance as our principal activity but to

Robert Johanson, chairman of Bendigo Bank, 2006–.

also provide other forms of financial accommodation to our existing client base'.[18]

Notwithstanding the energy that Thomas displayed during the 1980s in developing tools such as electronic banking and branch expansion, there was on the surface at least no aping of the banks' strategic intent, nor—given the regulatory framework within which building societies operated—interest in growth plans beyond the home state of Victoria. Although in the late 1980s the society began complying with the banking sector's operational protocols, it insisted that there were no plans to seek a bank licence. The society was simply anticipating the likelihood that the state government would impose similar regulatory standards on building societies to those the Commonwealth required of banks. Bendigo Building Society simultaneously lobbied the state government to deregulate building societies in line with the federal government's deregulation of banks, complaining that in the post-Campbell era, building societies were constrained by more red tape than were the banks. The society applauded the *Victorian Building Society Act 1986* for partially rectifying that imbalance. In reality, as the society's directors well knew, state regulation of building societies was 'largely ineffective' for those inclined to push the envelope.[19] Guy said bluntly of the holes in the Victorian regulatory framework that unscrupulous operators 'drove trucks through that'.[20] It would take a scandal and the loss of millions of dollars of investors' funds to make the building society industry and the state government fully acknowledge this reality. Prior to the looming crisis the government had initiated a regulatory review that included two industry representatives (the then president of the Building Societies' Association, Robert Farrow, and Hunt). Unfortunately this review was only in its early stages when the crisis hit.

The building society scandal began in Geelong in June 1990, and soon enveloped the entire industry. As Bendigo Building Society noted in its annual report that year, it too was 'unfortunately caught up in this reaction'.[21] Robert Farrow had co-founded the Geelong-based Pyramid Building Society in 1957. From small beginnings, it grew rapidly during the 1980s and by the end of the decade was riding high, briefly the largest building society in Victoria and one of the largest in the nation. Its parent company, Farrow Corporation, had assets exceeding three billion dollars, and its six-storey headquarters on the Geelong waterfront was nearing completion. In May 1990, Farrow, basking in 'a reputation as one of the most aggressive players in the market',[22] talked up the likelihood of Pyramid obtaining a banking licence in order to expand even faster and further. He shrugged off rumours that his companies' underlying finances were at sixes and sevens (which at the start of the year had caused depositors to take fright and withdraw $100 million in a matter of days). After all, he pointed out, in mid February Victorian Treasurer Rob Jolly and Attorney General Andrew McCutcheon had issued a joint statement reassuring investors that Pyramid was solid. Their information, drawn from the ineffective regulatory watchdog then in place, was incorrect. In late June 1990 Pyramid and the entire Farrow Group collapsed.

Pyramid had been a paper tiger, its apparent growth underpinned by debts of over two billion dollars. Gradually there emerged publicly what concerned insiders had suspected for years: the Farrow Corporation's spectacular growth was built on sand. Federal Treasurer Keating acknowledged that he suspected something of Pyramid's financial difficulties even as the Victorian government reassured investors in February. State government advisers subsequently confirmed that fundamental problems in the Farrow Group had been evident—although not brought to the attention of the state treasurer—as early as 1988. Bendigo Building Society had sensed possible disaster when Pyramid, desperate for hard cash, offered it a large parcel of mortgages on what seemed to be attractive terms, and Bendigo—after sifting through the documentation and reappraising the paper values—was only prepared to offer cash for a third of them. When Farrow expressed gratitude for even for this level of support, Bendigo's management responded that it was in no one's interest for Pyramid to 'fall over'.[23]

The flaw in Pyramid's business plan was basic: attract investment funds by offering depositors higher rates than the bargain basement interest rates that were simultaneously being offered to attract borrowers. Pyramid could make money from the high up-front payments it charged borrowers, but this made it dependent upon ongoing and solid growth rates. As Johanson commented, Pyramid's approach could deliver spectacular short-term results by tapping into the 'great wash of liquidity that suddenly became available' from overseas, post-Campbell, but in the longer term 'their model just was not sustainable. There was no way that you could lend at less than you're borrowing and yet they needed to do that to maintain the momentum on both sides'. He added, 'even Mr Micawber could work out that doesn't really compute'.[24] His predecessor as chairman of Bendigo Bank, Richard Guy, had also scratched his head over the maths when he visited Melbourne and saw huge advertising signs by Pyramid on two sides of the iconic Southern Cross Hotel, on Exhibition Street in the heart of the city centre. The advertisement 'on one big glass window . . . said "Ask about our seventeen and a half per cent deposit rates", and around the corner on the next window it said "Try our home loans at fifteen and a half per cent". Now that meant they were buying money at seventeen and a half and lending it at fifteen and a half, and I thought "How do you make money doing that?"'[25]

Geelong and the south-western region of Victoria were especially hard hit by Pyramid's collapse, both in savings lost—notwithstanding a partial repayment package to depositors by the state government—and in community self-belief. Saturation coverage in the national media was sustained by revelations of bad practice and mountainous debt that were uncovered by Farrow's administrator, and by public sympathy for the efforts made by the Friends of Pyramid to put pressure on the government to appoint a royal commission to uncover the truth and recover their lost investments.

The immediate issue for other building societies was survival. Confidential news of Pyramid's collapse was conveyed to building society leaders at an emergency Sunday evening meeting in Melbourne, called by the state government just before the announcement that Pyramid would not open its doors for the next working week. It was a tense occasion, with building society heads unhappy that the government had previously assured investors that Pyramid was safe, and government ministers expressing consternation at the evidence that was starting to emerge about the business practices that had brought Pyramid down, and demanding assurances that the entire building society sector was not similarly compromised. Bendigo's representatives pushed hard for the government to guarantee deposits in the state's surviving building societies, and the government undertook to provide liquidity support through the Building Societies' Guarantee Fund that had been built up over the preceding years from annual levies on building societies. The Fund had been designed to support building societies and reassure depositors should an event like this occur. Pyramid's collapse nonetheless 'sparked the largest and most prolonged run on non-banking financial institutions in Australia's history',[26] and building societies tapped deeply into the Fund to meet the demands of panicking depositors.

In preparation for Pyramid's likely collapse, Bendigo Building Society had bundled up $25 million parcels of its own mortgages and had them checked and verified by potential buyers, including St George, the Australian sector leader. Bendigo now sold these paper assets in order to honour the rush by its depositors to withdraw their funds. There was a black humour in the process, because Bendigo's managers realised that the cheques they issued, and which often were later reinvested in the society, 'would have failed too' had the society gone under.[27] That scenario, they were confident, would not happen, but they were alert to the risk of take-over attempts while the society's paper assets were downvalued. Many long-term customers, for their part, apologised for drawing upon their deposits, and explained that they had to be prudent during the financial crisis.

Hunt assembled a 'war cabinet' to coordinate the society's response to the crisis. His 'mainstay' during this emergency was Johanson, whom he relied upon heavily for strategic direction.[28] In order to reassure investors they worked urgently to obtain a public letter from the Governor of the Reserve Bank, Bernie Fraser, that endorsed the business practices of the remaining Victorian building societies and their ability to meet their obligations to depositors. Fraser's letter also made plain that the banking system would 'assist the building societies in maintaining liquidity' and that the Reserve Bank would 'provide any necessary liquidity support to the banks involved'.[29] The Reserve Bank's statement would play a crucial role in stemming the emergency. In the short term, however, staff confidence began to sag as investors continued to withdraw their savings, and regular meetings were held to reassure them. The staff were told—and so it came to pass— that the run would shortly end, that deposits would be reinvested, that the crisis had strengthened Bendigo relative to its competitors, and that stricter regulation of the industry held no fears for solidly and transparently run businesses such as themselves.[30] The society undertook a searching review of its loan portfolio, and also energetically countered exaggerated commentary in national news coverage that the whole building society industry employed the same operating procedures that had brought Pyramid down. The society launched an advertising programme with the theme, 'Safe Since 1858'.[31] Large advertisements in the Melbourne *Sun* announced 'It's business as usual at the Bendigo Building Society as it has been continuously for 132 years. We are still a "traditional" Building Society. Over 80% of our loans are on residential homes, the best type of security. In every year of our history we have made a profit and this year we will exceed last year's profit . . . We assure you that your Society is safe and secure'.[32] Gradually customers heeded that message. The trust endured that had been built up over time.

This was a critical moment for the organisation. Hunt concluded that 'difficult as [the] times were, I felt this was when the Bendigo "came of age"':

> It demonstrated an inner strength and confirmed the substantial competencies embodied in the Group—but it also confirmed the uniqueness of the organisation and its strong and robust connection with the public it served. For me, it reinforced my view that this was an extraordinary organisation that had the capabilities to handle almost anything the market tossed at us. The effort by all of the people across the organisation was outstanding. The young people in the branches and departments—who didn't have the intricate knowledge of the issues (like the leadership team and the board)—remained focused and diligent despite the daily questions about the organisation's strength and ability to handle this period of uncertainty. This showed great faith and trust in the leadership group and, for me, the strength shown by the entire leadership team, and the commitment to the organisation while under attack, was outstanding.[33]

With survival assured, the next challenge for Bendigo Building Society was the future regulatory framework for building societies in Victoria. As the Melbourne

Age newspaper commented, 'the Pyramid disaster [had triggered a] crisis of public confidence in the financial system', and Attorney General Jim Kennan therefore had no choice but 'to reregulate the industry and replace the totally inadequate, unsophisticated and under-resourced regulatory and supervisory arrangements that played such a role in the Pyramid collapse'.[34] Kennan's department shared responsibility with Treasury for overseeing the building society sector, and the attorney general moved quickly to tighten the regulatory framework. He pointed out, however, that no amount of legislation could prevent poor commercial judgement, and he insisted that the people running commercial institutions had to take the blame as well as the praise for the business decisions they made. Although the Melbourne *Herald* congratulated the government post-Pyramid for establishing a new Australian benchmark for protection of depositors,[35] the worry for building society conservatives was that Kennan might re-regulate them out of existence. Jim Sweeney, head of St George, publicly backed the Victorian government's reform agenda. Bendigo Building Society also accepted that the support package it had wrung from the government came at a cost: inevitably stricter regulation under the Victorian Building Societies Act, perhaps forced mergers, and possibly even transfer to federal control or conversion to a single bank under Reserve Bank control.

Hunt became chairman of the Victorian Building Societies Association in 1990, replacing the discredited Farrow, in order to lead negotiations with the government about the future of their industry, and where necessary 'to counter attempts by banks and sections of government to have societies taken over by banks or transformed into banks'.[36] Many times Hunt travelled to Melbourne 'in the wee hours of the morning' for crisis meetings as he and Johanson sought to rebuild government and media confidence in the industry, before returning to Bendigo by late morning to resume the task of directing his own society.[37] Hunt later acknowledged that Kennan had been 'fantastic' during the crisis, and correct to demand fundamental reforms.[38] Endorsing accountants KPMG Peat Marwick's report, commissioned by the state government, which called for stricter regulation and accountability of the sector, Hunt declared, 'I've said for a long time we need to move in line with banking standards.'[39] However, when strict new Australia-wide regulations were introduced in 1992, administered locally by the Victorian Financial Institutions Commission (VFIC) and overseen by the Australian Financial Institutions Commission (AFIC), the Bendigo organisation, through its chairman Richard Guy, voiced 'major concerns regarding the costs to the industry and individual societies' of having now 'to provide vast amounts of information on a monthly basis'. In the following year Guy declared that the cost of reporting to the AFIC was proving to be 'unacceptably onerous'.[40]

The final issue for Bendigo Building Society to address in the aftermath of Pyramid's collapse was the restructuring of their business and the sector to ensure a sustainable future. The strong teamwork that had emerged between Johanson and Hunt during the crisis was of immense value throughout this rebuilding phase. Johanson dubbed their approach one of enlightened self-interest, for as he said of the building society sector, 'none of us could afford another one to go under'.[41] The society itself had emerged stronger. Brian Thomas (still a director) felt that the cost to Bendigo of the Pyramid disaster—some $150 million in lost deposits and several years' reduced earnings for shareholders—was a small price to pay to be rid of Pyramid.[42] Hunt drew lessons for the future:

> Clearly the Farrow Crisis saw the organisation reduce in size at the time but, in my view, it built and strengthened both the organisation and its credibility. This period certainly gave me confidence to move forward with the objective that this organisation could develop and implement a quite different range of strategies from the rest of the banking industry—and to do so successfully for all stakeholders. While developing forward strategy, one can never know what every turn in the road will unveil. However belief in the organisation demonstrated by customers, staff and the board through this time confirmed the organisation had something quite special and unique to offer, certainly something worth further developing.[43]

Senior manager John Perrow later remarked candidly, 'during Pyramid we just worked at whatever we had to [in order] to keep surviving. Then we started this mopping up afterwards, I guess, when we did mergers, takeovers, depending on the act at the time'.[44] The mergers and takeovers that Bendigo Building Society embarked upon after Pyramid had not been part of Thomas' earlier expansion plans, but were forced on the society because of the government's expectations of better business practices, and because the obvious difficulties that were being experienced by other societies were harming the credibility of the entire sector.

Kennan made plain that the price of government support during the depths of the Pyramid crisis was that the sector reinvent itself. The government contemplated voluntary mergers to create larger and more viable building societies, and even for the sector to coalesce into a bank. Kennan emphasised that the agreement reached with building society representatives during the first crisis meetings after Pyramid's collapse 'required those societies to make arrangements to sell, merge or restructure within 12 months in exchange for the provision by the government of liquidity support' from the Building Societies' Guarantee Fund.[45]

Bendigo Building Society took the lead in responding to the government's expectations, and when it met with the Victoria Savings and Loan Society (VS&L), and the Capital and Compass building societies, the four societies agreed to merge and become a bank. One strategy for doing so was to buy an existing banking licence. The State Bank of Victoria held a spare licence, that of the old Australian Bank, so a large delegation comprising representatives from the four building societies and the state government visited the bank. Its CEO was distracted and dismissive. The reason the building societies' proposal had seemed 'a distraction' to him was revealed only days later when the news broke that the once omnipotent State Bank was itself in financial trouble and was being sold to the Commonwealth Bank.[46]

While continuing to explore the possibility of bank conversion, Bendigo Building Society also pursued the more immediate object of building society mergers. Hunt and Johanson's preferred option, the merging of a number of societies, would work best if a merger with the well-run Ballarat based VS&L was first achieved. However, this fell through when St George made a better offer late in 1990. Bendigo next concentrated on the Capital Building Society, which had also been identified as a partner in the proposed larger industry grouping. Capital had been formed in Geelong in 1971, and at the time of Pyramid's collapse in June 1990 had built up a network of 26 branches (nine of them in and around Geelong, and another 17 in Melbourne) and over 300 agents throughout Victoria. However, the Pyramid disaster had 'very severely wounded' Capital.[47] As its directors acknowledged in their annual report for the financial year ending 30 June 1990, Pyramid's closure and the resulting collapse of investor confidence in Geelong had put the society under 'intense pressure'.[48] Soon voluntary redundancy packages were being offered, followed by retrenchments, in an attempt to reduce staff numbers. In the following year the society's new chairman, Kevin Roache, conceded that because Pyramid and Capital were both Geelong based, the collapse of the former 'had a bigger impact on Capital than on other societies' in Victoria.[49]

Although Capital's managing director, Brian Thom, was 'tight-lipped' when asked by the *Geelong Advertiser* in September 1990 about merger options, he 'admitted having talks with a number of parties'.[50] When the State Treasury bluntly told the society in 1991 that it 'had no alternative but to merge', Capital's board of directors conceded in May that they 'needed to consider the Society's future'.[51] Treasury suggested a takeover by the Bank of Melbourne, and GIO Australia, Australian Eagle, and IOOF were also considered. With no resolution in sight, the society decided in June 1991 to approach Bendigo Building Society. Neither society was unreservedly enthusiastic about the prospect, but Bendigo in particular recognised that it was a positive way forward both for Capital and for the sector. Bendigo's senior management were confident that Capital enjoyed strong local support and was essentially a well-managed organisation, but they were deeply suspicious that Capital's finances—because the society had sought to match the dazzling same-town rates that Pyramid had offered—did not add up. As merger negotiations proceeded, Bendigo staff double-checked the real value of Capital's loan book, and obtained protection on some of Capital's loans through the Building Societies' Guarantee Fund. Bendigo was nevertheless determined that if Capital were to merge, it should not, as had already happened with VS&L, be absorbed by another competitor. Richard Guy headed off the Bank of Melbourne by telling its head that there was a 'big hole' in Capital's financial position because of bad loans, but that Bendigo Building Society could absorb these because of the funding support made available through the government and the Building Societies' Guarantee Fund to assist such building society mergers. That funding, Guy asserted, would not be available to a bank.[52]

Whereas Hunt and Johanson were satisfied that, with support from the Building Societies' Guarantee Fund, the merger would be a success, Capital clung to the hope that it could trade its way through the crisis, and in August 1991 Thom announced that 'the best option for all parties involved is [for Capital] to remain an independent building society'. Thom added, 'Unfortunately [the] Government holds another view and we have been forced to further discussions of takeover or merger'.[53] At Capital's annual general meeting in October, Roache expressed optimism that with the return of investor confidence following Pyramid's collapse, the society could anticipate a profitable trading year.[54] Capital's management was slow to admit that they retained neither the funds nor the consumer confidence to survive another year. When they asked the state government for an extension of its financial support scheme to the end of 1991, Kennan agreed to support their request only on 'the understanding that Capital will, without further delay, enter into serious negotiations with a number of parties to ensure that it is merged with or taken over by a stronger financial institution'.[55] Capital continued to fume that it 'was being isolated' by those who were rebuilding the building society industry, and complained that it was having 'continually [to] resist . . . pressure from Treasury for the likes of Capital and Compass "to go away"'.[56] However, in late April 1992, Capital's directors yielded to the inevitable and agreed to merge with Bendigo. The difficulty of their decision was mediated by the goodwill that quickly built up on both sides, and determination to make the merger work.[57] The takeover was formalised on 30 April 1992. Thom became a general manager at Bendigo Building Society, and Roache joined the Bendigo board.

While the merger with Capital was still unfolding, Bendigo Building Society set out to takeover the struggling Dandenong based Compass Building Society before it too collapsed. Bendigo, carrying the building society brand, could not afford any failure or difficulty within the industry at this time. The initial negotiations were tense and conducted in secret; the government was anxious to smother rumours of another collapse that would again trigger investor panic, and Compass' management were unenthusiastic about a merger. Compass nonetheless agreed in early August 1992 to allow Bendigo staff to check its books, and Perrow recalls being 'smuggled' into Compass' offices to go through the accounts and loans books.[58] However, Compass stalled Bendigo while it engaged in parallel merger talks with Metway Bank and the Over 50s Friendly Society, which management hoped would propose 'an attractive alternative' to that being offered by Bendigo.[59] The state government initially refused to provide the required financial support from the Building Societies' Guarantee Fund for Bendigo to realise the merger, urging Bendigo to absorb Capital instead before thinking about other acquisitions. Johanson and Hunt continued to work on options to achieve the merger, in line with their original restructure plan to strengthen the industry. But in October 1992 the Kirner Labor Government was defeated and Jeff Kennett formed a new Liberal-National Party Government. Following a board meeting with Bendigo directors, the chairman, Richard Guy, was asked to phone the incoming treasurer, Alan Stockdale, about the mounting difficulties at Compass. When told that another building society was on the verge of closing its doors Stockdale agreed to let Bendigo Building Society take Compass over, and that if the Building Societies' Guarantee Funds of Compass, Capital, and Bendigo were insufficient to cover the debts involved the government would 'chip in' with extra funding.[60] Bendigo Building Society went ahead with the takeover and, as Guy put it, 'cleaned the mess up'.[61] The old Compass board met for the last time on 29 September 1992.

The Capital and Compass takeovers, together with the collapse of Pyramid and the conversion of RESI-Statewide and Hotham building societies into banks, left Bendigo Building Society as the giant in the Victorian building society sector ('we were the only one left standing in Victoria', recalls Johanson),[62] and one of the largest societies in Australia. As a result of its acquisition of Capital and Compass branches in Geelong, Melbourne's south-eastern suburbs, and Gippsland, together with its leadership role in negotiations with the government throughout the Pyramid crisis, Bendigo Building Society viewed very different horizons late in 1992 from those it had in June 1990. The society's board met outside Bendigo for the first time in its history when, in November 1992, its directors assembled in Geelong, and in March 1993 they met for the first time in Melbourne. After the Capital merger, which added $343 million to Bendigo Building Society's balance sheet, the society had 66 branches and assets of $1.4 billion. The acquisition of Compass added another $173 million to the business, and at the end of 1993, after rationalising overlapping infrastructure, Bendigo Building Society had increased its Victorian network to 74 branches. Moreover, as Guy and Hunt noted in their annual report for 1994, the acquisition of Capital and Compass broadened the company's business competencies by requiring it to take on 'loans of a different character to those traditionally handled by the Bendigo'.[63]

Guy had announced in Bendigo's 1992 annual report, and again in the following year, that having weathered the Pyramid crisis and continuing to trade profitably despite recession, unemployment, and banking deregulation in Australia, 'our Society can certainly hold its head high'.[64] The Pyramid crisis had nevertheless fundamentally changed the thinking of the society's senior management. The Bendigo, with its now enlarged business and customer base and with the mergers well advanced, had decided to convert from a building society into a bank. Perrow, who became one of the project managers for the process of bank conversion, believed that bigger building societies 'like us didn't fit in . . . where building societies were any more'.[65] Changing external circumstances had finally convinced the proto-bank to formalise the role that many of its customers felt it already performed. As Perrow reflected, 'we operate so much like a bank and have for so many years that people in Bendigo often say "I'm going down to the bank" when they were going to one of our branches when we were a building society'.[66]

The change in thinking was due in part to a pragmatic reassessment of the new operating climate for building societies post-Campbell and post-Pyramid. Brian Thomas, who had retired as managing director but was still a member of the board, maintained that the Pyramid 'screw-up' had produced such legislative 'overkill' that the operating climate for building societies had become unbearable, and he fumed at the heavy additional costs of regulatory compliance that 'told [us] how to run our own business'.[67] Hunt, his successor as managing director, and Guy also drew attention to the onerous nature of the new compliance processes required by the AFIC and the VFIC, and pointed out that banks now operated in a much freer regulatory environment. They complained that building societies now 'find themselves at a competitive disadvantage' to banks despite 'the supposed deregulation in the finance industry'.[68] Guy said privately that the regulatory changes 'really forced us into becoming a bank'.[69] Hunt had always felt that stronger regulation was required, and that it was only a matter of time before the Bendigo became a bank.

The decision to seek to become a bank was not simply a defensive reaction to external pressures. Senior executives drew lessons from the Pyramid crisis as they planned for the future. The society's growth, they realised, would be restricted if they remained a building society, but if they became a bank, not only would they operate in a kinder regulatory environment, but they would also have access to a wider range of markets, thus accelerating their growth. The building society sector's reputation had been tarnished by Pyramid, they acknowledged, but by converting to a bank they could escape that stigma and put in place new protocols that, as Johanson put it, would make them 'a more transparent public company than [they] had been'. Explaining that point of view, Johanson said that as a result of the Pyramid crisis 'we learned a lot about the nature of the customer relationships we had, and the fragilities of the business'. Reflecting further, he explained that 'the building society brand which had survived so well for such a long time was, we felt, really damaged by . . . this whole process . . . There had been regulatory failure, there'd been market failure, and so we started on the path of saying "well, we've got to get ourselves into a better framework"'.[70]

In June 1995 Bendigo Building Society delivered two large volumes of documentation to Federal Treasurer Ralph Willis in its application for the Reserve Bank to grant it a banking licence. Guy, Hunt, and Johanson also travelled to Sydney to present a copy of the application to the governor of the Reserve Bank, Bernie Fraser. The application had been prepared in record time, after the board had formally resolved on 30 January 1995 to seek a licence. Much of the preparation had already been done during the Pyramid crisis, when Victorian Attorney General Jim

A momentous occasion – Robert Johanson and Rob Hunt watch company secretary Andrew Long sign Bendigo's new Banking Authority on 1 July 1995.

Kennan was pushing the bank conversion agenda. The process was assisted by the recruitment of experienced banking staff, such as Malcolm Bishop and Greg Gillett, who moved from the NAB to become senior managers in the Bendigo structure. Many experienced bankers joined over the years, each finding the unique style of banking offered by Bendigo Bank different from what they had experienced, but likely to appeal to customers across Australia. Bendigo Bank was formally launched—with simultaneous celebrations in five centres around Victoria—on 1 July 1995, after 137 years of operations as a building society. Guy was chairman of the new bank, Johanson its deputy chairman, and Hunt its managing director. It held assets of over $1.5 billion, and operated 74 branches and over 400 agencies in Victoria and southern New South Wales. Its last year as a building society produced a before-tax profit (and before adjustments for bank conversion) of $18 million, and as a bank this has progressively improved over subsequent years.

Consolidation

In 2005, marking its tenth anniversary as a bank, Guy and Hunt acknowledged that, in 1995, Bendigo Bank had been a tiny institution with a limited product range and no national distribution capacity, and was overly dependent on home lending funded by retail deposits to sustain future business growth.[71] By 2005 its 74 branches had grown to over 300 spread across the nation, its assets had increased to over $13 billion, and it posted an after-tax profit of over $87 million for the year to 30 June 2005. Its activities had expanded to include a wide range of business banking, insurance, and wealth creation services, and in addition it had massively increased its community banking activities.

This widening scale and range of activities had dated from the beginning of its banking operations, with the introduction of telephone banking and the purchase of the National Mortgage Market Corporation (NMMC) in 1995. NMMC, a mortgage securitisation finance company, operated throughout Australia as a third-party service provider and manager of loan portfolios. Its purchase marked Bendigo Bank's first substantial move into activities beyond those of a traditional deposit-taking retail bank. In 1997, in a still more significant step, Bendigo Bank bought the

The initial Community Bank directors conference was held around the Bendigo board table. Ten years on 600 delegates packed into Bendigo's biggest function centre to celebrate the movement's first decade.

Australian subsidiary of the Italian bank, Banca Monte dei Paschi di Siena, a provider of commercial financial services to Australia's large Italian community, and relaunched it as Cassa Commerciale Australia Limited. In 1998 Bendigo Bank bought the financial planners Worley Securities and, in the following year, the Victorian Securities Corporation, a Ballarat-based debenture and investment company. These acquisitions gave the bank new business-service capabilities and foreign-exchange skills, as well as an office presence in all mainland capital cities and in another prominent regional centre.

Bendigo Bank's retail banking services were reinforced also by the introduction of internet banking in 1998 and the launch of its Community Bank programme. In 1999 it bought the branch network of the IOOF Building Society and formed a business alliance with the IOOF Group to establish Bendigo Investment Services (its IOOF share was purchased by the bank in 2002, and in 2006 it was restructured as Bendigo Financial Planning). In June 2000 Bendigo Bank announced a friendly merger bid (formally realised in October) for Queensland's First Australian Building

Society (an amalgamation of four older regionally based building societies), which comprised 48 branches, 20 agencies, 430 staff, and controlled assets of some $1.5 billion. In the same year, Bendigo Bank's joint venture with Elders Australia Limited led to the formal establishment of Elders Rural Bank, which delivered rural finance products through Elders' national network of 220 agencies. Bendigo Bank also established GuildBanking in 2000, an alliance with the Pharmacy Guild of Australia to provide specialist financial services to pharmacists. In November 2000 Bendigo Bank's partnership with Tasmanian Trustees resulted in the opening of their first joint retail bank branch, at Burnie in Tasmania. Guy and Hunt announced confidently that 'Bendigo has transformed itself from a regional company primarily servicing Victoria into a bank with growing national presence'.[72]

The following years saw their confidence confirmed. The early and mid 2000s were years of consolidation and further expansion. First Australian was integrated into the business (resulting in one-quarter of the bank's shareholders being resident in Queensland) and, in consequence, the Queensland-based mortgage insurer, Sunstate, was also acquired. Online share trading was launched. A single wealth management division was established, made up of Sandhurst Trustees, Victorian Securities Corporation, Worley Securities, and Bendigo Investment Services. By the mid 2000s Bendigo Bank's pre-tax profit had jumped above $100 million for the first time and it joined the list of Australia's 'Top 100' companies. It took over Oxford Funding to strengthen its services for business customers.

By 2007 Bendigo Bank had, with the opening of its first branch in the Northern Territory, become a fully national bank with branches in every state and territory. In March 2007, however, a 'predatory' takeover proposal was announced by its slightly smaller Queensland competitor, the Bank of Queensland, which suggested that a merger would create Australia's first 'big small bank'.[73] The offer was rejected and in August a better formulated merger proposal, this time with Adelaide Bank, was announced simultaneously in Bendigo and Adelaide. The merger was realised on 30 November 2007. The first meeting of the new Bendigo and Adelaide Bank Group, with Johanson as its chairman and Hunt the managing director, took place in Adelaide on 4 December 2007.

In rejecting the Bank of Queensland's takeover offer in the previous year, Bendigo Bank had pointed out that the two banks represented very different business models and philosophies. Although at first sight Bendigo Bank's development since 1995 mimicked the conventional business logic of its larger competitors, significant points of difference were evident from the beginnings of Bendigo Bank. These became still clearer with the passage of time. Johanson recalls that when Bendigo became a bank in 1995 'we had a lot of people who said you can't call yourselves Bendigo any more. You've got to call yourself, you know, you beaut bank, but our response was no, we want to anchor ourselves in the business that we have, we'll do ourselves more damage by disenfranchising the people who care for us'.[74] Guy and Hunt stressed in the 1996 annual report that, as a result of a strategic rethink that accompanied the transition to a bank, they had formed 'a clear vision of our identity as a regional community bank', and that although they would develop business banking activities, they were committed also to investing heavily in their retail banking arm.[75] The new bank's leadership group recognised that if it came to competing head to head with Australia's largest banks 'we haven't got a hope', and so the conclusion was seemingly simple: 'we play to our strengths'.[76]

But what were these strengths? Four external factors influenced the bank's thinking on this crucial question. The first was the Pyramid crisis, which drew attention to Bendigo Building Society's historical strengths in transparent business practices and close relationships with its customers. The second was the Wallis Review. In May 1996, following the defeat of Keating's Labor Government in March by a Liberal-National Party coalition headed by John Howard, incoming Federal Treasurer Peter Costello set up the Financial System Inquiry, thereafter known as the Wallis Review after its chairman, the businessman Stan Wallis. The Inquiry was asked to review the course of financial deregulation and the effects of new technologies, and to suggest an appropriate regulatory framework for the evolving sector. Wallis delivered the final report in April 1997. It endorsed deregulation (and indeed supported further consolidation of the biggest banks, a proposal that the Howard Government rejected), and proposed a new regulatory framework whereby the Reserve Bank would shape monetary policy, a new Australian

Prudential Regulatory Authority (hived off from the Reserve Bank) would regulate financial institutions, and the Australian Securities Commission would ensure consumer protection. The government's adoption of most of the Wallis Review's recommendations later in 1997 ensured that the momentum of the financial deregulation which had followed the release of the Campbell Report in 1981 would continue. Bendigo Bank sought to carve out a niche for itself in this landscape by emphasising in its submission to the Wallis Review 'the leading role [that was being] played by regional community banks in servicing regional communities and in providing competition and product innovation'. The bank claimed for itself 'a unique position as the only regionally-based Australian bank'.[77]

The third external event which shaped Bendigo Bank's direction was the sharp reduction in the bank's revenue line and the impact of this on the new bank's profits after the Commonwealth Bank slashed home-loan interest rates in 1997, which as Hunt noted 'severely dented the profitability of housing lending'.[78] Hunt conceded that housing loan margins had been subsidising many other customer services, and that such cross-subsidisation could not be sustained. Guy fretted that Bendigo Bank 'was too slow in responding to official interest rate falls', and when its annual report was released, he conceded that the interest rate cuts had 'reduced the bank's margin by a third' and sliced its profits by 13 per cent.[79] As Guy and Hunt formally admitted in the 1997 annual report, 'Traditionally a strength of the Bendigo, our reliance on home lending (89 per cent of loans by security at June 1996) thereby exposed us to substantial reductions in income once prices fell'.[80] The *Australian* announced that Bendigo Bank had resolved to restructure its activities in order to reduce its traditional dependence on home lending.[81] Hunt acknowledged during 1998, as the bank's profits recovered, that as a result of that reorientation 'we had re-shaped our business to grow profit on reduced home lending margins', and had 'beefed up [the bank's] business book' in order to reduce dependency on home-loan income.[82] In developing business banking, Hunt and his colleagues had no intention of abandoning their traditional roots in communities, but they determined to develop a more sophisticated and comprehensive approach to community banking than had sufficed when the bank was a building society.

The fourth external development was the accelerating pace of branch closures by the major banks during the 1990s as pre-Campbell concepts of savings banks and retail banks faded, and as banking strategy became driven more and more by the dictates of the bottom line. Branch closures were accompanied by mounting public anger that the major banks, in pursuing this strategy and relying increasingly on new electronic banking technologies, had seemingly abandoned any notion of a social service role for banks in communities. Bendigo Bank felt that the industry had under-estimated the importance of the branch in supporting local commerce and local communities. Bendigo Bank staffers witnessed local anger first hand from 1996 onwards as they began to develop Community Bank. Bendigo Bank saw in these developments 'a clear opportunity to establish a uniquely Australian bank—one able to respond to the obvious desire for a bank that would "do the right thing" . . . We determined to build a different bank'.[83]

Community wrath at the crude way in which the major banks were using deregulation to cut their operating costs and maximise profits confirmed strategic thinking at Bendigo Bank during the mid 1990s about what they should not do, and how they should position themselves in order to be perceived as a bank that would do the right thing and generate strong growth in shareholder value at the same time. It was therefore relatively easy to say in 1995, notwithstanding the strong tide of market deregulation, that Bendigo Bank would 'set out to establish a clear point of difference'.[84] While some saw these statements as being merely good marketing spin, Bendigo Bank rejected this and went on to declare, a decade later, 'Ours is not a brand that has been built on product, feature or price, because [these] are easily replicated by larger competitors. Instead, we have built brand awareness and respect through our willingness to place the interests of our customers and communities first—in the knowledge that promoting success for them will see us rewarded by their loyalty and increased custom'.[85] Hunt told the sceptics that it was actual deeds that were being judged, and that it was these deeds that the bank's customers valued. But in making these claims, how could Bendigo Bank distinguish itself from other new banks, such as the Bank of Queensland, which also had strong regional client bases? And how could it differentiate itself from the new but much larger St George Bank, which had helped Bendigo Bank through the Pyramid crisis, and which argued in similar terms that its close customer relationships distinguished it from other banks?

Guy provided a partial answer when he explained in 1998 that, as a result of financial deregulation, non-banking institutions were now able to offer services previously monopolised by banks, and that the banks were therefore being forced to reposition themselves. Some of them, said Guy, were striving to become global players, and some sought to provide the cheapest product. Guy contended that amid all this repositioning, Bendigo Bank was able to draw on two unique strengths: firstly, it was Australia's only regionally based bank, and was therefore better placed to understand regional banking needs; and secondly, it was 'close to the communities we serve'.[86] Claiming a distinctive 'banking empathy' based on a long history of neighbourhood financing, in 2001 Bendigo Bank pointed to the consistent strength of its retail deposits (then 88 per cent of total deposits) as a sign of that closeness to communities and as a guarantee of the bank's stability, and pledged that in using this strong deposit base to develop its business, the bank would continue to be guided by its close relationships with its clients: 'family, community, a sense of belonging, are the most important things for our customers and . . . the actual banking services we provide are simply tools for achieving those ends'.[87]

It was Hunt, however, who best articulated the approach that set Bendigo Bank apart from its competitors. Since his appointment as chief executive officer of Bendigo Building Society in 1988, Hunt had thought long and hard about the mounting economic and social pressures being experienced in regional Australia, and also about the future role for his business as it converted to a regional bank. Reflecting on the historical elements that had contributed to the success of Bendigo Building Society, and that could perhaps inform the new bank's operations, he attached special importance to the building society's participation in supporting the consolidation of neighbourhoods and communities during the late nineteenth and early twentieth centuries. By 1994 Hunt had identified a set of elements that, in both the past and the present, he thought underpinned robust and resilient communities. He began to expound a demand side vision of banking practice that was alert to these elements and responsive to community needs, as an alternative to the supply side model of banking services that had dominated the Australian financial sector since deregulation. Hunt started to talk about a bank that built community prosperity rather than feeding off it. He believed that Bendigo could build a successful bank whose operations reinforced the 'local aspirations, local endeavour, local capital, and . . . local vision' that had sustained communities in the past but that had been weakened by the concentration of capital and the centralisation of investment decision-making as the Australian banking, stock exchange, compulsory superannuation, and capital trust systems were transformed during the late twentieth century.[88]

In a letter to Deputy Prime Minister John Anderson in 2000, Hunt expanded upon comments that he had recently made to Anderson when they bumped into each other at Melbourne Airport. They had discussed community sustainability in regional Australia, and Hunt's suggestions about the role that banking could play to 'begin the community change process'. Hunt now explained that Bendigo Bank initiatives such as its Elders Rural Bank joint venture and the first stage of Community Bank were only entry points for enacting his larger vision of banking and community development:

> Over a number of years now, Bendigo Bank has recognised that one of the reasons for rural decline is the individual communities' inability to manage the capital generated in their region. I think it is acknowledged that most country districts export capital (in fact much beyond 'financial' capital) and, given we are the only regionally-based bank, we felt compelled to sit down and develop a new banking model to ensure access to essential banking services and a solution which enabled us to unite, involve, and engage community in solving the problem. In effect this is using 'demand side' strategy (the community's buying power in banking) to secure a co-operatively spirited venture—but using very solid commercial principles.

Hunt argued that this model had 'the capacity . . . not only [to] secure banking services but to generate local profit, regain employment, and instil a "can do" attitude in many districts'.[89]

These principles had begun to be applied by Bendigo Bank in the late 1990s in schemes that went beyond narrowly conceived banking practice. They were evident in part in Bendigo Bank's support for regional business development. In 1997, for example, the bank became a major shareholder in the revitalisation of the Bendigo Stock Exchange (BSX) as an internet-based alternative equity market, which hoped to tap into superannuation funds in order to redirect some of the flows of investment capital into small and medium businesses in regional areas. In 2005 BSX amalgamated with the Newcastle Stock Exchange as NSX Limited, establishing a single national alternative investment market for small to medium-sized enterprises (including share dealing in listed Community Bank companies). Although the BSX has achieved limited success to date, Bendigo Bank continues to maintain a minority interest in it and the NSX today. A growing number of smaller businesses have joined the exchange, and a solid number of Community Banks and other bank-sponsored Community Enterprises have been listed on the exchange over the years.

Bendigo Bank was also a major partner in the 2000 launch of Community Telco Australia (CTA), which sought to bridge the funding gap between investment in advanced telecommunications infrastructure for regional and metropolitan businesses. CTA was envisaged as a community-based initiative that aggregated regional demand for telecommunications services through locally owned companies. A pilot company, Bendigo Community Telco, was established in August 2000. Bendigo Bank was the largest of 14 shareholder organisations sponsoring the company, which was hailed as Australia's first locally owned telecommunications company, and which was credited with boosting the business competitiveness of the Bendigo region. A second company, iTEL Community Telco, was launched in Ipswich, Queensland, in 2002. By 2007 CTA was supporting the delivery of locally owned telecommunications services in eight communities in Victoria, Queensland, New South Wales, and Tasmania.

These incubation schemes for regional business were paralleled by community development programmes. The best known is Lead On, a community youth project that harnesses local business sponsorships to support the participation of young people in community organisations and events. Lead On was established in

Community Telco sought to provide regional communities with a bigger say in the provision of telecommunications.

Boasting Bendigo Bank as its major sponsor, Lead On is a programme aimed at engaging young people – tomorrow's leaders, as Hunt says – into community life.

Bendigo during 1999 with support from the Victorian government. It was expanded, with federal and Queensland government backing, into other Victorian and Queensland regional centres during 2003. By 2004 twelve cities and towns in eastern Australia were participating in the programme, and Western Australia joined in 2007. Another initiative, begun by Bendigo Bank in May 2000, is its Ethical Investment Fund, Australia's first ethical bank deposit scheme. In 2002 it launched Community Sector Banking (CSB), a joint venture between Bendigo Bank and Community 21, a company representing an alliance of organisations in the not-for-profit community sector. The main purpose of CSB is to improve the cash management of participating organisations and thus boost their client services. A micro-finance partnership between CSB and the Brotherhood of St Laurence, begun in 2003, assists low-income earners to buy household goods.

In addition to these social development schemes, the bank introduced a number of ecologically progressive products and programmes. During 2002, it began to offer discounted Green Home Loans for five-star rated environmentally sensitive homes, and Green Personal Loans to encourage householders to install energy- and water-efficient products. In 2006, Bendigo Bank began a bio-diesel experiment with farmers in the Wimmera and central Victoria to operate heavy farm machinery. The bank also began carbon-offset programmes, starting with the bank's car fleet in 2005 and staff air travel in 2006, and broadening out early in 2007 with a

Generation Green programme to help its customers and community partners to reduce their carbon footprint. The programme's first product, Bendigo Carbon Offset, enables participants to offset their carbon emissions.

Bendigo Bank's initiatives in regional business development, community and social equity programmes, and environmental sustainability were recognised by awards such as *Ethical Investor Magazine*'s inaugural Sustainable Business of the Year award in 2002 (won again in the following year, together with a merit award in 2003 for Community/Social Initiatives), and Victoria's Good Corporate Citizen award in 2003. In 2005 Bendigo Bank achieved the highest rating of any bank in an A.C. Neilsen survey of customer satisfaction, and in 2008 its customer satisfaction tallies continue to lead the industry. These results support Bendigo Bank's claim that '"good community" and good business are not mutually exclusive'.[90]

The growth of Bendigo Bank since 1995 has rested on its investment in what Hunt calls its 'point of difference' from other banks in Australia.[91] Although the bank prides itself on its close relationships with its customers, maintained for 150 years, the point of difference goes further to include its partnerships with communities to build prosperity and social wellbeing. Hunt argues that all banks offer similar products but Bendigo Bank's history of community engagement sets it apart and gives it a unique capability to apply into the future the socially responsible banking strategies that it developed in the past.

When Bendigo Bank was established from Bendigo Building Society, Hunt asked his staff to look hard at the historical role played by banks, and also at the history of Bendigo Building Society, so that they could define themselves in the present and project that role into the future. He maintains that 'banks were originally formed in my view to feed into prosperity. And they prospered in a prosperous village'. In Hunt's opinion, the more innovation the early banks fostered, and the more social capital they generated, the stronger their business became. He also believes that in modern Australian history a similar relationship is discernible in the growth of the city of Bendigo and its building societies. That shared history produced a 'core value system' in Bendigo Building Society that Bendigo Bank is now applying across Australia.[92]

chapter

2

Grand boulevard: Pall Mall, Bendigo, postcard, c. 1918. On the right of the picture is the Beehive Store and Mining Exchange, and behind it a large sign 'Abbott' marks the business premises of Joseph Abbott. The hulking Shamrock Hotel is visible beyond it. On the left side of Pall Mall are the Law Courts, Post Office, and the chimney and poppet head of Hustler's Royal Reserve mine. In the foreground stands the Alexandra Fountain in Charing Cross. LA TROBE PICTURE COLLECTION, STATE LIBRARY OF VICTORIA.

Neighbou

rs

Australians today equate banking with impersonal corporate strategies and global scale, rather than with the comprehensible across-the-counter passbook transactions and the conversations that they remember as having characterised banking in the past. Banking then seemed to revolve around the immediacies of financing the family home or business. Banking now, apparently, centres on boardroom negotiations and the pixellated abstractions of computer screens that track international money markets. Although Bendigo Bank is a significant player in today's Australian financial sector, the core responsibilities and accountabilities of the bank's antecedents during the nineteenth and twentieth centuries were small-scale and neighbourly. Its clients were local investors, home-buyers and small businesses. They were neighbours, most of them living in and around Bendigo, and others scattered across small communities in an ever-widening region of business operations that extended through Victoria and eventually across the nation.

External developments periodically intruded on these local relationships, transforming both the scale and spread of operations. The original building society concept of mutual benefit through local association was itself an import from England. The local founders of these building societies had settled in Bendigo during the 1850s as a result of another global phenomenon: the international movement of people triggered by the discovery of gold in California, the Australian colonies, and New Zealand. The subsequent development of Bendigo's building societies into a national bank was determined in part by the long-running effects of the Victorian gold-mining boom that began in 1851, and by the peaks and troughs through which that boom was played out and through which it gradually diminished over the following century. The ongoing development of Bendigo's building societies was also influenced by the surge in Victorian rural settlement from the

1870s into the 1920s. It was shaped as well by drought, by the economic depressions of the 1890s and the 1930s, by two world wars, by the deregulation of the national banking sector during the 1980s, and by the meltdown in the Victorian financial system in the early 1990s.

Although these broader events contributed significantly to the transformation of Bendigo's local building societies into a national bank (albeit remaining anchored in regional Australia), these external crises and opportunities would not have translated into this remarkable outcome had it not been for the persistence since 1858 of the original village dynamics of localism and neighbourliness. Two overlapping elements explain this: the capacity for open-ended regional growth that could be harnessed by the active participation of neighbours within local communities; and the strong ethical conditioning factor of local accountability upon which this business growth depended. This nurtured an enduring sense of social responsibility in business. Bendigo Bank argues that its origins in 1858 'began [with] the philosophy of community obligation' and that this character continues to underpin its operations.[1] Corporate social responsibility is a feature that is frequently attributed to Bendigo Bank today. In 2001, for example, *Ethical Investor Magazine* named it 'Sustainable Company of the Year' and in 2003 the bank won Victoria's Good Corporate Citizen award. It is less often remarked by outside financial commentators that this characteristic is grounded in the bank's neighbourly origins as a Bendigo building society in 1858. However, Bendigo Bank itself is today acutely aware of this history, and has concluded that a successful bank does not simply feed off the prosperity of a given moment but has a role to play in building the many communities in which it operates nationally and, indeed, internationally.

9 July 1858. A winter's evening in Bendigo, and at Abbott's Hotel on Pall Mall a crowd is assembling. Joseph Abbott directs them to a large function room. Upwards of 100 men jam inside. James Sullivan (a municipal councillor, trustee for the new Bendigo Savings Bank, and later Victorian Minister for Mines) is elected chairman. He explains that the meeting has been called to consider establishing a building society. James Burnside proposes a motion that a building society be formed, 'enabling shareholders of such a society to become possessed of freehold and leasehold property, and other benefits'.[2] *Other speakers support the proposal. The motion is carried unanimously. A provisional steering committee is elected, and a membership list is compiled of around 70 names.*

Just over three weeks later, a still larger meeting takes place at Abbott's. About 170 new shareholders cram into the hotel. The society's draft rules are discussed and endorsed, and votes are tallied for a permanent committee of directors. George Fletcher (Bendigo's town clerk), Abbott, Robert Burrowes (later MLA for Bendigo, Minister for Mines and Minister for Public Works), and William Vahland (soon to establish himself as Bendigo's best known architect) are among those elected. Burnside is elected Secretary.

A month later, and the society meets again at Abbott's Hotel, this time for its first sale of shares. A batch of four is offered. Bidding starts at £5. Morris Philips wins the prize with a bid of twelve guineas. He opts to pay in instalments over the next 12 months. The operations of the Bendigo Land and Building Society have properly begun.

The Bendigo Land and Building Society was the earliest among a cluster of local financial associations in Bendigo established between 1858 and 1901, whose collective histories have in common not only an abstract historical link with the creation of Bendigo Bank in 1995 but also the enduring characteristic of mutual benefit through local association. Their participants were neighbours in a regional community. The founders of the Bendigo Land and Building Society had something else in common: they were recent immigrants. Abbott was a native of Birmingham, the English birthplace of the building society movement, and had lived in Bendigo for just five years. Burrowes, a Canadian, and Vahland, from Hanover, had also arrived in 1853, and Sullivan, an Irishman, in 1854. The newcomers pooled their resources to establish themselves in a new land.

22 January 1980. A midsummer day on the flat lands of Melbourne's sprawling western suburbs. At 227 Barkly Street, just down the road from the Italian and Vietnamese stalls that crowd central Footscray's fruit and vegetable market, a small celebration is taking place. It marks the opening of a full-time branch office of Bendigo Building Society. A model gold mine provides a quirky Bendigo reference point in this metropolitan multicultural working-class community. The newly appointed branch manager, Leon Bates, gives an up-beat speech. He is a popular local sportsman, and as a real-estate agent has already acted as a property valuer for Bendigo Building Society in the western suburbs. The branch is opening, he says, to meet the strong local demand for home finance, and it will strengthen the network of local agencies that the society has built up across the western suburbs over the past 40 years. Bates has plans for the new branch to sponsor the Footscray District Football League, but that will be a good news announcement for a later day. Today he has another headline grab: he tells Melbourne journalists that the new branch is the very first to be opened outside Bendigo.

The history of localism that sustains Bendigo Bank is not limited to Bendigo. Its clients also comprise neighbours in Melbourne. This is in small part an historical illusion: the record books of various early independent Melbourne building societies were merged into the archives of Bendigo Bank through the record-keeping effects of successive business takeovers. The actual expansion of Bendigo's building societies into Melbourne is a much more significant feature of Bendigo Bank's history. It was highlighted by the opening of Bendigo Permanent's Footscray office in 1980, which was operated by Bates and three female support staff. This was the first full branch to be established outside Bendigo by any of that city's building societies, and in common with the establishment of the Bendigo Land and Building Society in 1858, many of the participants in the Footscray launch were immigrants. Footscray, an industrial suburb in Melbourne's inner western region, had been heavily settled by Italians and other non-English-speaking immigrants after the Second World War, and Bendigo Permanent responded to the newcomers' desire to buy and renovate homes in the district. This makeover of an old suburb was only the latest development in a long-running engagement by all Bendigo's building societies in Melbourne's housing market. During the 1910s and 1920s, when Melbourne was the federal capital of Australia, the Bendigo societies had participated significantly in financing the building of new suburbs in Melbourne. In the capital city, as in the regional city, the building societies' key business was with neighbours.

1 September 2005. Hundreds of delegates are attending the first day of Bendigo Bank's annual Community Bank National Conference in Bendigo. The last session before lunch *is called 'Australia all over', and gives snapshot updates of local banking activities in communities right across the nation. Presentations throughout the morning and afternoon provide supporting detail. The manager of the thriving Wentworth Community Bank, in south-west New South Wales, describes a model of business success that all the delegates are determined to emulate. Some $30 million worth of business, he says, has been generated in Wentworth during the past year. Representatives from Bendigo Bank's network of Western Australian branches explain how the profits from business growth there are being ploughed back into local communities to build public swimming pools and support ambulance services. The chairman of the new Cooroy and Tewantin branch in Queensland's Noosa Shire outlines the social problems that simmer beneath the prosperous veneer of his district, and describes how the new branch is already bolstering family support services through donations and voluntary labour. Representatives from Cummins on South Australia's Eyre Peninsula report on the loss of life and widespread property damage caused by the devastating bushfire that shocked the nation in 2005. Jeff Pearson, the branch treasurer, describes how the community of Cummins had thrown itself into the reconstruction effort, and how assistance from the national bushfire appeal and Bendigo Bank's Community Foundation are being applied to get the community back on its feet. Pausing, Jeff ponders for a moment why there are no branches of the major banks left in Cummins. Their departure, he concludes, has empowered the community to take greater control of local affairs.*

In the history of Bendigo Bank, the neighbourhood energy displayed in building the village is a feature not only of Bendigo's emergence as an important regional city, and of suburban growth and revitalisation in metropolitan Melbourne, but is also symptomatic of grassroots activism in building and sustaining communities throughout the nation. The history of Bendigo Bank connects with local histories of building the village right across Australia. Some of these associations are the result of mergers with parallel organisations in other places. The Mildura-based Sunraysia Permanent Building Society, for example, merged with Bendigo Permanent in 1985 and Geelong's Capital and Dandenong's Compass building societies were absorbed during 1992. In 1997, Bendigo Bank took over Monte Paschi Australia

Limited, which supplied financial services to Australia's Italian community, and relaunched it in every mainland capital city as Cassa Commerciale Australia Limited. In 1999, Bendigo Bank bought the IOOF Building Society (an offshoot of the Independent Order of Oddfellows), and in 2000 it absorbed Queensland's First Australian Building Society (itself an amalgamation of four earlier Queensland building societies). The Bank's broad community base is also a result of the expansion of Bendigo's building societies across regional Victoria and into southern NSW during the late nineteenth and early twentieth centuries. These links have been consolidated since 1998 by the expansion of Bendigo Bank's network of Community Banks throughout the nation. As the Bank's 1998 annual report noted, 'Bendigo Bank was founded on a sense of community' and it continues to articulate it.[3] Throughout its history of expanding geographical engagement, Bendigo Bank's business has been to facilitate grassroots banking among neighbours.

In the following chapter I describe that history in relation to rural communities from the late nineteenth century to the present day. In chapter four I explain the origins of the Community Bank movement in 1998 and its subsequent development. However, here I narrow my focus to Bendigo Bank's neighbourhood origins, from the establishment of the Bendigo Land and Building Society in 1858 to the merger of the Sandhurst Trustees with the consolidated Bendigo Building Society in 1991.

Genesis of the Building Society Movement

The building society was a concept imported from Britain. Its essence was neighbourliness and mutual benefit. Building societies in Britain began as one expression of the broader friendly societies movement, and were originally regulated by the Friendly Societies Acts of 1793 through to 1834, before the first Building Societies Act was implemented in 1836. Friendly societies provided members and their families with sickness, old age, and bereavement support, drawn from the accumulated contributions of each society's members. Building societies assisted members to save, with the goal of home ownership in mind. Savings banks, the first of which were established in England during the 1790s, likewise encouraged thrift and self-improvement. Friendly societies, building societies, and savings banks all sought to maximise the social well-being of the working classes. Building societies were a product of Nonconformist mutualism in the English Midlands, the first societies being established in Birmingham during the 1770s. By 1800 at least 50 societies had been established in the Midlands, Lancashire, and Yorkshire, and a decade later they had spread to London and Scotland. They spread rapidly thereafter; during the 1830s, 1840s, and 1850s there were probably at any given time between 2000 and 3000 building societies operating across Britain.

These building societies were all small-scale and short-term. They characteristically had no more than 20 members whose regular subscriptions, loan repayments, and the accumulating interest thereon were sufficient—over a period of 10 to 15 years—to provide all members with finance to build a house. A different approach was offered by Bowkett and Starr-Bowkett building societies. Bowkett societies, the first of which was established by Dr Thomas Edward Bowkett in the London parish of Clerkenwell around 1850, helped working people obtain low-cost housing by offering loans free of interest. Starr-Bowkett building societies, which were begun by Richard Benjamin Starr around 1859, attempted to overcome the financial weakness of such societies by requiring borrowers not only to repay advances, but also to contribute a small weekly membership subscription. Starr-Bowkett societies were very popular and over 1000 had been established by the time of Starr's death in 1892. The distribution of loan funds in all types of building society was usually determined either by auction, at which members bid for the next allocation of investment capital, or by ballot, in which members' names were drawn from a box or barrel. In both cases borrowers were allocated shares whose paper values were paid off by monthly repayments. Although home borrowers made up the majority of building society shareholders, most societies also competed with savings banks by allowing investing members to accumulate savings and interest.

All these early societies were terminating building societies. Once all borrowing members had paid off their homes, the society closed, generally after 10 to 15 years, although they were often quickly reinvented for the benefit of new members. London's 1852 New City Mutual Building Society, for example, was re-established as the Second City Mutual in 1856, and as the Third City Mutual in 1860.

From the middle of the nineteenth century, a new style of permanent building society began to develop. The main architect of the 'Permanent plan' was Arthur Scratchley, whose *Treatise on Benefit Building Societies*, first published in 1847, was enlarged over successive editions between 1851 and 1891. Scratchley's idea was that, although individual members would belong to a society for a finite period while saving to buy a house, the society itself would be ongoing. The first such society was created in 1846 and the idea rapidly took off in and around London. The North and Midlands were much slower to adopt the permanent principle.

Notwithstanding the rapid growth of the building society movement throughout Britain during the nineteenth and early twentieth centuries, the establishment of a national association, and the gradual conversion of societies from terminating to permanent structures, British building societies remained local in orientation and methods before the First World War. The first international congress of building societies, held in London in 1914, was a hesitant affair. Thereafter, inter-war and post-Second World War growth transformed the building society sector in Britain and consolidated the movement's international networks. Nevertheless its essence remained local empowerment. It has been called 'one of the most socially significant movements in British history'.[4]

These origins were proudly acknowledged and their memory perpetuated by the building societies in Bendigo. In 1933, for example, the year of the Fourth International Congress in London, Richard Abbott—Chairman of the Sandhurst Mutual Permanent Investment and Building Society (and the son of Joseph Abbott)—celebrated the 'many useful co-operative efforts' that had originated in Birmingham to improve social well-being. These were capped, he said, by the building society movement, which championed 'the idea that an Englishman's house was his castle, and . . . [this] desire to own his own house and home [has become] an almost national characteristic of the British race'. Abbott declared that as a result of the building society concept, wherever 'colonists from the mother country migrated this persistent principle of self-help was carried [with them] and became a most important factor in pioneering new lands'.[5]

British colonists had established building societies in North America during the 1830s and in the Australian colonies during the 1840s. They also established friendly societies, often as branches of British parent organisations. The Independent Order of Oddfellows (IOOF), for example, established its first Australian lodge in Sydney in 1836. Manchester Unity began in 1840 as a Melbourne lodge of the IOOF. It merged in 1993 with the Australian Natives Association (ANA), which had begun in Melbourne during 1871 offering membership benefits to Australian-born men. The histories of both the ANA and the IOOF would overlap with that of Bendigo Bank. The first savings bank in Australia was established in Sydney during 1819 and government-backed savings banks were established in New South Wales in 1832, South Australia in 1847, and Victoria (subsuming the first savings bank, which began in Melbourne during 1842) in 1853.

Australia's earliest building societies, like their Birmingham models, were terminating associations. So too were the first societies in Bendigo. They gave advances to home borrowers from the accumulated funds of their members that had been invested in return for shares. Most investing shareholders accumulated shares with the aim of trading them for a home loan of equivalent value. At the monthly meetings of Bendigo's early building societies, the national anthem and a concert customarily preceded an auction of shares whose paper value could be translated into finance for a new home. If the bidding failed to reach the nominated share value, the shares were sold by ballot. They could be paid off in full or by monthly repayments (lower cost fortnightly repayments were introduced between 1881 and 1901) over 12 years. Any lapses in repayments were punished with fines, although members could apply for suspension of payments on the grounds of sickness or unemployment.

From the 1860s, Australian building societies evolved into permanent organisations with continuing processes for raising and retaining investment capital, and profitably reinvesting their accumulating funds in the expanding markets for home and small-business finance. In Melbourne, one of the first such societies was the Metropolitan Permanent Building Society, established in 1863. In Bendigo, the transformation from terminating to permanent structures was played out between 1858 and 1911. This transition meshed with the city's evolution from a frontier settlement to a large city. In Bendigo and Melbourne settlers were literally building the village from scratch. Australian colonial governments invested massively in building public infrastructure for these new societies, trading banks funded the growth of rural production, and share markets raised capital for mining and other public companies. But building societies supplied the loan capital for home building in the new communities.

The transformation of Bendigo's building societies from terminating into permanent form was driven not only by the need to build the village, but also by the social aspirations of immigrants to achieve more than had seemed possible in the Old World. Thus the building societies' goal broadened: 'assisting . . . citizens in acquiring their homes upon easy and convenient repayment terms in keeping with their earnings, and, at the same time, providing a profitable form of investment for the thrifty investor'.[6] As was also happening in Britain, Australian building societies evolved to meet the interests of investors as well as home borrowers, but in gold-rich Bendigo the opportunities and returns for thrifty investors were manifestly greater. It was the resulting interest in creating local investment pathways, more than it was unmediated borrowing of ideas from Britain, which led building societies in Bendigo to adopt permanent structures and experiment with long-term capital mechanisms to generate and maintain a secure capital base.

Over the first 70 years of Bendigo's history, these adaptations to local conditions were significantly influenced by the energetic and innovative qualities of the immigrant gold-rush generation and their children. These qualities are clearly evident in the entrepreneurial abilities and longevity of the office holders who drove the growth of Bendigo's early building societies well into the twentieth century. Joseph Abbott, for example, one of the founders of Bendigo Permanent in 1858, was also a foundation director of the Sandhurst building society in 1881 and its chairman from 1888 until 1894, and a major foundation shareholder in Sandhurst Trustees during 1888. In addition he was a successful businessman, municipal councillor (and mayor in 1891), parliamentarian (representing the northern province in the Victorian

PALL MALL, LOOKING SOUTH.

LINE OF REEFS

PUBLIC OFFICES

JOSEPH HY ABBOTT ESQ MAYOR

BROKERS ON CHANGE

TOWN HALL

SCHOOL OF MINES & MECHANICS INSTITUTE

VIEW POINT

Legislative Council from 1889 until 1904), and pioneer of the Hospital Sunday movement. Vahland, another founding director of Bendigo Permanent and its Chairman from 1876, became its inaugural managing director in 1891 and retained that position until his death in 1915. At the society's annual meeting in 1914, he reflected that 'he had been a member of the board without interruption for 49 years & he hoped to be spared to see its Jubilee' in the following year. He died just four months short of the event.[7] Angus Mackay junior, co-owner of the *Bendigo Advertiser*, was a director and then chairman of the Bendigo and Eaglehawk Star Permanent Society from the early 1900s until the late 1940s. The building societies' secretaries and managers were equally remarkable. The record for longevity in office lies with Ralph W. Brown, who joined Bendigo Permanent as an office boy in 1877, became company secretary in 1890, and continued in that position until his death in 1916. Pride of place in terms of influence probably lies with Edward Thomas, manager of the Star from 1901 to 1929. He was not only instrumental in founding the society and guiding it until the Great Depression, but he engineered his son Edward Travis Thomas to succeed him (as he did in turn for his own son in 1964).

The characteristics of the gold-rush generation and their children are also evident in the broader constituency of shareholders, depositors, and borrowers that the societies represented. Their active participation in the societies' long-term development demonstrates that the societies' remarkable growth cannot be explained simply by the wealth generated by gold mining, but must also take into account the resilience engendered by living in a water-scarce and gold-dependent community. The beginnings of Bendigo Bank are as much about the hardships of a mining community that used the assets accumulated during the booms to ride out the bad times, as they are about the uninterrupted pathways to fortune that were followed by a few. In 1927, on the eve of the Great Depression, one struggling local borrower vowed that 'he was doing his best to keep payments going. He promised to keep payments up with reduction of his arrears if possible. He is [a] railway employee on [a] small salary & from payments made appears to be making an honest attempt to keep going'.[8] Doing one's best did not guarantee a safe ride

Opposite page: City Father: Joseph Henry Abbott, from a woodcut, 'The City of Bendigo', in the *Illustrated Australian News*, 1 August 1892. LA TROBE PICTURE COLLECTION, STATE LIBRARY OF VICTORIA.

through the hard times. In 1885, for example, one woman wrote to the Sandhurst Mutual Permanent Investment and Building Society 'stating that in consequence of her Husband's decease she is unable to continue the repayments and desires the society to dispose of her property and relieve her from further responsibility'. The house and furniture were sold.[9] Bendigo Bank's archives are peppered with letters from borrowers during the nineteenth and early twentieth centuries seeking suspension of their repayments owing to unemployment, accidents, illness and, at the turn of the century, because of sojourns in the Western Australian goldfields. Community building in a new region of European settlement provides a context for, but does not fully explain, the growth of Bendigo's building societies. Where did Bendigo's lending money come from? How was this capital mobilised as a continuing and dependable resource as Bendigo's building societies evolved from terminating to permanent structures? Where did the money go? What demands were being met? In an instant community, the conditions of capital supply and demand differed from those in Britain where building societies had originated. In answering these questions it is helpful to divide the development of Bendigo's building societies into two periods of roughly 70 years: from 1858 to the start of the Great Depression in 1929, and from the 1930s to the emergence of a single building society in 1991. This whole period can be characterised as an evolutionary period of proto-banking in the history of Bendigo Bank.

Early Development, 1858–1929

The history of Bendigo (or Sandhurst as it was officially styled until 1891, in opposition to local idiom) from the discovery of gold in 1851 to the commencement of the Great Depression is one of extremes: from the massive growth triggered by gold mining and the transition from shallow alluvial to company-based quartz reef mining between the 1850s and the 1870s; to the gold-mining industry's collapse during the First World War; and cycles of boom and drought-induced bust in the rural economy of the surrounding region. Gold mining made Bendigo an instant city, the third largest in Victoria after Melbourne and Ballarat. The three cities were linked by railway in 1862. But Bendigo was not simply a hothouse of riches and open-ended opportunities. The city and its institutions were also shaped by forced adjustments to hard times. Although the city weathered the catastrophic depression of the 1890s better than most of Victoria—owing to the continuing profitability of company mining that had pursued the quartz reefs to great depths—by the turn of the century Bendigo's building societies conceded the difficulties of operating amid 'the general depression prevailing'.[10] Thereafter, as the directors of the Star granted glumly in 1915, the city's economy was buffeted 'by the triple evils of war, drought, and a diminished gold yield'.[11] By 1920 the Star acknowledged that during its 19 years of existence 'more than ordinary vicissitudes have had to be met and faced by the whole community', and that 'In 1914 we experienced the strain of a severe drought and towards the close of that year the great war spread its baleful influence over practically the whole world. Added to these evils, we in Bendigo, have witnessed the decline of what was once our staple industry of gold mining'.[12] By 1927, well before the onset of the Great Depression, most of Bendigo's mines had already closed, and none were paying dividends to investors.

The population of the district had surged with the first rush for gold in 1851, and peaked during the 1880s. Settlement included not only central Bendigo, but also a wide arc of neighbourhoods nestled in surrounding gullies and flats, such as Golden Square, Kangaroo Flat, California Gully, Eaglehawk Gully, and White Hills. Some 30,000 people lived in the district during the early 1850s and, when the Bendigo Land and Building Society was established in 1858, there were perhaps 33,000, of whom a third lived in the central township. Over 36,000 people lived in Bendigo city and Eaglehawk when the Sandhurst building society was founded in 1881. Thereafter population growth stalled, declining to 34,000 in 1891 and dropping further in the early twentieth century. By 1929 Bendigo's population had barely recovered to the level of 1891.

The origins of Bendigo Bank are to be found in the Bendigo Mutual Permanent Land and Building Society (originating in 1858), the Sandhurst Mutual Permanent Investment and Building Society (1881), Sandhurst Trustees (1887), and the Bendigo and Eaglehawk Starr-Bowkett Building Society (1901). These institutions have parallel and often intersecting histories that coalesced between 1858 and 1991 into

Beginnings: Sandhurst in 1857. Engraving by J. Tingle based on a painting by S.T. Gill. A poster advertising a government land sale hangs from a fence in the left foreground. RARE PRINTED COLLECTION, STATE LIBRARY OF VICTORIA.

Gold rush city: Sandhurst, looking north from the Masonic Hall, c. 1875. LA TROBE PICTURE COLLECTION, STATE LIBRARY OF VICTORIA.

that of the Bendigo Building Society and eventually Bendigo Bank. Sandhurst Trustees, which concluded this process of amalgamation by merging with Bendigo Building Society in 1991, was one of a number of trustee companies that developed in Australia during the late nineteenth century. The first such company, the Trustees, Executors, and Agency Company, began in Melbourne in 1879. They offered trustworthy and prudent administration of financial assets and businesses while their owners were away, and executor services for wills and deceased estates. Like Sandhurst Trustees, the three Bendigo building societies began as small local elements within a broader colonial framework. Victorian building societies operated under a common regulatory framework, initially the *Friendly Societies Act 1865* and later the *Building Societies Act 1874* and *1890*—the operations of which were tightened further by the *Companies Act 1896*—and the *Building Societies Act 1928*. The Bendigo societies did not join the Melbourne-based Victorian Association of Building and Mortgage Societies, established in 1889, but in 1932 they enthusiastically supported the creation of a new industry body, the Building Societies Association.

Bendigo's early building societies were all modest in membership and decision-making. Only 10 shareholders, for example, attended the 1928 annual shareholders' meeting of Bendigo Permanent (the largest of these societies, and the second largest in the state), notwithstanding the inducements of 'light refreshments' (an initiative that began with the society's 1915 Jubilee celebrations). Most of the society's annual meetings over the previous 50 years had attracted only a handful of members—never more than 50. Annual meetings of the smaller Sandhurst during the late nineteenth century were attended by between 10 and 16 at a time when membership was around 90 to 100. Twelve shareholders attended the society's annual meeting in 1929 and at the Star, just six shareholders attended the society's annual meeting that same year. The small core of active participants in all three societies was largely male. A scattering of female investors and family members did attend society functions, but their roles were largely symbolic. At meetings of the early Star, for example, women sang songs and were asked to draw the ballot. Men monopolised the directorships and the positions of secretary or manager. Bendigo Permanent's rules stipulated: 'Females and minors shall be entitled to hold Investing Shares in this Society, and to vote at all its meetings; but they shall not be qualified to hold any office, neither shall minors under fourteen years be allowed to vote'.[13]

The societies had tiny staffs and makeshift office accommodation. Bendigo Permanent appointed an assistant to the secretary in 1877, but in 1884 the secretary pleaded for a second assistant on account of 'the great strain I have this year been subjected to by extra work', adding that his son had been helping him in the office for 12 months without pay.[14] The society's staff had grown to four in 1889, and to five (the secretary, plus two male and two female support staff) by 1929. The Sandhurst did not appoint an assistant manager until 1903 (at five shillings per week), and the Star made do with a secretary manager and one female assistant. Meetings of the earliest society, the Bendigo Land and Building Society, were held for the first two and a half years at Abbott's Hotel. The society's minutes first record a meeting being 'held at the Society's office', rather than at Abbott's, in

Regional metropolis: Bendigo from the Old Chum poppet head, 1905. LA TROBE PICTURE COLLECTION, STATE LIBRARY OF VICTORIA.

February 1861.[15] Its successor, Bendigo Permanent, held committee meetings in the Temple Court Hotel from 1865 until 1870, and then rented office space in Bull Street. It moved to new rooms in Bath Buildings, Mitchell Street, during 1872, and in 1877 moved back to Bull Street, renting larger premises in Thomas Gould's Buildings, which it purchased in 1883. Annual meetings of shareholders continued to be held in hotels until 1919, a righteous motion against this practice being rejected by a large margin in 1880. The Sandhurst in 1928 finally bought the office building in View Street that it had occupied since its establishment in 1881. The Star rented an office in the Sandhurst Trustees' View Street headquarters until the 1930s, and held its annual meetings nearby in the ANA Hall until 1916; thereafter they were held at the society's View Street office. Neither the Star nor the Sandhurst opened sub-offices, and it was not until 1906, almost 50 years after the society was formed, that Bendigo Permanent opened its first (short-lived) 'branch' office at Eaglehawk. The Sandhurst responded by installing an eye-catching brass plate on the front of its Eaglehawk agency.

Bendigo's building societies maintained cordial relations despite their competition for local business. In 1885, for example, the societies met to set a uniform interest rate on deposits; in 1897 they jointly lobbied Parliament to amend the new Companies Act, which was hurting their home lending; and in 1931 the three societies acted in concert to seek modification of federal income tax regulations. Such collaboration was grounded on personal friendships and overlapping responsibilities. When in 1895, the Sandhurst Trustees organised a meeting with Bendigo building societies to lobby parliament against pending land and tax legislation, it was Joseph Abbott—closely linked to the Trustees and to the Sandhurst and Bendigo Permanent building societies—who undertook to table their petition in the Legislative Council.

Bendigo's building societies

Bendigo Permanent was the largest of Bendigo's building societies. Its origins can be traced back to 1858. In July of that year the Bendigo Land and Building Society was established. It was set up as a terminating society, and once its objective of a home for all its members was met it was wound up in August 1863. However, its operations were interwoven with two other Bendigo societies that operated alongside it from 1860 and continued after its close until 1868.

The first of these was the Bendigo Permanent Land Building and Investment Society, which was established in November 1860. It had directors in common with the Bendigo Land and Building Society and James Burnside was secretary of both. The two societies worked in close association, initially sharing office space at Abbott's Hotel, using the same bookkeeping and jointly purchasing a safe. Notwithstanding the Bendigo Permanent Land Building and Investment Society's ambition to endure as a permanent building society, it faltered and was wound up in September 1861.

The second society was the Sandhurst Land, Building and Investment Society, which was established in November 1862.[16] It also operated in close association with the Bendigo Land and Building Society, holding its committee meetings in the latter's office. Burnside was secretary of both societies, and several other key stakeholders were joint directors. Like the 1858–1863 society, it was a terminating society and was wound up in January 1868. Unlike the 1858 society (but in common with the failed permanent society, whose advertising it copied), it promoted property investment as well as home ownership. With an eye to developing these strategies long term, the society resolved in October 1864 to establish a permanent society. This was achieved in November 1865 when the common pool of directors and shareholders who had participated in the three earlier building societies formed a new board of directors to launch the Bendigo Permanent Land and

First Annual Report of the Committee of Management of The Bendigo Permanent Land and Building Society November 5th 1866

The Committee in submitting this the first annual report have to state that when the Society was started twelve months ago one hundred and sixtyfour shares were taken up, but on a number of these, only the entrance fees were paid which were eventually for-feited to the Society. The Committee however are glad in being able to say the Society has progressed very satis-factorily the number of invested shares is now one hundred and thirty three and of shares advanced seventy one and one fifth. the amount of money advanced by the Society being £3555.– the total number of share now taken up is 204 a result that proves that the Society is meeting with increased favor and steadily

Bendigo Permanent Land and Building Society, hand-written first annual report, 1866.

Building Society. Although the society initially measured its growth from 1865, holding its Fiftieth Jubilee celebrations in 1915 and its Diamond Jubilee in 1925, it became generally accepted that Bendigo Permanent 'was first started as a terminating society in 1858'.[17]

A small core of men guided the development of Bendigo Permanent through its establishment and early years of consolidation. At the society's Diamond Jubilee celebrations in 1925, it was emphasised that the list of its early directors and trustees was studded with the 'well-known names of early citizens'.[18] These included Abbott, Robert Burrowes (an early advocate of municipal government, and MLA for Bendigo from 1866 until his death in 1893), William Steane, Edward Holten, and Vahland (all of whom had also been directors of the earlier societies that preceded Bendigo Permanent), the politicians George Aspinall and John Holmes (both of them mayors of Sandhurst), and Robert Clark (a mining union leader, city mayor, and MLA for Sandhurst), the Bendigo district Mining Registrar Horatio Busst, and the businessmen Jacob Cohn, Alexander Cook, Thomas Milroy, and George Darnton Watson. The closed nature of decision-making within this network did at times generate resentment across the wider membership of the society. When George Victor Lansell, eldest son of Bendigo's 'Quartz King', George Lansell, was nominated by the directors in 1909 to join the board, many shareholders objected. They claimed (correctly) at the society's annual meeting that the multiple votes controlled by the largest shareholders allowed 'dummyism' when votes were cast, and they noisily rejected being 'bossed' by a clique.[19] Lansell nonetheless became a director in 1911. A prominent businessman, philanthropist, and soldier, he was elected to the Victorian Legislative Council in 1928.

The position of secretary was equally important to the society's success. Burnside was Bendigo Permanent's first secretary until shortly before his death in April 1878. He was succeeded by Solomon Herman, from Poland, who served until November 1890. His replacement, Ralph W. Brown, had joined the society as a junior clerk in April 1877. At the time of his death in February 1916 this 'genial and popular Secretary' had served the society for almost 40 years.[20] His was a long and successful career that almost did not happen. Brown's first opportunity

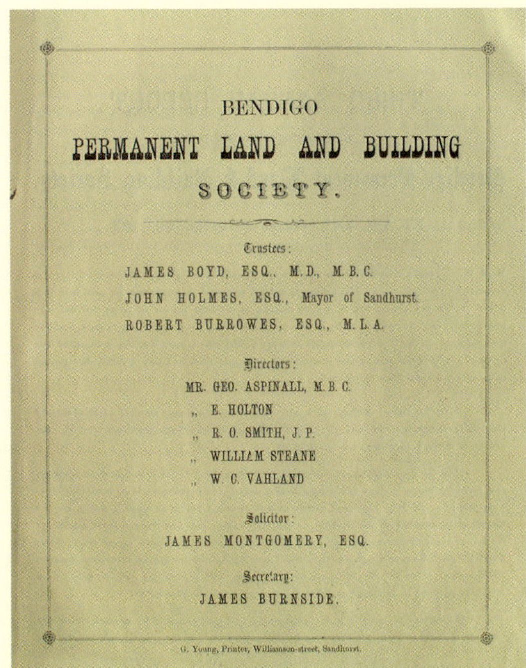

BENDIGO

PERMANENT LAND AND BUILDING

SOCIETY.

Trustees:

JAMES BOYD, ESQ., M.D., M.B.C.

JOHN HOLMES, ESQ., Mayor of Sandhurst.

ROBERT BURROWES, ESQ., M.L.A.

Directors:

MR. GEO. ASPINALL, M.B.C.

„ E. HOLTON

„ R. O. SMITH, J.P.

„ WILLIAM STEANE

„ W. C. VAHLAND

Solicitor:

JAMES MONTGOMERY, ESQ.

Secretary:

JAMES BURNSIDE.

G. Young, Printer, Williamson-street, Sandhurst.

Above: William Vahland, foundation director, and inaugural managing director of Bendigo Permanent, 1891–1915.
Left: Bendigo Permanent, cover page, first printed annual report, 1868.

Bendigo Permanent staff, 1925. The secretary, Andrew Balsillie, is seated in the centre, holding a copy of the society's annual report.

had come with the directors' decision in 1877 to 'appoint . . . a lad for the office' to assist Burnside. The directors stipulated in the job description 'a youth to assist in office at a salary of 12/6 per week, that he must be well educated and write with a fair hand'.[21] When five years later Brown requested a salary increase to two pounds per week, the directors asked 'whether a lad at less cost would not be sufficient'. However, Herman replied that it was impossible for Brown to live on less than one pound a week, and that it would be an unreasonable burden on the secretary to have to train a new office boy 'from scratch'.[22] Herman argued that 'it would not be possible for him to conduct an increasing business with any new lad, as it had taken him several years to train young Brown who now had a practical knowledge of the books and was exceedingly useful'. The directors remained unconvinced, and it was only Chairman Vahland's casting vote that saved Brown's career with Bendigo Permanent.[23] On Brown's death, another long-serving officer, Andrew Balsillie, was appointed secretary. Balsillie had joined the society in 1896 and became its cashier and accountant. He would remain secretary-manager for 30 years. Meanwhile in April 1929 his eventual replacement, T. Frank Perrow, then an office boy of 16, 'completed his month's probation & has given every satisfaction & his appointment to the Permanent Staff is now confirmed'.[24]

Bendigo Permanent was initially a miniscule financial institution. Its total funds in 1866 were barely £3000. By 1884, when Bendigo Permanent renamed itself the Bendigo Mutual Permanent Land and Building Society, it had become one of the largest regional building societies in Victoria and had accumulated some £57,000 in shares and deposits. By 1886 its total funds had reached £100,000. However, the 1870s and 1880s were challenging times for the society, with investor frenzy for mining shares alternating with the flow-on effects of recession in the mining industry, both of which put pressure on the society's ability to attract depositors and borrowers. To survive these times, the society developed cautious business policies. These were reinforced in 1890 when Herman—swayed by the wild speculation in mining shares—was found to have made massive defalcations on the society's funds. The scandal stung the society into reviewing its management structures and it created the new position of 'Managing Director, to take the general supervision of all business in and outside the Office'.[25] It also reinforced a conservative approach to risk management, the society 'confining . . . business to the strictest lines of safety' at a time when other lending institutions in the colony were overextending themselves. When the property bubble burst in Melbourne, the society was better placed than most to ride the storm. The directors reported in 1893 that notwithstanding 'a period of unexampled disturbance in financial circles throughout the colony', the society had recorded a 'very satisfactory outcome', and it maintained some £153,000 in funds.[26]

The debilitating effects upon Victoria of the 1890s depression intensified the society's fiscal caution, and thereafter it built up a substantial reserve fund 'to meet any sudden loss that may arise'.[27] Bendigo Permanent survived the depression, whereas many of its larger metropolitan competitors either failed or had their business massively eroded, to emerge in the early twentieth century as one of the largest building societies in Victoria. The society boasted in 1897 that it was 'by its age and magnitude by far the foremost institution out of Melbourne'.[28] By 1918 it was ranked sixth in the state and by 1924 when its assets passed the quarter-million-pound mark its directors expressed satisfaction that 'the Society now ranks as the most popular Institution in Northern Victoria both with Investors and Borrowers'.[29] In the following year, when the society celebrated its Diamond Jubilee as a permanent society, the directors went still further in their claims and asserted that 'Whilst in actual figures the Society now ranks about the fourth largest Building Society in the State, it is easily the leading Society outside the metropolis'.[30] On the eve of the Great Depression, chairman Busst reported that Bendigo Permanent, with well over £400,000 in available funds, had become the second largest building society in Victoria.

The Sandhurst Mutual Permanent Investment and Building Society (whose name persisted unchanged, notwithstanding a vote by its directors in 1895 to change Sandhurst to Bendigo)[31] was a much smaller undertaking; by 1929 its total funds were little more than a quarter of those mobilised by Bendigo Permanent. The Sandhurst was established in September 1881. Like Bendigo Permanent, it replaced an older terminating society, the Sandhurst Building Society, which had begun in 1871. The overlaps and continuities between the two societies were so close that the new Sandhurst took over 'the old Society's' furniture and safe.[32] Continuity was also a characteristic of the Sandhurst's key personnel during this foundation period. Henry van der Heyde, the society's first manager, was replaced by Henry North as acting manager in July 1888 (he was confirmed as manager in December 1889). North finally retired in October 1916. He was succeeded by Arthur Palmer, who remained manager until December 1931. The society's solicitor, Charles Cohen, held the post from the society's inception in 1881 until his death in 1924. The first Chairman of Directors, Joseph Abbott, served from 1881 until 1894 (he died in 1904). Upon his resignation the vacant directorship passed to his son Richard. William Neill was chairman for a remarkable 31 years, from early 1898 to the end of 1928. Richard Abbott replaced him as chairman. Leonard V. Lansell was a director from 1915 to 1928. The architect and city councillor (and several times mayor of Bendigo during the 1930s) George Garvin became a director in 1920 and replaced Abbott as chairman in 1936.

Richard Hartley Smith Abbott, chairman of Sandhurst Building Society, 1928–1936.
REPRODUCED FROM A 1929 PHOTOGRAPH OWNED BY THE NATIONAL LIBRARY OF AUSTRALIA, NLA.PIC-an22355128.

In the Sandhurst, Bendigo Permanent had a rival, a permanent building society that energetically set about catching the eye of local investors by advertising investment shares that could be paid off for as little as one shilling per fortnight. The Sandhurst was not Bendigo Permanent's only competitor. The Eaglehawk Building Society also converted from a terminating into a permanent society during 1881, and scared its adversaries by adopting 'the lowest tariff of any Building Society in the colony'.[33] By 1891 three permanent societies remained in the city: Bendigo Permanent, Sandhurst, and the Commercial Permanent Land and Building Society. The Sandhurst was Bendigo Permanent's only serious competitor.

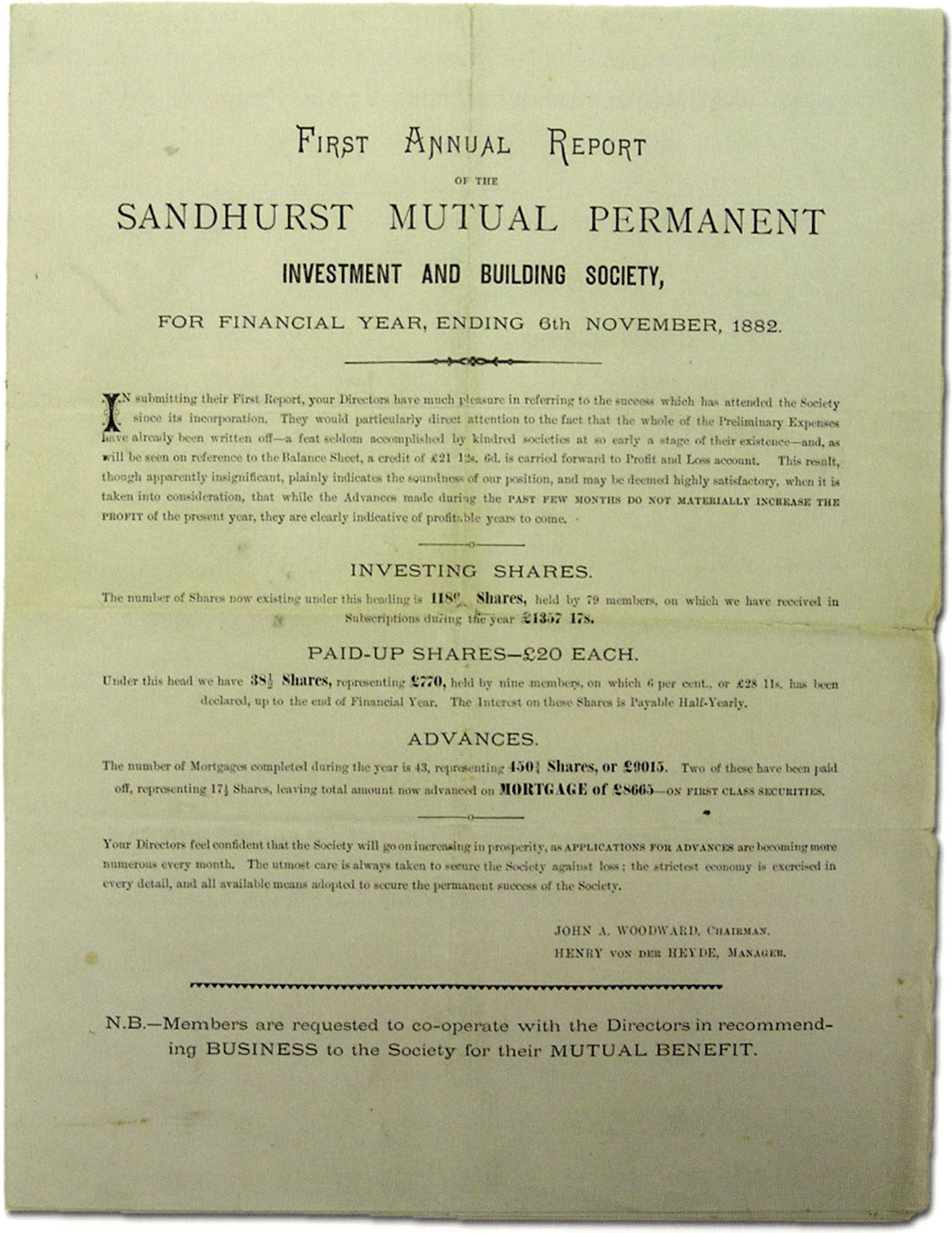

FIRST ANNUAL REPORT

OF THE

SANDHURST MUTUAL PERMANENT

INVESTMENT AND BUILDING SOCIETY,

FOR FINANCIAL YEAR, ENDING 6th NOVEMBER, 1882.

IN submitting their First Report, your Directors have much pleasure in referring to the success which has attended the Society since its incorporation. They would particularly direct attention to the fact that the whole of the Preliminary Expenses have already been written off—a feat seldom accomplished by kindred societies at so early a stage of their existence—and, as will be seen on reference to the Balance Sheet, a credit of £21 12s. 6d. is carried forward to Profit and Loss account. This result, though apparently insignificant, plainly indicates the soundness of our position, and may be deemed highly satisfactory, when it is taken into consideration, that while the Advances made during the PAST FEW MONTHS DO NOT MATERIALLY INCREASE THE PROFIT of the present year, they are clearly indicative of profitable years to come.

INVESTING SHARES.

The number of Shares now existing under this heading is **118^{9} Shares,** held by 79 members, on which we have received in Subscriptions during the year **£1357 17s.**

PAID-UP SHARES—£20 EACH.

Under this head we have **38½ Shares,** representing **£770,** held by nine members, on which 6 per cent., or £28 11s. has been declared, up to the end of Financial Year. The Interest on these Shares is Payable Half-Yearly.

ADVANCES.

The number of Mortgages completed during the year is 43, representing **450¾ Shares, or £9015.** Two of these have been paid off, representing 17½ Shares, leaving total amount now advanced on **MORTGAGE of £8665**—ON FIRST CLASS SECURITIES.

Your Directors feel confident that the Society will go on increasing in prosperity, as APPLICATIONS FOR ADVANCES are becoming more numerous every month. The utmost care is always taken to secure the Society against loss; the strictest economy is exercised in every detail, and all available means adopted to secure the permanent success of the Society.

JOHN A. WOODWARD, CHAIRMAN.
HENRY VON DER HEYDE, MANAGER.

N.B.—Members are requested to co-operate with the Directors in recommending BUSINESS to the Society for their MUTUAL BENEFIT.

Sandhurst Mutual Permanent Investment and Building Society, first annual report, 1882.

It redefined building society practice in Bendigo by introducing the mutual principle to the city, by which the Sandhurst channelled back a hefty slice of profits as interest and bonuses to all members. The Sandhurst could thereby offer radically low interest rates to borrowers, forcing Bendigo Permanent to restructure itself as a mutual society as well. The latter's more cautious lending policy was vindicated in 1889 when the Sandhurst lost heavily after being judged in the county court and later in the supreme court to have lent on the security of an incorrect certificate of title.

Sandhurst Building Society, cover page, 1893 annual report.

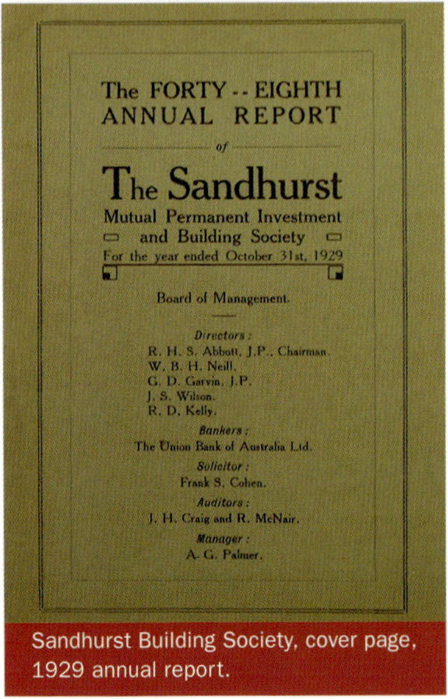

The FORTY - - EIGHTH
ANNUAL REPORT
of
The Sandhurst
Mutual Permanent Investment
and Building Society
For the year ended October 31st, 1929

Board of Management.

Directors:
R. H. S. Abbott, J.P., Chairman.
W. B. H. Neill.
G. D. Garvin, J.P.
J. S. Wilson.
R. D. Kelly.

Bankers:
The Union Bank of Australia Ltd.

Solicitor:
Frank S. Cohen.

Auditors:
J. H. Craig and R. McNair.

Manager:
A. G. Palmer.

Sandhurst Building Society, cover page, 1929 annual report.

This adverse finding seemed at the time to be a temporary hiccup, and the Sandhurst's accumulated funds reached £48,000 in 1890. Thereafter the society's position crumbled and it struggled to survive the 1890s depression, notwithstanding, or perhaps because of, its reputation as the most progressive building society in Bendigo. With the local branches of the Commercial Bank and the London Chartered Bank having already closed their doors, the society called an emergency meeting in 1893 for 'consideration of the Financial Position of the Society, in the event of the stoppage of the Society's Bankers'.[34] In 1894 the directors' fees and the manager's salary were slashed, and in 1895 the directors accepted North's offer to cut his salary further. The society clawed its way back to profitability during the first decade of the twentieth century, in 1910 regaining the funding base that it had lost after 1890. Thereafter the Sandhurst maintained steady growth, reaching £100,000 of accumulated funds in 1928–1929, more than 40 years after Bendigo Permanent had reached that milestone.

Sandhurst Trustees Limited (known until 1985 as the Sandhurst and Northern District Trustees, Executors and Agency Company) began on the initiative of John Neeson, a local mining manager and accountant, in December 1887. Neeson was also a director of the Sandhurst building society (he was a director from its establishment in 1881 until his death in 1901). Speaking on behalf of 'a number of influential gentlemen', Neeson pointed to the 'great success' of trustee operations in Melbourne and the recent successful launch of a trustee company in the rival gold-mining centre of Ballarat. He predicted that 'a similar result may be looked for here as the operations of this Company (including as it would do the whole of the Northern District) cover quite as large a field as that of the Ballarat Company'.[35] At a meeting convened by Neeson on 12 December, provisional directors were appointed (including Dr James Boyd, one of the foundation trustees for Bendigo Permanent) and Neeson was made secretary in order to form a local trustee company and advertise for shares. The share float was greatly oversubscribed, and shareholders met on 9 February 1888 to formally launch the company and appoint its board of directors. One of the largest shareholders was Joseph Abbott, a co-founder of both the Bendigo Permanent and Sandhurst building societies and currently chairman of the Sandhurst. Neeson was confirmed as manager of the new trustee company. William Davis, manager of the Colonial Bank's Bendigo branch, was elected chairman, and Boyd vice-chairman.

Dr James Boyd, a foundation trustee of Bendigo Permanent, and foundation vice-chairman of Sandhurst Trustees in 1888.

The new company was an immediate success and quickly established itself in agency work and as trustee, executor and administrator of wills and estates. In November 1891 it could afford to spend £4000 to buy the handsome former Sandhurst Post Office in View Street. The building was progressively enlarged and its main office and boardroom decked out with lush blackwood panelling. In 1895 the company became trustee for the large real-estate fortune accumulated by the late Reverend Dr Henry Backhaus, the first Roman Catholic chaplain appointed to the Victorian goldfields. Administering the Backhaus estate represented 'a significant source of basic income' for the company.[36] James McQuie became manager of Sandhurst Trustees after Neeson's death in 1901 and retained that office until 1926. J.H. Abbott junior was chairman of the company from 1912 until shortly before his death in 1946.

The Bendigo and Eaglehawk Star Permanent Society began in August 1901 as the Bendigo and Eaglehawk Starr-Bowkett Building Society. It was a minnow; its funds were a fraction of Sandhurst Permanent's, let alone those of Bendigo Permanent. It was, moreover, initially a terminating building society, though like its older and larger competitors it offered the benefits of the mutual system to its

Sandhurst Trustees office (formerly Sandhurst Post Office, 1869–1887), View Street, 1890s.

members. Its first chairman, from 1901 to 1929, was Garrett John Sweeney, an Irish immigrant who had become Bendigo's biggest timber merchant. Angus Mackay junior, co-owner of the *Advertiser* newspaper, became a director in 1904, and was chairman through most of the 1930s and 1940s. Other important early participants in the society were John B. Young and James Curnow (a mayor of Bendigo, auctioneer and businessman). However it was Edward Thomas, an accountant and Wesleyan lay preacher, who was the key mover in establishing the society and overseeing its development. Thomas acted as secretary and manager from 1901 until his retirement in 1929.

The society initially applied Starr-Bowkett principles, advising working people that 'the first and great advantage [of membership] is the right to a loan of £100 per share free of interest, which is obtained by ballot'.[37] Membership was available to 'thrifty persons' in return for an entrance fee of one shilling per share sought and a weekly subscription of one shilling per share. Members had the choice of paying their subscriptions and waiting for the luck of the draw in the regular ballot for home loans, or of bidding for additional enabling shares that were regularly offered for sale. However, at a packed meeting held at the ANA Hall in December 1910, members voted 102 to 72 to reconstitute the society as a permanent building society with investment shares, interest-fixed borrowings, and fortnightly repayments. Some members worried that under the proposed changes their hard-earned investments would be ferreted away and made inaccessible. However, George Garvin (later a director and chairman of the Sandhurst building society) responded on behalf of larger shareholders that members' capital 'was not being confiscated, but was simply being transferred from a non-earning position to an earning position'. One working man in the audience protested eloquently against these changes:

> The reason he had joined the society was because it was represented to him that he would—sooner or later—he might have to wait 14 years—get a ballot of £500 free of interest (Hear, hear). In the meantime he was to pay 1/- per week per share. He was quite satisfied to go on and pay his 1/- until his turn came . . . [The change] was going to press very hard on the working man. (Hear, hear). Many a working man

Minutes of Special General Meeting of the members of the Bendigo and Eaglehawk Starr-Bowkett Building Society held in the Masonic Hall on Friday Nov. 1st 1901

The Chairman of Directors Mr G. J. Sweeney occupied the chair and called upon the Secretary to read the minute of the Directors Meeting authorising the calling of the Special General Meeting to consider a notice of motion by Member Francis Davey viz ~~"That a~~

"That rule No. 5 be altered by the addition of the following words to paragraph 1, viz. 'Any member whose subscriptions from the date of entry shall be three fortnights in arrear on the date of the Ballot Meeting, except as provided for in rule 6 shall be deemed to be unfinancial and shall not participate in the Ballot'."

Motion — Mr Davey moved that standing in his name which was seconded by Mr J. D. Gilbert and after a short discussion carried nem. con.

Confirmation of Minutes — On the motion of Messrs Davey & Gilbert

The Meeting then closed

Confirmed Nov. 1st 1901

G J Sweeney Chairman

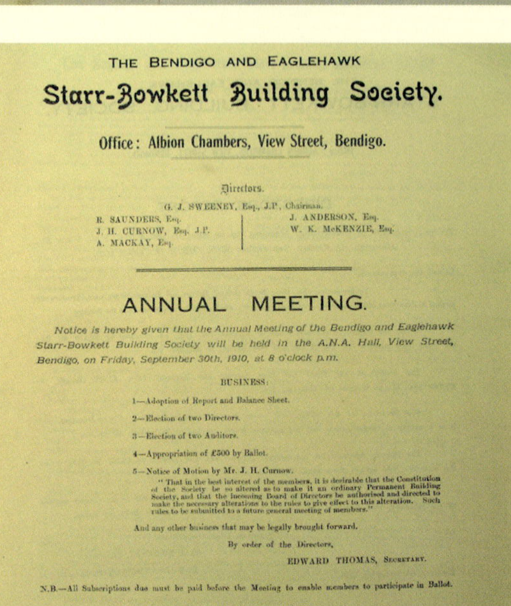

THE BENDIGO AND EAGLEHAWK

Starr-Bowkett Building Society.

Office: Albion Chambers, View Street, Bendigo.

Directors.

G. J. SWEENEY, Esq., J.P., Chairman.

R. SAUNDERS, Esq.
J. H. CURNOW, Esq. J.P.
A. MACKAY, Esq.

J. ANDERSON, Esq.
W. K. McKENZIE, Esq.

ANNUAL MEETING.

Notice is hereby given that the Annual Meeting of the Bendigo and Eaglehawk Starr-Bowkett Building Society will be held in the A.N.A. Hall, View Street, Bendigo, on Friday, September 30th, 1910, at 8 o'clock p.m.

BUSINESS:

1—Adoption of Report and Balance Sheet.

2—Election of two Directors.

3—Election of two Auditors.

4—Appropriation of £500 by Ballot.

5—Notice of Motion by Mr. J. H. Curnow.

"That in the best interest of the members, it is desirable that the Constitution of the Society be so altered as to make it an ordinary Permanent Building Society, and that the Incoming Board of Directors be authorised and directed to make the necessary alterations to the rules to give effect to this alteration. Such rules to be submitted to a future general meeting of members."

And any other business that may be legally brought forward.

By order of the Directors,

EDWARD THOMAS, Secretary.

N.B.—All Subscriptions due must be paid before the Meeting to enable members to participate in Ballot.

Above: Minutes of the Bendigo and Eaglehawk Starr-Bowkett Building Society, 1 November 1901.
Below: Bendigo and Eaglehawk Starr-Bowkett Building Society ballot barrel.
Left: Turning point: notice paper for the Bendigo and Eaglehawk Starr-Bowkett Building Society's annual meeting, 1910.

went into this simply because he thought he would have a chance of getting a loan which would enable him to put up a home of his own, and now they wanted to compel these people to pay interest for the money if they wanted it, and give them 5 per cent. on the money they had paid in. (Applause).[38]

The directors conceded that 'the founders honestly thought it was possible to establish a Starr-Bowkett Society by which every man or woman would get a ballot in 12 . . . or 14 years. But unfortunately, the directors had found the position was altogether different' and that members who clung to that hope were living in 'a fool's paradise'. Curnow warned 'that it was absolutely impossible to be able to give anything like a third of the members a ballot within 14 years, and they also honestly believed it was impossible to give the whole of the members a ballot within 30 or 40 years from now'. What false kindness was that, he asked, for 'the poor working man' to be made to pay fortnightly instalments for 14 years and then have those contributions lie idle for another 30 or 40 years in the 'hope of getting money free of interest? If these proposals were carried shares would be given bearing interest straight away'.[39]

The new structure and the name change to Bendigo and Eaglehawk Star Permanent Society took effect from 1911. The directors conceded at the end of that year that the society's 'drastic change' in character had resulted in 'some considerable displacement of Funds',[40] but the restructuring was quickly shown to be a fillip for capital growth and in 1920 the Star, with some £35,000 of capital to draw upon, was in a position to buy the smaller Commercial Permanent Land and Building Society. In 1929 Thomas retired as secretary and became a director of the society, the position of secretary being taken over by his son Edward Travis Thomas. As father and son changed places on the eve of the Great Depression, the Star had built up its capital reserves to over £50,000, about half that of Sandhurst and almost one-eighth that of Bendigo Permanent. At Bendigo Permanent, Balsillie in 1928 said of the Star and the Sandhurst that '[their] combined funds are slightly over one third of ours'.[41]

Structural change

As the Star's soul-searching in 1910 highlights, two of the most significant developments in Bendigo's early building societies were their structural shift to permanency and the subsequent adjustment of their capital management processes to support this shift. Both changes reveal a widening division of expectation between low-income investors, whose lifetime goal was saving to buy a modest home, and higher-income investors who wanted a clear return on their money. The changes also reveal how the broader dynamics of private capital investment in Australia during the nineteenth and early twentieth centuries were played out in an important regional community. During the nineteenth century, private investment capital in the Australian colonies was sourced both from Britain and locally, and was mobilised by governments, banks, and the building and friendly societies. Most of the capital for government public works was raised on the British money market, and British investment capital also flooded into the emerging Australian banking system. Trading banks dominated British and local private capital investment. But as building societies metamorphosed into permanent financial organisations, they competed fiercely with savings banks for the remaining share of Australia's capital market. Building societies were decimated by the 1890s depression and thereafter wary small investors preferred the government-protected savings banks. State savings banks and the Commonwealth Savings Bank, established in 1912, grew rapidly during the early twentieth century, eclipsing building societies and rivalling trading banks for deposits. Trading banks and savings banks underpinned Australian economic growth by lending to pastoralists, farmers, and mining companies. However, building societies controlled residential financing until the 1890s depression, a

Bendigo Permanent's headquarters, 1887.

period during which investment in home building was a major driver of domestic private capital accumulation, and of improvements in housing quality which translated into high and widely shared levels of social well-being for Australians.

The shift by Bendigo's building societies to a permanent structure necessitated the creation of permanent reserves to guard against emergencies. Bendigo Permanent had learned the need for a substantial permanent reserve fund when it was under financial pressure during the 1870s as a result of being drained of capital by the investment boom in mining shares, and later in the decade when a trough in the mining and wool industries, and drought, hurt the general economy and undermined the local building industry. Vahland spoke gloomily in 1878 about 'the depressed state of the district', and he and his fellow directors resolved to set aside each year a slice from the society's profits to build up a contingency or reserve fund.[42] The collapse of Melbourne banks and building societies during the 1890s depression reinforced the society's determination to build up its reserve fund in order to 'weather' such 'wave[s] of financial trouble',[43] and from 1893 onwards the society maintained more capital in reserves than it committed to borrowers. The society's efforts to drought-proof itself further entrenched this thinking. Vahland commented in 1896 that 'the continued bad seasons had necessitated the strengthening of the Contingent Fund for probable losses'.[44] His successor, Busst, claimed in 1928 that this 'careful building up of its reserves' over the years was 'making the Institution a Gilt edged investment'.[45] Bendigo's other building societies imitated Bendigo Permanent. The Star drew attention in 1920 to its transformation from a terminating Starr-Bowkett society 'without capital' into a permanent business with a secure reserve fund 'as a base of operations'.[46]

Behind this quest for permanent structure and permanent capital reserves lay the development of processes to mobilise a dependable supply of investment capital sufficient not only to secure defensive reserves, but also to deliver attractive profits and sustain continuing business growth. As the debate in 1910 over the Star's restructuring dramatised, the methods of terminating building societies, aimed at the short-term mobilisation of investment capital, were incapable of permanently marshalling and harnessing investment capital. The problem facing Bendigo's building societies was how to generate a dependable flow of investment capital to meet local demand for home building and business growth. Vahland had early recognised this challenge when he conceded to shareholders at Bendigo Permanent's annual meeting in November 1879 that local demand for advances 'still greatly exceeds the power of your Directors to supply'.[47] In order to escape from this impasse, the building societies experimented with four strategies for raising capital: maturing shares, bank overdrafts, fixed-term and at-call deposits, and permanent shares.

Medium-term maturing shares were a carryover from the practices of terminating building societies. Maturing shares evolved into two types: 'contributing' and 'prepaid' (or 'paid-up') maturing shares. Contributing shares could be purchased with a small entrance fee and follow-up monthly or fortnightly instalments; shareholders received interest and could withdraw their accumulated capital. 'Prepaid' shares enabled investors to make an initial up-front payment in lieu of regular contributions. The method that Burnside (Bendigo Permanent's first secretary) devised for distinguishing between the interest payable on prepaid and contributing shares was challenged by an investor in 1883, and the case was resolved in the Supreme Court in April 1884. The case threatened the viability of Victorian building societies as investment institutions, but the Supreme Court—while acknowledging that Burnside's method corresponded more to the superseded Friendly Societies Act of 1865 than to the Building Societies Act of 1874 under which the society was now supposed to operate—ruled in favour of Bendigo Permanent. The court ruling nonetheless required that building society rules be revised, elaborated, and strictly followed.

Thereafter Bendigo Permanent offered contributing shares that could be purchased by paying an entrance fee of two shillings and sixpence per share and monthly subscriptions of five shillings per share, the balance being redeemable at any time on one month's notice. Once subscriptions and accumulating interest reached £50, over about six years, the shares matured and were paid out. Members not wishing to commit to monthly payments could instead choose prepaid maturing shares, paying £30 per share up front, and watching the interest accumulate until the share reached £50 in value and matured. The society's 1892 annual report, using the eye-catching headline 'TO INVESTORS! / HOW TO BECOME RICH', calculated that one contributing share purchased in 1865 and thereafter reinvested in prepaid shares would by 1892 have required payments of £162 and returned a profit of over £572.[48] The attractiveness of these shares to potential homebuyers suffered as a result of the 1896 Companies Act, which halted building societies' previous practice of offering home loans against the future maturing value of contributing shares. As Bendigo Permanent acknowledged in its 1898 annual report, the amount invested in contributing shares had fallen and the shares were more frequently withdrawn. However, maturing shares remained popular with small investors. In 1916, under the headline 'Systematic Saving the Surest Source of Wealth', the society recalculated the return over 51 years of six pounds per year invested in contributing shares, and declared a profit to the canny investor of £3162.[49]

The Sandhurst also offered contributing and paid-up shares, capped at £20 per share and maturing over approximately 10 years. In 1924 Richard Abbott called the contributing shares 'a specially good method for any one desiring to put away ten shillings or a pound a fortnight, or any other small odd sums'.[50] They were popular with members, and together with paid-up shares comprised between 70 and 80 per cent of the society's share capital throughout this period. They were, however, an unpredictable capital supply. When Abbott spoke glowingly of them in 1924, maturing shares as a proportion of deposits in the society had dropped to a low point of 23 per cent compared to a high point of 51 per cent in 1907, and in 1929 they made up 39 per cent of all deposits in the society. The first large batch of shares matured in 1891 as the society celebrated its tenth anniversary and they were hailed as having 'proved a really good investment'.[51] Another large parcel of shares matured in 1903. The directors boasted that they represented a 'safe and profitable investment which was unrivalled',[52] but as the shares matured the challenge facing the society—and evident in all three societies' public pronouncements about handsome investment returns—was to induce shareholders to reinvest their profits. Although maturing shares generated ample capital inflows, they were volatile. The investment capital was not reliably locked in.

'Mining Revival at Sandhurst—the Beehive', *Illustrated Australian News*, 16 May 1883. The landmark Beehive Store and Mining Exchange in Pall Mall opened in 1852 and was rebuilt in 1871. LA TROBE PICTURE COLLECTION, STATE LIBRARY OF VICTORIA.

E HIVE

Bendigo Permanent had confronted this problem from the outset of its operations. In 1867, and again in the following year, the directors expressed 'regret that the profits are not quite so large as was anticipated which is mainly attributable to the large number of investing shares that have been withdrawn' because of competing investment opportunities. The directors were so worried that this was eroding capital growth that they halved the secretary's salary and their own fees.[53] The society's woes intensified during the 1870s as a result of the drain on investment capital caused by the boom in gold-mining shares. At Bendigo Permanent's annual meeting of shareholders in November 1871, the directors reported that the previous 12 months had been 'marked by great speculation in mining, which naturally caused a number of investing shares to be withdrawn'.[54] In 1880 Secretary Herman warned that the society would need to increase its bank overdraft in order to make up for the capital about to be lost by the maturing of another large batch of shares.

Bank overdrafts negotiated with the local managers of the trading banks were the second means used by building societies to raise short-term capital and underwrite the sustained growth of their loan advances. However, their ability to use this strategy to expand their business was constrained by two tensions: the capping of overdrafts by each bank's head office in Melbourne, and the tight margin between the interest rate charged by the banks and that charged by the societies for loans. These frictions resulted in the continual lobbying of local bank managers and threats to move business to rival banks as the societies sought to increase their overdrafts and obtain easier terms. In 1878 the directors of Bendigo Permanent resorted to the high-risk strategy of signing personal guarantees in order to increase the society's overdraft from the Colonial Bank. This strategy was imitated during the 1880s by their colleagues in the newly formed Sandhurst. Less sanguine about personal guarantees, and irked by the 'monstrous interest' payable on their overdraft,[55] the directors of Bendigo Permanent switched business to the Commercial Bank in 1880, lured by the offer of a £10,000 overdraft, but they continued to urge reductions in the bank's interest rate. Exasperated, in 1883 the Commercial Bank requested the society 'to make other arrangements for the society's Banking arrangements, owing to the numerous demands made upon the Bank and regretting that occasion should have arisen for the severance of business connections between the two institutions'.[56] The society's directors then flirted with a third bank, the Union Bank, but shied away from its demand for personal guarantees from the directors in order to secure an overdraft. The society resumed its relationship with the Commercial Bank, and indeed maintained it (notwithstanding the Bank's temporary closure during the 1890s depression) for the next century. On the eve of the Great Depression, the society maintained a £25,000 overdraft with the bank in Bendigo and smaller overdrafts in Melbourne and Geelong. The Sandhurst and Star building societies both operated overdrafts through the Union Bank and, like their larger competitor, frequently negotiated with the bank and its rivals to secure better terms. The associated stresses perhaps contributed to the hesitation of all Bendigo building societies to over-extend their loan making. As the directors of Bendigo Permanent reported to shareholders in 1892, they 'continued to conduct the society on the strictest lines of safety, and have rather restricted than extended the business during the year, preferring to keep a substantial credit balance than have an overdraft at our Bankers'.[57]

Raising capital: cover page of Bendigo Permanent's 1887 annual report.

Short-term and at-call deposits were the third and most important source of capital for Bendigo's early building societies. At the Sandhurst, for example, term deposits and deposits at call represented 51 per cent of all deposits in 1929, and during the early 1920s they had accounted for close to 70 per cent of deposits. They enabled building societies to tap into what Busst called in 1915 'the weekly savings of the thrifty, [and] the riches of the wealthy'.[58] Bendigo Permanent had since 1870 systematised this essentially ad hoc form of investment, targeting those who did not like the regular share payment instalments normally required by building societies, by offering interest-bearing fixed-term deposits for periods of three to 12 months. The other societies followed Bendigo Permanent's lead. By inviting periodic investments drawn from the 'saving[s] of the working classes', Bendigo Permanent argued as early as 1867 that it offered working people greater benefits than could savings banks.[59] In pursuing this strategy, building societies were, in fact, beginning to operate as proto-banks, and indeed by the 1870s and 1880s Victorian building societies rivalled savings banks as savings institutions. This rivalry had been played out in Bendigo since the creation of permanent building societies. Castlemaine and Bendigo were the first goldfield communities in Victoria to open savings bank branches when the Victorian Government established the Commissioners of Savings Banks in 1855. Moreover, in 1865 the government established a Post Office Savings Bank as well, copying from British precedents, which enabled post offices to accept deposits in communities that had no savings bank of their own. In 1870, when Bendigo Permanent began to offer term deposits, they accounted for only 11 per cent of investments in the society, the other 89 per cent coming from shares. However in 1886 Bendigo Permanent began to compete directly with savings banks, expanding its principle of fixed deposits 'to a small degree' by establishing a 'Savings Branch' where small-scale depositors could open at-call accounts with a minimum balance of one pound.[60] Thereafter, at-call and fixed-term deposits always comprised (with the exception of 1893, in the midst of the 1890s depression) at least half of investments in the society. In 1929 they formed 63 per cent of investments, as against 37 per cent from shares. Bendigo Permanent's savings accounts had by 1892 accumulated over £20,000 in deposits, which was about half the total investments that year in the rival Sandhurst society. By 1911 the savings accounts had attached chequebooks 'as in Banks'.[61] The Sandhurst and the Star likewise established 'Savings Bank' accounts during 1908 'in which large or small sums may be placed as Deposits at Call'.[62]

The Star had argued since its establishment in 1901 'that the society acts as a savings bank, the subscriptions of the members being ultimately returned to them, together with a proper share of any profit that may be earned by the society'.[63] This was a necessary stance to adopt in response to fierce competition from the savings bank sector. In 1897, reacting to the financial meltdown in Melbourne during the depression, the Victorian Government guaranteed depositors in savings banks and amalgamated the Commissioners of Savings Banks with the Post Office Savings Bank, creating a single entity that in 1912 was renamed the State Savings Bank of Victoria. It was energetically led between 1897 and 1929 by George Emery, a Castlemaine-born second-generation product of the gold-rush revolution. Emery's energy was sorely needed for the State Savings Bank to compete not only with the trading banks and building societies, but also with the new Commonwealth Savings Bank that Prime Minister Andrew Fisher established in 1912 as a national savings bank.

Notwithstanding the volume of investments that they generated, Bendigo building societies' fixed-term and at-call deposits were a still more volatile method of raising and retaining capital than were maturing shares. The societies worried especially that large-scale investors could at any moment withdraw their funds to obtain better returns elsewhere. In 1887, for example, Herman advised that

Mining metropolis: Bendigo from the New Chum mine, *Illustrated Australian News*, 26 May 1888.
LA TROBE PICTURE COLLECTION, STATE LIBRARY OF VICTORIA.

dissatisfaction with the interest rate being offered on fixed deposits was translating into a drain on funds, and warned that several large deposits were in jeopardy. At the Sandhurst, Abbott raised concerns in 1894 about 'the stability of the Society' if prominent local businessman John B. Young were to withdraw a deposit of some £4000.[64] The uncertainty surrounding the reliability of fixed-term deposits was highlighted in 1896 when the Victorian Parliament, responding to the financial crisis in Melbourne, challenged the very basis of Victorian building societies' ability to take deposits. Alarmed, Bendigo Permanent and the Sandhurst put strong counter arguments to the Legislative Council select committee appointed to consider proposals 'to deprive Building Societies of the right of taking Deposits'.[65] Although that possibility was averted, the 1896 Companies Act did impose significantly tighter restrictions on building society deposits.

Permanent shares were the fourth means of raising capital. In order to maintain investments and build business, Bendigo's permanent building societies had to tap local capital in more enduring ways. It was a slow transition. Bendigo Permanent drove the change, stung in part by the flow-on effects of the downturn in mining and the retraction in Bendigo property values during the late 1870s and early 1880s, and in part by the competition it faced from the newly established Sandhurst building society. The change was hatched in 1883 by Vahland and Herman, who urged upon the directors the need for 'liberalising' the society in response to the 'great falling off in the local industries', and identified the creation of 'a permanent capital' by issuing permanent paid-up shares in place of maturing shares as the chief instrument for doing so.[66] Shareholders could sell their permanent shares to other buyers, but they could not withdraw their value from the society. Opinions about this proposal were divided, and after lengthy discussion by the directors a final decision was deferred. It was not until September 1884 that the society agreed to issue £5000 worth of non-withdrawable £10 'permanent paid up investing shares', to be paid off by fortnightly instalments, in order 'to strengthen the stability of the Society'.[67]

Herman, keen to extend the society's permanent capital, regarded this share issue as only a first step. He visited Melbourne's building societies during 1887 to study the best means of further 'permanentizing . . . the society's invested capital', and in 1888 proposed a bold plan to give 'a back bone to the society' by converting its share capital into two-thirds permanent and one-third maturing shares. Herman conceded that 'if it were not for the fact that I think it best to encourage the small investors because they are factors in recommending loans, & generally making the society popular, the best mode would have been to fix the capital entirely in permanent shares' targeted at large investors who wanted the peace of mind of a regular dividend.[68] Herman's proposal was postponed. In 1894, arguing the case for a further issue of £10 permanent paid-up shares, Vahland echoed the words of the now-disgraced Herman, contending that they 'formed the backbone of the society and could not be withdrawn. A large sum was payable annually for the ordinary matured contributing and prepaid shares, the greater portion of which was generally re-invested in the society in new shares or deposits. [However] if the matured shares were all taken away, the balance at the bank would

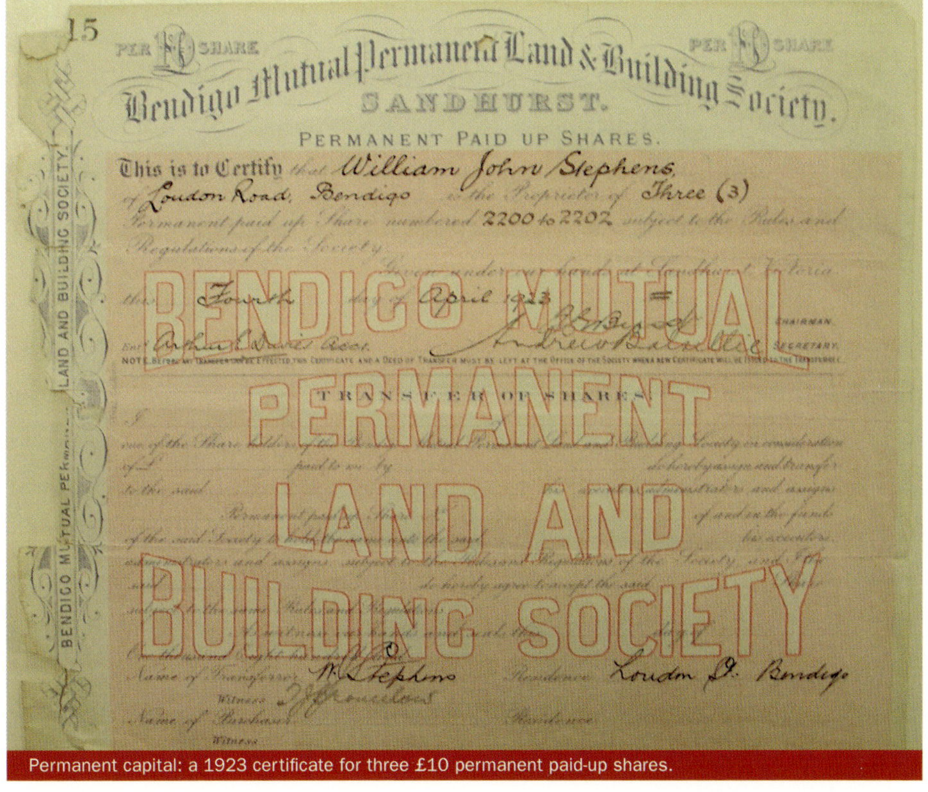

15

PER £10 SHARE

Bendigo Mutual Permanent Land & Building Society.

SANDHURST.

PER £10 SHARE

PERMANENT PAID UP SHARES.

This is to Certify that William John Stephens of Loudon Road, Bendigo is the Proprietor of Three (3) Permanent paid up Shares numbered 2200 to 2202 subject to the Rules and Regulations of the Society.

this Fourth day of April 1923

CHAIRMAN.

SECRETARY.

TRANSFER OF SHARES.

Name of Transferror W. Stephens Residence Loudon St. Bendigo

Witness

Name of Purchaser Residence

Witness

BENDIGO MUTUAL PERMANENT LAND AND BUILDING SOCIETY

BENDIGO MUTUAL PERMANENT LAND AND BUILDING SOCIETY.

Permanent capital: a 1923 certificate for three £10 permanent paid-up shares.

disappear'.[69] There was no immediate consensus. Opposing the issuing of further permanent shares in 1925, Lansell countered 'that the Contributing Shares should be encouraged as this had been a great incentive to encourage thrift'. Other directors responded that 'the conversion of withdrawable capital into Permanent Capital' was essential for the society's long-term growth.[70] The society eventually resolved in 1927 to issue a further £25,000 worth of £10 permanent shares, and to halt the reinvestment of maturing shares beyond late 1929. As Bendigo Permanent noted in 1930, 'The Society for some years past has adopted a policy of stabilizing its Capital by permitting the conversion of withdrawable maturing Shares into Permanent Paid-up £10 Shares with beneficial results, and after the payment of this year's matured Prepaid Shares, there will remain a very trifling number to deal with'.[71]

Change was slower still at the Sandhurst. The society cautiously introduced a limited number of £5 permanent paid-up shares in 1885, but plans in 1890 to issue more were shelved with the onset of the depression. The Star's conversion into a permanent society in 1911, and the restructuring of its shareholder base in favour of £5 permanent paid-up shares rather than maturing shares, were watched with interest by the Sandhurst. In 1912 Richard Abbott suggested a further issue of Sandhurst permanent shares, but it was not until December 1914 that the society finally agreed to offer 4000 permanent shares to investing members who wished to convert their maturing shares. In 1928, responding to Bendigo Permanent's latest share issue, the society moved to offer more permanent shares and to limit the number of maturing shares, which had grown strongly since the mid 1920s. As Abbott explained, 'Nearly all building societies were finding it necessary to increase their permanent capital, and to provide for these shares, if possible, to be converted into permanent capital'.[72] In 1929, the society capped the interest payable on its maturing shares, and offered incentives to convert them into permanent shares.

Notwithstanding this switch away from unsecured investment capital, by the time of the Great Depression Bendigo's largest building societies still depended on capital that could be easily withdrawn. In 1929, Sandhurst's investment capital was made up almost equally of deposits (£43,000 or 51 per cent) and shares (£42,000 or 49 per cent), almost 80 per cent of which were maturing rather than permanent shares. The proportions had been much the same in 1889, just before the 1890s depression, when deposits comprised 53 per cent of investments and shares 47 per cent (83 per cent of which were maturing shares). Permanent shares grew only slowly as a proportion of total deposits in the society, from around eight per cent in 1889 to ten per cent in 1929. Bendigo Permanent's much larger pool of investments was made up in 1929 of fixed-term and at-call deposits (representing 63 per cent of investment capital in the society) and shares (37 per cent). In spite of Herman's and Vahland's efforts, this represented a slight erosion of the position 40 years earlier, just before the 1890s depression, when deposits formed 59 per cent and shares 41 per cent of investments.

Although Bendigo's building societies had succeeded in harnessing significant local investment flows as they evolved from terminating into permanent organisations between 1858 and 1929, by the Great Depression their operations remained tied to the volatilities of short-term investments. The Star's funds more than doubled from £23,000 in 1911 to £52,000 in 1931. Sandhurst's increased from some £43,000 before the 1890s depression to £103,000 when Wall Street crashed in 1929. Bendigo Permanent increased its investment funds from under £4000 in 1870 to £31,000 at the time of Sandhurst's launch in 1881, £165,000 when Star Permanent was launched in 1911, and £407,000 by 1929. But as all three societies made advances each year to borrowers, cautiously exceeding their annual inflow of investments, the uncertain equilibrium between neighbourhood investment supply and borrowing demand was a source of anxiety for all of Bendigo's building societies.

Using capital locally

What happened to the local investment capital that was mobilised by Bendigo's early building societies? There was no business logic in moving beyond the immediate horizons of terminating mutual benefit societies, and accumulate permanent capital reserves and generating open-ended flows of capital, unless this pooled investment capital could be harnessed to generate significantly increased profits for the business and to deliver clear social benefits to members. Thus the key issue that faced the managers of Bendigo's building societies was to match their capital supply with local business demand. There was an important social issue to be faced as well. Bendigo's building societies were distinguished from savings banks less by interest rate benefits than by neighbourly mutualism. There was no neighbourly logic in investing locally if locally generated capital was not employed for local social benefit. The *Bendigo Advertiser* complained in 1858 that all deposits in the local savings bank were sent to Melbourne for reinvestment, 'thus depriving the district of the advantages which should result from its own economy'.[73] Could building societies do better, combining robust business growth with the delivery of sustained local social benefits?

For home affordability, the answer seemed to be yes. Building society capital was primarily reinvested in land purchase and home building, and in 1894 Vahland emphasised that 'Since its establishment [Bendigo Permanent] had paid £88,200 in dividends, and enabled thousands of families to build or purchase houses, so that the society had done a deal of good for the district as well as the members of the society'.[74] In 1909 Bendigo Permanent again drew attention to the 'good that [was being] done to the district by keeping the savings of the people in our midst'.[75] Loans were secured against property or the value of the borrowers' building society

'This would be a typical home in 1865'. Bendigo Permanent, *Diamond Jubilee, 1865–1925: Sixtieth Annual Balance.*

shares. Borrowing shares were offered at £20 each, payable over ten to 12 years at 2/6 per share per fortnight. Payments could be suspended during periods of sickness or unemployment. The Bendigo societies built up a large home-loan business from tiny beginnings. In 1866, its first full year of operations as a permanent building society, Bendigo Permanent advanced barely £3000 to borrowers. In 1881, the year in which Sandhurst became a permanent society, Bendigo Permanent had £31,000 in advances on its ledgers. By 1911, the Star's first year as a permanent building society, Bendigo Permanent's advances had risen to £169,000 and by 1929 its loans were nudging £425,000. The combined loans of its competitors were less than a third of that amount. The Sandhurst's loan accounts in 1929 totalled £90,000 and the Star's stood at around £50,000. The Star's lendings had roughly doubled since it became a permanent society in 1911. Forty-three of the Sandhurst's members (about half its total) had loans from the society in 1882; five years later that number had increased to 164 members. The society's loans peaked at £63,000 during 1891, but halved by 1897 and did not exceed its 1891 record until 1913.

There had been three impediments to building society lending growth during these years. Firstly, the Building Societies Act of 1874 limited each building society's advances to three times its paid-up capital (a restriction which further influenced Bendigo Permanent and the Sandhurst to enlarge their share capital). Secondly, the 1896 Companies Act prevented investing shareholders from borrowing more than nine-tenths of the paper value of their shares, thus removing an important incentive for membership of building societies. Thirdly, building societies faced fierce competition from the State Savings Bank of Victoria after George Emery took the bank's helm in 1897. As Sandhurst's directors conceded in 1928, the 'society had a strong competitor in the State Savings Bank, which had a lot of money under its control, and was in a position to advance moneys at lower rates of interest than anyone else'.[76] Residential construction was nonetheless one of the most important elements driving the Australian economy and increasing the social well-being of its members, and its major funding source came from the building societies.

At the time of the First World War, Bendigo Permanent released an advertising booklet with the cover title 'Own Your Own Home. Stop Paying Rent', which

'A popular present-day home', 1925. Bendigo Permanent, *Diamond Jubilee, 1865–1925: Sixtieth Annual Balance.*

claimed that since 'the inception of this Society over 14,000 persons have accomplished the desire of owning their own homes'.[77] During its Diamond Jubilee celebrations in 1925, Bendigo Permanent calculated more conservatively that since 1865 it had financed the purchase or construction of some 8000 homes, and that over 1000 borrowers were currently purchasing or building homes through the society.[78]

In 1891 the society's annual report had drawn attention to 'How a Building Society helps a man to purchase a House for Himself', and in 1902 its advertisements asked 'WHY PAY RENT, when you can purchase the house you occupy, or build a new one, and the fortnightly repayments will be no heavier than your former rental?'[79] Borrowers were advised in 1916 that a home loan would 'PROVIDE A HOME FOR YOUR FAMILY' and by breaking the cycle of rent payments would put borrowers 'on the road to prosperity'. They were reminded in 1918: 'WHY DO YOU PAY RENT? When with the Society's assistance you can apply your rent to the purchase of a *home*, and thus become *your own landlord*.'[80]

'Nice cottages. . . for 10/- per week. . . Why Pay Rent?' Sandhurst Mutual Permanent Investment and Building Society, *23rd Yearly Balance. 31st October, 1904.*

The master of home-loan advertising, however, was the smaller Sandhurst. During the early twentieth century it showcased how its loans made every style of home affordable to its members, as the advertisements reproduced here graphically illustrate.

The Sandhurst's trump card in the home-lending market was the mutual

THE SANDHURST MUTUAL PERMANENT INVESTMENT AND BUILDING SOCIETY

VIEW POINT, BENDIGO

Comfortable homes, containing 4 rooms, bath, front and back verandahs, 11/3 per week, paying principal and interest.

Why Pay Rent?

'Comfortable homes, . . . 11/3 per week. . . Why Pay Rent?' Sandhurst Mutual Permanent Investment and Building Society, *23rd Yearly Balance, 31st October, 1904.*

THE SANDHURST MUTUAL PERMANENT INVESTMENT AND BUILDING SOCIETY

VIEW POINT, BENDIGO

Nice homes like this, five rooms, front and back verandahs, 12/6 per week, paying principal and interest.

Why Pay Rent?

'Nice homes. . . , 12/6 per week. . . Why Pay Rent?' Sandhurst Mutual Permanent Investment and Building Society, *23rd Yearly Balance, 31st October, 1904.*

THE SANDHURST MUTUAL PERMANENT INVESTMENT AND BUILDING SOCIETY

Handsome houses, similar to engraving, 5 rooms, bath, with front and back verandahs, 13s. 9d. per week, paying principal and interest.

Why Pay Rent?

'Handsome houses, . . . 13/9 per week. . . Why Pay Rent?' Sandhurst Mutual Permanent Investment and Building Society, *22nd Yearly Balance, 31st October, 1903.* [81]

system. The society had introduced the system to Bendigo on its establishment as a mutual permanent building society in 1881. The mutual system was copied from Melbourne, and corrected the discrimination by early permanent building societies against borrowers in favour of investors. In the older system only investing members shared in a society's profits, but under the mutual system all members were shareholders and thus the borrowing member was also recognised as 'a partner'[82] and participated in the distribution of annual bonuses. The Sandhurst thus spoke with credibility when it proclaimed: 'Become your own *landlord*, and prove that *rent* is *double* what you pay in *interest for a loan!*'[83] Speaking at the annual meeting of shareholders in December 1920, Richard Abbott astutely noted that the mutual system was well suited to the aspirations of 'young people anxious to begin making a home of their own', and he emphasised that thanks to the bonuses the society paid back to its members 'there are instances where the interest charge for the year has been entirely wiped out'.[84] The principle of mutual benefit was taken still further by the Star between 1901 and 1910, when it promised all its shareholders 'the right to a loan of £100 per share free of interest, which is obtained by ballot'.[85] The Star's advertisements were eye-catching: 'Makes advances to Members FREE of INTEREST by Ballot!'[86] The society's radical nature was wound back when it became a permanent society in 1911, and its 'ballot loans' were phased out in 1919.[87]

In 1884 Bendigo Permanent also adopted the mutual system, albeit reluctantly, in response to the Sandhurst's competition. In doing so it explicitly copied from its newer, smaller rival. Herman and Vahland had proposed the change in 1883 but the other directors were hesitant. In 1884 Herman asked them to reconsider the matter, pointing out that the society was losing business to the Sandhurst, which was growing rapidly because of the 'hold the system has taken of the public mind'.[88] Vahland again backed his secretary, explaining that the mutual system would 'popularise [the Society] among all classes of people requiring accommodation on the easiest terms'.[89] At a special meeting of shareholders in September 1884, the proposal was formally accepted by the society, which also endorsed a change of name to the Bendigo Mutual Permanent Land and Building Society.

But even the new mutual system could not entirely solve a nagging problem that was beginning to perplex the managers of Bendigo's permanent building societies: how to generate sufficient borrowing demand for the investment capital on hand. In recommending reform in 1884, Herman had also pointed to a downturn in Bendigo's economy and a corresponding dip in loan applications. Despite its advertising pitch to homeowners, Bendigo Permanent had always offered loans to investors in residential property as well as to owner-occupiers. Even so the society struggled to match capital supply with local demand for housing. During the 1890s and the early 1900s especially, as a result in part of protracted drought and declining gold yields on the local economy, Bendigo Permanent found itself with more funds than it could employ. The society sought to rein in investments by reducing interest rates on deposits, and urged shareholders to help the society find new business. Vahland warned shareholders in 1898 that 'considerably more money had come to hand than could be disposed of to borrowers', and in subsequent years as the Federation Drought worsened, he reiterated his concern that too much 'cash in hand' was hurting the society's profitability.[90]

The problem Vahland faced was more fundamental than a passing recession in the local economy. The supply of capital being raised through shares and deposit accounts in Bendigo was greater than could be profitably re-employed to meet the local demand for housing. This imbalance was highlighted by the turn-of-the-century difficulties faced by the Sandhurst, the building society that had introduced to Bendigo the concept of mutual reward for investors and borrowers. The society reluctantly refused to accept new deposits 'in consequence of our inability to find an outlet for money offered on deposit', bewailing the fact that 'the estimation in which the society is held by capitalists has led to the supply being considerably in excess of demand'.[91] Such deposits, the society realised, represented 'idle money'.[92] The Sandhurst also reduced its interest rate on repayments, offering the cheapest loans in the district in order to generate more business. From 1911 onwards, as deposits continued to outstrip demand, the society began to invest considerable sums in state and Commonwealth debentures. At annual meetings throughout the 1920s, Sandhurst's directors urged shareholders to recommend its home loans to their acquaintances in order to expand advances.

The social benefit to Bendigo from neighbourhood investment in housing was not translating into robust business growth for the city's building societies. They responded to the ceiling in home loan demand by simultaneously seeking additional local markets for investment capital. Bendigo Permanent's predecessor, the Sandhurst Land, Building and Investment Society, had granted non-residential loans to local businessmen during the early 1860s. As Bendigo's building societies transmuted into permanent investment societies, they necessarily became significant lenders to both small and large businesses, happily playing second fiddle to the bankers and share brokers who supplied capital to mining and industry. Bendigo Pottery, for example, regularly borrowed from and invested in the Sandhurst. Lending to local shopkeepers and publicans quickly became an important business avenue for all the Bendigo building societies. In this way they continued to lock local investment capital into the sustained development of Bendigo and its immediate region. It was said of the Sandhurst in 1886 that its investment activities had 'undoubtedly [acted as] powerful aids to prosperity and progress, by keeping capital in the district'.[93]

However local diversification of their client base still left the Bendigo building societies dependent on the health of the local economy. Moreover, the capital needs of local home building and the investment opportunities in business development, even combined, did not match the Bendigo building societies' successes in generating investment capital. As the Sandhurst's directors reported in 1905:

> The want of suitable securities has been keenly felt. The Society's resources are such as can supply all the demands which the district may make, but the absence of applications such as the Directors could see their way to accept has limited the business of the year. The Directors will be very glad of the assistance of members in the introduction of new business.[94]

Expansion into Melbourne

The only lasting solution to the constraint imposed on the Bendigo building societies by local business opportunities was to expand their investment horizons

Melbourne's early growth corridors: Yarraville railway station, postcard, 1890. LA TROBE PICTURE COLLECTION, STATE LIBRARY OF VICTORIA.

beyond Bendigo, and by the early twentieth century their gaze began to turn to Melbourne where many of the gold-rush generation had moved after retiring.

Bendigo Bank's apparently early associations with Melbourne derive in part from the activities of independent Melbourne building societies whose archives have been incorporated into those of Bendigo Bank as a result of subsequent business mergers. The Standard Building and Investment Society (later the Standard Mutual Building Society), for example, was established in 1872 and, in 1904, was subsumed within the new Federal Building Society. The County of Bourke Permanent Building and Investment Society was formed in 1875. Both societies would combine in 1959. The Argus Permanent Building and Investment Society was established in 1888 (and became the Colonial Mutual Permanent Building Society in 1980). All these Melbourne-based building societies were eventually taken over by the Geelong-based Capital Building Society, which in turn was taken over by Bendigo Permanent in 1992. The records of all these societies are now stored in the archives of Bendigo Bank.

Bendigo's building societies quickly developed their own direct links with Melbourne. Some were the result of the personal associations there of many of the societies' directors, several of whom retired to the capital city. Burrowes, Clark, Joseph Abbott, and Lansell were elected to parliament and acted as intermediaries on behalf of the building societies. Occasionally Bendigo-based business clients provided business opportunities in Melbourne. In 1887 Bendigo Pottery, a close business partner of the Sandhurst, obtained an advance on property it held in Melbourne. Sometimes Melbourne business clients approached the Bendigo societies for loans. In 1919, for example, the Sandhurst approved a large loan of £3250 for a 'Motor Garage and 2 storey brick shops, workroom etc in course of construction, at Glenferrie Road, Malvern'.[95]

Moonee Ponds, c. 1925. RUTH HOLLICK COLLECTION, STATE LIBRARY OF VICTORIA.

The bulk of the societies' loans in Melbourne were for home building. The rapid expansion of Melbourne's suburbs during the inter-war period was largely financed by the State Savings Bank. By the mid 1920s the Bank had become the largest home builder in Victoria, but even it was struggling to meet the growing demand for suburban homes. The Star and the Sandhurst quickly acted upon this new neighbourhood demand for housing, responding in part to inquiries about home loans from Bendigo locals relocating to Melbourne. Both societies began to generate significant home and business lending in Melbourne during the 1910s and 1920s, especially in the high-growth north-western suburban band of Northcote,

Brunswick, Coburg, North Carlton, Moonee Ponds, Essendon, Ascot Vale, Newmarket, Footscray, and Yarraville. In 1910 the Sandhurst began to advertise regularly in Melbourne's *Age* newspaper and appointed a well-connected Melbourne agent, the MLC W.H. Edgar. In 1912, and again in 1919, the Sandhurst carefully reviewed the extent of its investments in city and suburban Melbourne property to assess 'the advisability of doing business and extending operations in Melbourne & suburbs'.[96] In addition to their core business in the working-class western and northern suburbs, both societies also developed significant business across the eastern middle-suburban ring in Kew, Malvern, Armadale, Caulfield, St Kilda, Elwood and Brighton.

Ascot Vale, postcard, c. 1906. LA TROBE PICTURE COLLECTION, STATE LIBRARY OF VICTORIA.

Bendigo Permanent did not enter the Melbourne market before the Great Depression, perhaps in part because it sought to steer clear of its larger building society rivals who were headquartered in the capital city. However, Bendigo Permanent was also looking beyond neighbourhood transactions in Bendigo, and in 1925 it not only established agencies on the fringes of Melbourne (at Werribee and Healesville), but also expanded confidently into the city of Geelong. It was a

Home lending opportunities in Geelong: construction of the Ford Motor Works, 1925.

calculated move, because during that year the Ford Motor Company began large-scale car body assembly at Geelong. Chairman Busst visited Geelong in 1927 and confirmed that the district was 'attracting many large Industries & factories all of which are making Geelong a very large industrial centre and large amounts of Capital are being invested in these industries'.[97] Whereas in 1928 the Sandhurst ruled out any prospect of establishing an agency in Geelong, Bendigo Permanent's secretary Balsillie inspected the city during the same year and reported favourably on business prospects, noting that Ford was already employing 800 people and expected to increase its workforce.[98]

Consolidation, 1930–1991

Bendigo today is a thriving regional city of almost 95,000 people. However, for much of the period between 1930 and 1991 it was a city on the edge. Its staple industry, gold mining, had collapsed during the First World War and, although there was a muted revival in company mining during the 1930s, only a fraction of the mines returned a dividend to investors. The Second World War snuffed out any lingering hopes of a gold-mining revival. Few of the mines reopened after the war and the last one closed in 1954. Bendigo's economy gradually readjusted to other staples: manufacturing and service industries for agricultural, sheep, and cattle producers in northern Victoria. It began from a low base; in 1947 the effects of the Great Depression and the worst drought in the twentieth century, followed by the Second World War, had reduced the city's population to 31,000 people. Gradually, however, the readjustments turned the city around. When the last mine closed in 1954, the city's population had increased to almost 37,000 inhabitants, much the same as it had been in 1881 before the gradual decline in deep reef mining. Bendigo's population thereafter rose slowly, to 40,000 people in 1961, some 55,000 by 1981, and over 60,000 by the time of Bendigo Building Society's merger with Sandhurst Trustees in 1991.

The well-developed neighbourly preoccupations of Bendigo's early building societies were reinforced during the 1930s and 1940s by the city's experiences of world depression, debilitating drought, and world war. They were further ingrained during the subsequent decades of readjustment and sluggish growth. Arthur Bolton, a leading Bendigo businessman and Sandhurst shareholder, congratulated the society at its 1936 annual meeting for being 'not merely a financial institution but a business which was genuinely helping along the progress of humanity', and Garvin, now chairman of directors, responded that 'the

'Bendigo: The Golden City', Victorian Railways poster, c. 1920.
REPRODUCED WITH THE PERMISSION OF THE KEEPER OF PUBLIC RECORDS, PUBLIC RECORD OFFICE VICTORIA, AUSTRALIA. PROV, VPRS 12903/P1, BOX 608/02.

Pall Mall, 1968.

directors had endeavoured to obtain personal contact with borrowers. During the depression, this aspect had been very much emphasised, with the result that the society had been able to find a way out for borrowers who had been faced with the difficulty of meeting payments'.[99] The great drought of 1937–1939 strengthened these sentiments, Bolton noting in 1937 that 'People appreciated the personal contact they were able to make with the management of the society'.[100] These were times of hardship for all. As the Sandhurst glumly conceded in 1938, the effects of the drought would 'necessarily fall heavily on the people with whom the society transacted business'.[101]

Frank Perrow, Balsillie's assistant at Bendigo Permanent, recalled that during the Great Depression:

> Andrew Balsillie would give me a letter to take to [home loan borrowers] which said: 'We know you can't pay, but we would appreciate it if you would stay in the house for six months or so, when things might get better. Please do not vacate the house.' The fact was that we had too many empty houses on our hands—people used to just walk into the office and leave the keys; I can remember a row of keys hanging on hooks. But Andrew's letter built our reputation for being friendly.[102]

Balsillie's attitude combined pragmatism with neighbourly social responsibility. His grandson remembers him calling in on struggling home borrowers during Sunday walks, and bending over backwards to help them. It was 'a friendly society type of thing' to do. But he added that Balsillie's support was conditional on the borrowers' behaviour not jarring with his dour Presbyterian values. If they had a reputation as ne'er-do-wells or pub-goers, 'out they went'.[103] Perrow carried on the social support that Balsillie had offered during the Depression. Indeed he was known to top up some home loans out of his own pocket. It was truly a neighbourly sort of thing to do, and that was how Perrow wanted Bendigo Permanent to operate. He had no interest in extending its operations beyond Bendigo, remaining 'more than happy for it to be the Bendigo Building Society located in Bendigo'.[104]

Balsillie's and Perrow's deep-seated sense of neighbourly social responsibility conditioned the society for the remainder of the twentieth century. The Great

Depression also instilled in Perrow an unrelenting fiscal conservatism. His goal was cautious: steady growth, rather than rapid and perhaps unsustainable expansion. John Perrow remembers with amusement the effort exerted by Bendigo Permanent staff to convince a farmer to invest a substantial deposit with the society. When he eventually agreed they asked him, '"What made you finally decide?", and he said . . . "I was here last time . . . and that old bugger," he said [pointing at Frank Perrow], "the little bloke . . . with the stomach; . . . he walked past . . . and he had . . . braces *and a belt* on and I thought anybody that conservative can look after my money!"'[105] Bendigo's austerity years—and perhaps Perrow's towering reputation—also taught the Sandhurst and the Star the benefit of the cautious policies that Bendigo Permanent had followed since the 1870s. They learnt the advantage of maintaining substantial capital reserves and of tempering their zeal for lending. As the Star acknowledged late in 1931, 'The past year has been a most difficult and anxious one' and in consequence the board 'have deemed it prudent to work on conservative lines'.[106]

Neighbourliness and caution were certainly ingredients for long-term business success. But over the next half century this came at the cost of insularity and hence missed opportunities for faster (although perhaps less secure) growth. With the coming of peace, and plans for post-war reconstruction to overcome the acute housing shortage and promote social well-being, Bendigo's building society managers held great hopes for the future. On the surface they had delivered impressive gains. Despite the hardships caused by the Great Depression, the cautious Bendigo Permanent emerged from it strengthened. Of the ten largest building societies in Victoria in 1930, only Bendigo Permanent had increased its total funds by 1934. It comfortably retained its position as the second largest society in the state, but notwithstanding its superior profitability (Balsillie reported proudly in 1935 that it was the 'highest earner' in the state[107]), the society was still well under a third the size of Victoria's largest society, the Fourth Victoria Permanent Property Building and Investment Society. The war further consolidated Bendigo Permanent's position as the second largest building society in the state (after Fourth Victoria). Its funds reached half a million pounds in 1942 (by comparison the Sandhurst's were

£194,000). Dr Albert Beischer, one of Bendigo Permanent's directors, calculated in 1950 that the society comprised some 500 shareholders and 1700 depositors, and had 1600 people buying homes. Its funds passed £1 million in 1954 (making it a 'one million show' as Lansell proudly described it) and £2 million in 1959 (by comparison, the Star's were over half a million pounds), an achievement that Beischer called 'a real milestone in our history'.[108]

By the time of Bendigo Permanent's centenary celebrations in 1965, its accumulated funds had reached almost £5.5 million and its directors—looking back over a 'Century of Progress'—characterised the society as 'now one of the largest Permanent Building Society's [sic] in Australia'.[109] Its funds had grown to over £19 million by 1970 (the Sandhurst and the Star, roughly equal in size by the early 1970s, were together about one-third the size of Bendigo Permanent, much the same as they had been before the Great Depression). But the news was not all good. Although Bendigo Permanent's assets had increased enormously during the post-war period and it continued to dominate in its chosen local markets, its relative position within the building society sector as a whole had deteriorated. In 1979, even after its merger with the Star, Bendigo Permanent's total funds of almost $113 million made it only the fourth largest building society in Victoria (although still the largest non-metropolitan society), and the 17th largest nationally among the 99-member Australian Association of Permanent Building Societies.

'A Century of Progress': Bendigo Building Society 1865–1965.

This was Perrow's legacy. He had poured most of his considerable energies into Bendigo Permanent, determined 'to make the Bendigo successful within what he saw as success. And that was never to be the biggest, to be the best ... He wasn't interested in just pure growth for growth's sake, he was more interested in growth that had some benefit, in other words it helped people and it made a profit for the shareholders. And he always seemed to match those pretty well'.[110] The other Bendigo building societies followed a similar path. Brian Thomas recalls that during his father's management of the Star 'the history of the Society [was] pretty much on a straight line'.[111] Throughout these decades Sandhurst Trustees had similarly, as its general manager Ian Mansbridge later conceded, 'just drifted along looking after estates and wills'. The Trustees 'never really grew very large', he said, because 'the business was just a spokes and wheels for trusts . . . and . . . we used to make about £10,000 a year or something like that; [it was] very small'.[112] When Allen Guy joined the board of Sandhurst Trustees in 1969 he was shocked to find it so 'old fashioned' with its 14 staff still perched on high stools and doing ledger work on sloping desks. He determined to introduce new business methods.[113]

The Trustees and the building societies undoubtedly worked hard during the post-war period, but they did so within narrow horizons. Length of service became more a feature of the building societies' leadership group than innovation. The young men who had built up these societies were now old men, and even their juniors were ageing. At the Star, E. Travis Thomas replaced his father as secretary in 1929 and retained the position until 1964 when his own son, E. Brian Thomas, became secretary. E. Travis Thomas was still not ready for retirement; he became chairman of directors in 1965 and finally resigned in 1974 because of ill health. The society's first generation of leaders had faded with the passing of John B. Young in 1938 and Angus Mackay in 1951. At the Sandhurst, Arthur Palmer resigned as manager in 1932 and was replaced by William Draper. He remained manager for the next 23 years, until his death in 1955. Draper's successor, Archibald Johnson, retired late in 1965 and was succeeded by Brian Guest. He retained this position until the merger with Bendigo Permanent in 1983, when he became a deputy general manager of the expanded society until his retirement in 1993. On the Sandhurst's board of directors, the experienced hands gradually departed. Richard Abbott resigned as chairman in 1936 due to ill health, and in the same year his predecessor as chairman, William Neill, died after serving for over 37 years as director and chairman. Abbott, Sandhurst's largest shareholder, continued to hold his directorship but was rarely present because of failing health. His position was finally declared vacant in 1938, his colleagues acknowledging his 44 years' service to the society. He died in 1940. Shortly afterwards in 1942 Garvin, the new chairman, died after 22 years as a director. J.S. Wilson and J. Mitchell served as chairman through the 1940s, 1950s, and 1960s. Allen Guy became chairman in 1969 but stood down in 1974 (being replaced by Winston Patten) in order to concentrate his energies on Sandhurst Trustees. He became its chairman in 1979, one of several (the others were George V. Lansell, William Cowling, and Harold Abbott) with close ties to Bendigo's building societies.

At Bendigo Permanent, Balsillie resigned as secretary in 1946 after a remarkable 30 years in the job (he died in 1949). Arthur Davies, a staff member with 27 years' prior experience in the society, was appointed to succeed him as manager but stood down in the following year because of ill health. Perrow, who had joined the society as an office boy 18 years earlier, replaced him. Thirty years later, in 1977, he finally stood down as manager and became a director of the society. His son remembers him as 'the last of our autocratic managers . . . [P]rovided everything was going fine, [the board] virtually left him alone. The board meeting was once a fortnight and it was a report of this is what I've done in the last fortnight and this is what I'm going to do in the next fortnight and they'd pass a motion approving it all'.[114] Perrow resigned in 1984, after 55 years in the society; he died in 1993. Perrow had hoped that his son would replace him, but John Perrow (who worked for the society from 1963 to 1976, and again from 1981 to 1995) had other priorities. The society's new manager, appointed in 1978 to oversee the merged Bendigo Permanent and Star building society, was the Star's secretary Brian Thomas.

Conservative but intensely energetic, Frank Perrow served Bendigo Building Society from 1929 to 1984. He was manager from 1947 to 1977, and a director between 1977 and 1984.

Generational change was slow among the board of directors as well. Horatio Busst had become chairman upon Vahland's death in 1914 and in ailing health (he left a fortune invested in the society on his death) he retired in 1936. His son John filled his directorship. Busst senior was replaced as chairman and managing director by George V. Lansell. Knighted in 1951, Lansell remained chairman of Bendigo Permanent until his death in 1959; he had been a director for 48 years, 23 of them as chairman. His replacement, dentist and long-serving Bendigo Permanent director Albert Beischer, died in 1961, and his successor, Bert Mundy, died only two years later. William Cowling, chairman of Sandhurst Trustees and a director of Bendigo Permanent since 1946, was the society's next chairman, serving from 1963 until failing health prompted him to resign in 1970. Eric Cohen, a respected solicitor and a director of the society since 1963 (he had previously worked actively as a director of the Sandhurst building society until being 'head-hunted' to join Bendigo Permanent[115]), then served as chairman until retiring in 1986. His nephew Richard Guy, a leading Bendigo businessman, became the next chairman. He would oversee the merger in 1991 with Sandhurst Trustees (which had been chaired by his father Allen Guy between 1979 and 1989) and also the society's launch as Bendigo Bank in 1995, before retiring in 2006.

Sir George Victor Lansell was a director of Bendigo Permanent from 1911 and its chairman from 1936 until 1959, as well as being chairman of Sandhurst Trustees between 1946 and 1958.

Eric Cohen was a director of Sandhurst Building Society during the 1950s and early 1960s, and was a director of Bendigo Permanent from 1963 and its chairman from 1970 until 1986.

As Cohen and the Guys exemplify, new blood did periodically renew the leadership of the three building societies and the Trustees.

Allen Guy was chairman of Sandhurst Building Society from 1969 until 1974; he was also a director of Sandhurst Trustees from 1969, and its chairman between 1979 and 1989.

Harold Abbott (Joseph's grandson) became a director of the Sandhurst building society in 1943 and, as its supervising director, guided the society through difficult financial times during the 1950s. In 1946 he had also become a director of Sandhurst Trustees and was its chairman in 1970–1971. Abbott found a natural ally at both institutions in Allen Guy, a successful local businessman and city councillor. Guy joined the Sandhurst building society during 1959, at about the same time as he achieved full control of, and began quickly to expand, the ice-works that his father had co-founded during the 1920s. Guy became the Sandhurst's chairman in 1969, but stood down in 1974 to focus his attention on Sandhurst Trustees. Guy's son Peter also joined the board of the Sandhurst building society. His other son Richard joined the family business in 1970, and further built up its handling and distribution into the Melbourne market for apple, butter, and egg producers in central and northern Victoria. He joined Bendigo Permanent's board in 1981.

Newcomers revitalised the societies' senior management as well. Brian Thomas' appointment to the Star and later (masterminded by Frank Perrow) to the enlarged Bendigo Permanent, energised both societies. Brian Guest likewise built up a reputation as a 'very smart bloke' on his appointment as manager of the Sandhurst building society,[116] as did Mansbridge at Sandhurst Trustees. John Perrow's two periods of employment with Bendigo Permanent introduced the society to fresh accounting ideas and practices. His early advocacy of computer processing was taken up by Rob Hunt who joined the staff of Bendigo Permanent in 1973 and became its chief executive officer in 1988.

However, the newcomers' energies were diluted by the leisurely conservatism of the business climate which they entered. Albert Beischer, for example, and later Allen Guy, were presidents of Bendigo's exclusive Sandhurst Club, and Sir George Lansell was reputed to be the club's best billiards player. He sat in the Legislative Council, representing the conservative side of politics, and travelled in a chauffeured Rolls Royce. He was a shy man. Perrow remembered him as 'a sincere, honest man—honest as the day. Never did any real work, of course, because he didn't need to. Never bossed anyone around either; he *asked* people to do things'. Edith Lunn, who worked for the society as a typist, clerk, and ledger keeper between 1925 and 1937, likewise characterised Lansell as a 'very nice . . . gentleman . . . I used to have to go to his place sometimes and get cheques signed'.[117] The society's operations were still being 'run on a very old style' during the early 1990s. In 1993 a new director marvelled at the board's slow-paced meetings that regularly took up a whole day, with a 'palatial lunch for two hours in between'.[118]

Ian Mansbridge was appointed to Sandhurst Trustees in 1977 and became its managing director in 1982. In the wake of Pyramid, it made 'logical sense' to bring the Trustees and Bendigo together. REPRODUCED WITH PERMISSION FROM THE PRIVATE COLLECTION OF IAN MANSBRIDGE.

The newcomers' energies were dissipated also by the continuation into the post-war period of the institutional impediments to large-scale operations that had characterised Bendigo's building societies during their early development. Staff numbers, for example, remained small until the 1980s. Bendigo Permanent's seven staff in 1930 increased to nine by 1940 and to 28 in 1974 (all in Bendigo, plus one valuer employed in Melbourne), 15 of whom were women. In 1979, after the merger with the Star, Bendigo Building Society's staff rose to over 50. The Sandhurst had just six staff in 1964: the manager, two senior staff, and three assistants. It increased to seven (three of them women) by 1972. Sandhurst Trustees employed a dozen staff by the late 1970s. The building societies' small staffs precluded office expansion, and all three societies continued to function essentially as single office operations.

Bendigo Permanent staff in 1965.

Bendigo Permanent's old headquarters, early 1960s.

Sandhurst Building Society headquarters, View Street, 1959.

Bendigo Permanent's office (the society's earlier ambition to open additional local branches forgotten) remained in a former hotel in Bull Street, which was expanded into the adjoining property in 1933. New purpose-built headquarters were opened on the same site in 1965 to coincide with the society's centenary celebrations, and a still larger office was completed in 1977, taking over another neighbouring property. However, Thomas regarded the enlarged office as 'a rabbit warren' when he joined the society in the following year.[119] The Sandhurst society sold its old View Street headquarters in 1959 and bought a larger office several doors down the street. In 1973 it bought and redeveloped a still larger site in Williamson Street as its headquarters, which were opened by the Victorian Premier, Rupert Hamer, in 1975. The Star moved from rented offices in View Street to Charing Cross during the late 1930s, and built a new office there during the early 1960s, on part of the site of Bendigo Bank's later Fountain Court headquarters.

Star Building Society headquarters, Charing Cross, 1964.

Star Building Society, general office, 1964.

Technological change came slowly to these offices. At both Bendigo Permanent and the Star, father-son 'brawls' took place as the younger Perrows and Thomases sought to convince their fathers to move with the times.[120] The societies began to experiment with electric adding machines during the late 1950s, copying innovations in the banking sector. Harold Abbott, supported by Allen Guy, argued in 1962 that manual calculations had become 'outmoded' and urged the 'desirability of transferring to machines',[121] but when John Perrow joined Bendigo Permanent in 1963, he was shocked to find that the society still had just one adding machine to assist with the 'nightmare' of manually balancing the deposit and loan ledgers. John Perrow wanted computers but Frank was unmoved. As the son says of his father, 'he was *that* conservative!'[122] All three societies had nonetheless installed accounting machines by the mid 1960s, and Bendigo Permanent introduced a computerised accounting system when it opened its new headquarters in 1977, over a decade after the banks began to adopt computer systems. On-line computer systems were beyond the Star's resources, and the cost of updating its systems and installing ATMs was an important consideration for Sandhurst during its merger talks with Bendigo Permanent.

New communications technologies were slowly adopted. Bendigo Permanent's first internal staff telephone system was installed in 1955. Although cars were used for property inspections from early in the century, it was not until 1960, after lengthy debate and consideration, that the Star decided to buy its first office car (a Holden Special), and the Sandhurst copied their choice of car in 1967. Bendigo Permanent had relied on train travel and car hire during the 1930s and 1940s, and bought a Ford during the 1950s.

Bendigo Permanent's directors considered advertising with a neon sign in 1933 but 'it was not considered that such [a] sign would be of any great advantage'.[123] The society began advertising in movie theatres during the mid 1940s, but not until 1955 was a neon sign finally installed outside the society's office. Frank Perrow was sceptical about the value of advertising, and it was left to his son John to implement a comprehensive advertising and sponsorship programme. The Star experimented with radio advertising in 1968 and, as television extended its coverage into regional Australia during the early 1960s, the Sandhurst initiated television advertising in the following year.

Close collaboration between the building societies and Sandhurst Trustees facilitated local business, but perhaps also fed complacency and insularity. In 1939 Garvin, once a leading shareholder in the Star but now chairman of the Sandhurst building society and mayor of Bendigo, applauded 'the good feeling that existed between the building societies in Bendigo'.[124] A Sandhurst board meeting during 1959 was interrupted when word was received of the sudden passing of Sir George Lansell, a prominent and highly esteemed resident of Bendigo, Chairman of a Sister Society and a Director of the Board of Directors of the Sandhurst Trustees Company. After reference had been made by Mr. Wilson, supported by Mr. Abbott and the Chairman, a moment's silence was observed. It was then suggested that letters of sympathy be forwarded to the Bendigo Building Society and the Sandhurst Trustees Company, expressing the sympathy of the Directors in the loss of such a fine citizen.[125]

The overlapping responsibilities and interests of key stakeholders made for co-operative working relations. This co-operation was cemented by churchgoing, Freemasonry and often family connections (for example, the journalist and historian George Mackay was a director of Bendigo Permanent between 1927 and 1946, during which time his brother Angus was chairman of the Star; the Mackays were also related through marriage to both the Cohens and the Guys, so that Richard Guy's grandmother was a Mackay and his uncle was Eric Cohen). Family ties were especially close between Bendigo Permanent and each of its smaller competitors. The Sandhurst and the Star, because they were more equally matched, at times 'didn't get on particularly well'.[126] The three societies discussed interest rates, without necessarily reaching agreement. Sometimes they partnered in order to engage more effectively with the outside world. During the early 1930s, stung by federal government income tax proposals, the three building societies participated in the establishment of the Victorian Building Societies Association, and Richard Abbott (chairman of the Sandhurst) and Balsillie (manager of Bendigo Permanent) attended Association meetings in Melbourne on behalf of all their colleagues in Bendigo. Balsillie was elected the Association's vice president in 1937, and Perrow was its president during the mid 1950s. Brian Thomas became its president in the 1980s. During the 1950s, 1960s and 1970s the three societies collaborated to influence the framing of new building society legislation designed to facilitate deposit taking and lending.

Collaboration and outside engagement could be triggers for innovation, but they were often coloured by political conservatism and resistance to change. The Bendigo societies resisted federal tax reforms during the early 1930s, watched anxiously the framing of state housing legislation during the late 1930s, and fretted during the 1940s over the inflationary effects of legislation for shorter working hours. They worried about the post-war consequences of wartime federal regulatory interventions, the restructuring of the Commonwealth Bank as a quasi reserve bank, and the Chifley Labor Government's attempt to nationalise the banking system. The Star complained in 1949 that 'Our commercial and financial institutions and our whole system of economics are becoming too frequently the sport of politics and the politician is more and more developing the itch to meddle unnecessarily with everything and everybody, with disastrous results to the natural laws which should be left to govern our national economy'.[127] Bendigo's building societies reacted with hostility to legislative reforms designed by the Whitlam Labor Government in 1974 to impose federal controls on building societies, and by Victoria's Cain Labor Government during the mid 1980s to tighten building society regulations.

Brian Thomas and Brian Guest faced formidable challenges in regearing the Bendigo building societies from small to larger possibilities when they were appointed to manage the Star and the Sandhurst during the mid 1960s. Ian Mansbridge faced a similar challenge when he was appointed to the Sandhurst Trustees in 1977. Guest had confronted the Sandhurst building society board head-on in 1971, asserting that

> just advertising in the 'Bendigo Advertiser' is not enough. The Society has an identity problem. Most people recognise the name of the Bendigo Building Society immediately. The Sandhurst does not enjoy instantaneous recognition. Nothing is more discouraging when you advise a person of where you work and they identify you with the Sandhurst Trustees or reply 'where's that'?[128]

When Thomas became manager of Bendigo Permanent in 1978 he encountered the same resistance to change, but on a larger scale, and quickly engineered a rule change to require the retirement of directors aged over 75. Guest continued to cross swords with the directors of the Sandhurst. In 1981 he complained that they had rejected every proposal to celebrate the society's centenary year, and put on record his 'concern . . . that the Society plans to do nothing to mark this occasion'.[129]

Brian Guest, manager of the Sandhurst Building Society, 1965–1983, became deputy general manager of Bendigo Building Society, 1983–1993, after the two societies merged.

Guest's frustration was intense because those 100 years of growth had been distinguished not only by the Sandhurst's strong local development since 1881, but also by the remarkable growth of the building society sector as a whole since the Second World War at the expense of the banking sector. Whereas the banks had been strictly controlled since the 1930s and 1940s by Commonwealth regulation, building societies were only loosely regulated by the states. Their massive growth peaked during the 1970s. Whereas the Sandhurst, to Guest's irritation, discountenanced these exciting years of development, Bendigo Permanent relished its long history—hanging portraits of its past directors on the boardroom's walls, and claiming for itself the title of the oldest operating building society in mainland Australia—but only in order to highlight how it persisted in its traditional ways. In 1972, celebrating the doubling of house finance approvals over the previous 12 months, its board noted (in guarded disapproval of the efforts by larger building societies to resemble banks) that the society had 'continued to make every effort to assist people in the obtaining of a home for their own occupation, thereby carrying out the true function of a Building Society'.[130]

Homes for all

Frank Perrow, an intensely energetic man, clung to that opinion throughout his long tenure from 1947 until 1977 as manager of Bendigo Permanent. He declared in 1952 that building societies 'are established for one purpose—to assist the man on a lower income to acquire his own home over a long period with a set, stipulated rate of payment'. Upon his retirement Perrow urged shareholders never to forget that the society had been formed to provide home loans.[131] That vision continued largely undiluted into the post-Perrow era. Bendigo Permanent reiterated in 1982 that 'the Society's principal objective must be the provision of shelter finance'.[132] It nurtured the neighbourhood dream of owning the ubiquitous quarter-acre suburban house block.

Bendigo's building societies continued to articulate the vision of neighbourly social benefit for their members, a vision that was reinforced by the external shocks of world depression and the wartime housing shortage, and was broadened in its application by the increasing prosperity of most post-war Australians. However, in consequence of Depression-bred social division, wartime mobilisation, and Cold War anxiety, the goal of social benefit was complicated by a conservative nationalist agenda to promote home ownership. During the late 1930s, Bendigo Permanent characterised home building as 'a national necessity' and, in 1938, Lansell described the society's long record of providing housing finance as having 'national importance as home ownership was a strong influence in creating better citizenship'.[133] In 1949, amidst the tensions between the Western coalition and the Soviet Union over the partition of Germany and the drawn-out Berlin Blockade, Lansell reiterated his goal 'to be able to assist people to become owners of their own homes; and thus become better citizens'. Perrow echoed that opinion in 1952, declaring that 'a home owner is a home-maker and a good citizen'.[134]

The Great Depression had briefly dimmed Australians' dream of home ownership. However, Bendigo quickly experienced a strong revival in the housing market, and Bendigo Permanent reported in 1934 that 'numerous bright modern homes are being erected with the assistance of the society's loans'.[135] The society's loan applications increased from 149 in 1933 to 332 in 1938. Demand evaporated during the Second World War, during which time military service and the gearing of all energies to wartime production resulted in what the Sandhurst called an 'extreme house shortage'.[136] However, the housing market rebounded strongly after the war. By 1954, Bendigo Permanent had around £1 million of loans on its books, Sandhurst had £398,000 of advances, and the Star another £248,000. By 1960

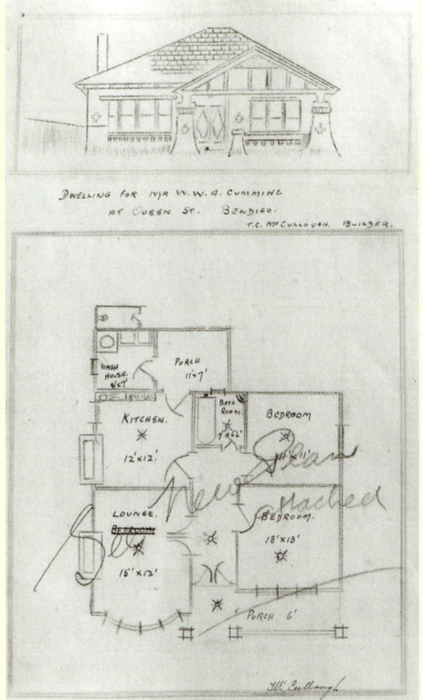

Left: Home-making, 1934. Builder Trevor McCullough's plans for a two-bedroom bungalow for W.W.A. (Bill) and Alice Cumming at 262 Queen Street, Bendigo, 21 September 1934. Bill Cumming obtained a £400 loan from Bendigo Permanent. REPRODUCED BY PERMISSION OF KEN CUMMING.

Below: The Secretary approves: letter by Andrew Balsillie granting insurance cover for the Cummings' property, 28 November 1934. REPRODUCED BY PERMISSION OF KEN CUMMING.

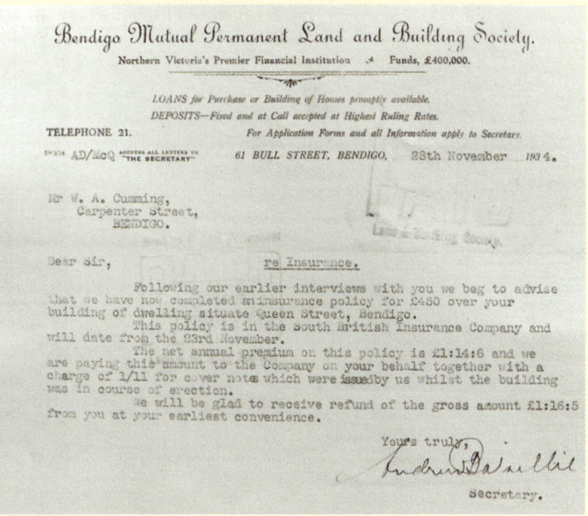

Bendigo Mutual Permanent Land and Building Society.

Northern Victoria's Premier Financial Institution Funds, £400,000.

LOANS for Purchase or Building of Homes promptly available.
DEPOSITS—Fixed and at Call accepted at Highest Ruling Rates.

TELEPHONE 21. *For Application Forms and all Information apply to Secretary.*

AD/McQ ADDRESS ALL LETTERS TO "THE SECRETARY" *61 BULL STREET, BENDIGO,* 28th November 1934.

Mr W. A. Cumming,
Carpenter Street,
BENDIGO.

Dear Sir, re Insurance.

Following our earlier interviews with you we beg to advise that we have now completed an insurance policy for £450 over your building of dwelling situate Queen Street, Bendigo.

This policy is in the South British Insurance Company and will date from the 23rd November.

The net annual premium on this policy is £1:14:6 and we are paying this amount to the Company on your behalf together with a charge of 1/11 for cover notes which were issued by us whilst the building was in course of erection.

We will be glad to receive refund of the gross amount £1:16:5 from you at your earliest convenience.

Yours truly,
Andrew Balsillie
Secretary.

The Cummings' new home, c. 1934.

Loans for home buyers, 1951. Bendigo Bank newspaper advertisement, 5 June 1951.

A helping hand for new home owners, 1969.

Dream homes: Bendigo Permanent annual report, 1967.

Sandhurst's loans had risen to £613,000 and Bendigo Permanent's to £2.3 million. Bendigo Permanent's loan portfolio expanded to over $18 million by 1970, $115 million by 1980, and $603 million by 1990.

This growth in housing finance continued to be supported not only by the Bendigo property market, but also by home lending in Melbourne, notwithstanding the continuing dominance of home finance by the State Bank and the rapid growth of new Melbourne-based building societies. The Sandhurst and the Star consolidated their early twentieth-century interventions in the Victorian capital, the Star focusing on up-market home lending in the eastern suburbs.[137] In October 1954, Melbourne borrowers accounted for between 12 and 14 per cent of the Sandhurst's total loans (Bendigo and district accounting for over one-quarter of the total). These Melbourne loans were almost entirely directed to the western metropolitan region, many of them to Italian migrants who were buying homes in suburbs such as Altona, Footscray, Yarraville, and St Albans. By October 1961, Melbourne loans had increased to almost one-third of the Sandhurst's total (concentrated in Altona, St Albans, Footscray, Yarraville, Newport, Sunshine, and

Post-war Melbourne suburbia: South Caulfield, 1945. FROM THE COLLECTION OF THE NATIONAL ARCHIVES OF AUSTRALIA, A1200, L900.

Williamstown) and borrowers in Bendigo and district accounted for another third of total loans. The Sandhurst resolved in 1963 to establish further agencies across the entire metropolitan region (although in 1969 it was decided to cancel the society's Geelong agency because the agent—one Robert Farrow—was judged to have been building up business for his own Pyramid Building Society rather than for the Sandhurst).[138] Brian Thomas, who became secretary of the Star in 1964, energetically expanded the society's home lending in Melbourne's eastern suburbs because he realised that the Bendigo home loan market was oversupplied. The Star so increased its agency business in Melbourne that in 1968 it decided to open a permanent Melbourne office. Thomas remembers 'long hours spent trailing backwards and forwards to Melbourne, doing inspections, talking to people, interviews and so on'.[139] During Allen Guy's chairmanship of the Sandhurst between 1969 and 1974, he also prodded it to further build up business in Melbourne, arguing 'that the Society did not have a spread of Agents'.[140]

Bendigo Permanent also ventured into the Melbourne home loan market during the inter-war years, Lansell remarking in 1942 that the society had 'extended its operations to the Melbourne Metropolitan Suburban Area with success'.[141] Whereas the Star's focus was up-market, Bendigo Permanent targeted smaller-scale borrowers.[142] The ramping up of the Victorian Housing Commission's 'slum' clearance activities in inner-suburban working-class suburbs such as Collingwood and Richmond during the mid 1950s made Bendigo Permanent vulnerable on some of its advances, and in response some of its lending was curtailed and its 'liabilities [were] reduced to a safe figure'.[143] Like the Sandhurst it increasingly focused on the immigrant western suburbs. Its 1965 centennial report commented that 'few people realise that [the society] does a very large amount of home finance in the metropolitan area'.[144] Richard Guy recalls that 'An enormous amount of lending was done in the western suburbs by Bendigo. It had a fine reputation, they'd done it for decades. Frank Perrow would get in his car and drive around and they'd do a kerbside valuation on all the houses and how much he'd lend. He knew as much about real estate down there as anyone did'.[145] By the early 1980s Melbourne had become Bendigo Permanent's largest market for home finance.[146]

Post-war inflation dented the hopes of many Australians of achieving home ownership. The *Argus* newspaper noted dourly in 1951 that 'Daily, as the cost of living soars merrily upward, the young family man's chance of ever owning his own home becomes more and more remote'. A decade later the *Age* was still complaining that it was becoming increasingly difficult for Australian families to achieve what is 'every Australian's right'.[147] Bendigo Permanent acknowledged during 1973 that notwithstanding the booming demand for home loans, the society was hard placed to meet the aspirations of many potential borrowers in 'the present climate of inflation'.[148] These pressures on credit supply were the result in part of the booms and recessions in a multi-sectored national economy. They were also influenced by the Commonwealth government, whose efforts to moderate or stimulate national economic growth sometimes meant pain for borrowers and lending institutions. During the 1950s the Menzies Coalition Government's credit squeeze was blamed for making it 'nearly impossible for the average worker to raise a . . . savings bank loan'. The early 1980s interest rate hikes triggered by Treasurer John Howard were labelled 'that substantial slug [that] will be the last straw' for many home loan borrowers.[149]

Government economic regulation sometimes provided unpleasant surprises for building societies as well. Menzies' credit squeeze caught out the Sandhurst, which in 1956 found itself overextended in its loan making and with the ANZ Bank alarmed at the blowout in the society's overdraft. Abbott, the supervising director, admitted that the society's position was 'dangerous' and further loans were suspended 'in an endeavour to consolidate the finances of the Society'. The society's predicament persisted into the early 1960s, the society conceding in 1961 that it had again 'over advanced' and that loans would once more have to be suspended.[150] Building societies overall were the indirect beneficiaries of Commonwealth financial regulation. Whereas banks were tightly regulated by the Commonwealth, building societies were loosely controlled by the states, and Victoria's Liberal-Country Party governing coalition was especially favourably disposed to boosting the sector's growth. Restrictions imposed during the 1930s and 1940s limited the borrowing capacity of building societies to three times the amount of their available capital, and capped the interest payable on deposits. Subsequent lobbying by the sector resulted in the loosening of these restrictions. Discussions during 1953 resulted in amendments to the Building Societies Act that were designed to give the societies 'much more scope' for growing their deposits and loans.[151] The Act was amended again in 1961 to increase the borrowing cap on building societies to five times their capital. This regulatory landscape enabled the sector to compete effectively with the banks both for home loans and for deposits.

Bendigo's building societies sustained their housing loans in the neighbourhoods of Bendigo and Melbourne by continuing to rely upon trading banks for large overdrafts. Mounting demand for home loans resulted in ongoing negotiations with the banks about increasing their overdrafts and limiting the interest charges owing on them. The case for expanding bank overdrafts caused disagreements within the boards of the building societies. At the Sandhurst, for example, Abbott—cautious after the society's financial woes during the 1950s—resisted increasing the society's overdraft, whereas Allen Guy argued that it was essential in order to expand the society's business. The wrangling sometimes generated significant friction with the banks as well. In 1974, for example, an exasperated Star resolved to transfer its banking from the ANZ to the Commercial Banking Company.

As they had before the Great Depression, the building societies also sought to mobilise capital by issuing shares, but this policy was quickly at variance with the actualities of neighbourhood capital mobilisation. In 1930, Sandhurst shares represented some 57 per cent of the society's deposits, but by the late 1940s they had shrunk to a little over one-third (made up roughly equally of permanent and maturing shares). At the Star, similarly, shares comprised some 59 per cent of its investment capital during the early 1930s, but by the late 1940s and the early 1950s that proportion had eroded to approximately one-third. Bendigo Permanent best illustrates the fundamental changes at work. Shares represented only 38 per cent of its much larger deposit base in 1930 and, by the late 1940s and early 1950s, they had diminished to approximately one-quarter. The cap on lending by the Building Societies Act was a powerful incentive for societies to increase their permanent capital by further issues of shares. The directors of all three societies wrestled with the question of whether these share issues should be offered as withdrawable or permanent stock. Richard Abbott advised Sandhurst shareholders in 1930 that the world depression had shown that 'In difficult times withdrawable shares, although popular, are undesirable. Your directors have ceased issuing any of these for more than two years past, and as they mature they will be paid out'.[152]

Bendigo Permanent reported in 1930 that, as a result of its pre-depression policy of encouraging the conversion of maturing contributing shares into permanent shares, the former category now comprised 'very restricted numbers'. In the following year the board celebrated that 'the gradual conversion of withdrawable shares into Permanent Paid Up Shares has greatly stabilized the capital of the Society'.[153] That aspiration did not mesh with the neighbourhood realities faced by depositors during the turmoil of world depression and war. Depositors wanted ready access to their savings. In 1936 Bendigo Permanent responded to client demand by reformulating its share structure, offering £10 permanent paid-up shares, and contributing shares that matured at £50 value per share. The society's rules were again rewritten in 1949, converting the £10 shares into £1 permanent paid-up shares and raising additional capital by offering existing investors the opportunity to purchase the new shares. Additional permanent share issues were successfully offered throughout the 1950s and into the early 1960s. With decimalisation in 1966, new $1 permanent paid-up shares were offered, together with $1 terminating paid-up shares (withdrawable with three months' notice) and $100 terminating contributing shares. Further issues of permanent paid-up shares were successfully offered throughout the 1960s and 1970s.

The Sandhurst and the Star went through a similar process. In 1930, Richard Abbott steered through a scheme designed to convert half the capital of the Sandhurst's contributing members into permanent £5 paid-up shares, and to issue further permanent paid-up shares to existing shareholders. However, in 1934 the society resumed issuing maturing £20 shares, acknowledging their popularity with members. In 1936 the Sandhurst issued more permanent paid-up shares in order to boost the society's capital base, but it also increased the 'class of terminating share'.[154] In 1938, with the demand for loans pushing the society towards its loan limit, the Sandhurst again attempted to boost its permanent capital base by offering paid-up holders of maturing shares generous terms for converting all or some of their shares into permanent paid-up shares. By the early 1940s, all paid-up shareholders had converted to permanent paid-up shares, but there were further issues of paid-up maturing shares during the late 1940s. The Star also issued paid-up maturing shares during 1948 to meet the demand for loans. In 1959 the Sandhurst, stung by the federal credit squeeze on the one hand and by the demand for housing finance on the other, again reviewed its share structure in order to maximise its capital base. The directors were divided in their opinions, but in February 1961 they resolved to convert all shares into permanent stock.

From building society to proto-bank

By the 1960s, however, shares of all varieties represented only a fraction of the societies' expanding capital base. A fundamental shift was taking place in the investment structure of Australian building societies. The societies had originally raised capital by issuing shares, but during the 1950s and 1960s capital raising switched decisively to deposit accounts. This change is most clearly evident at Bendigo Permanent, the oldest of Bendigo's building societies and whose policy had most single-mindedly sought to build up permanent shares. However, neighbours were simultaneously making investment decisions that were quite at variance with the views of the managers of the society. In 1960 Bendigo Permanent shares comprised only 17 per cent of the society's investment capital; deposit accounts made up the other 83 per cent. By the early 1970s these deposits—most of them from Bendigo and district—had grown to over 90 per cent of the society's investment capital, a proportion that remained relatively unchanged throughout the 1970s and 1980s. In 1990 deposit accounts formed almost 95 per cent of the society's investment capital.

Safe investments: Bendigo Permanent advertisement, 1959. Bendigo Bank newspaper cutting, 2 December 1959.

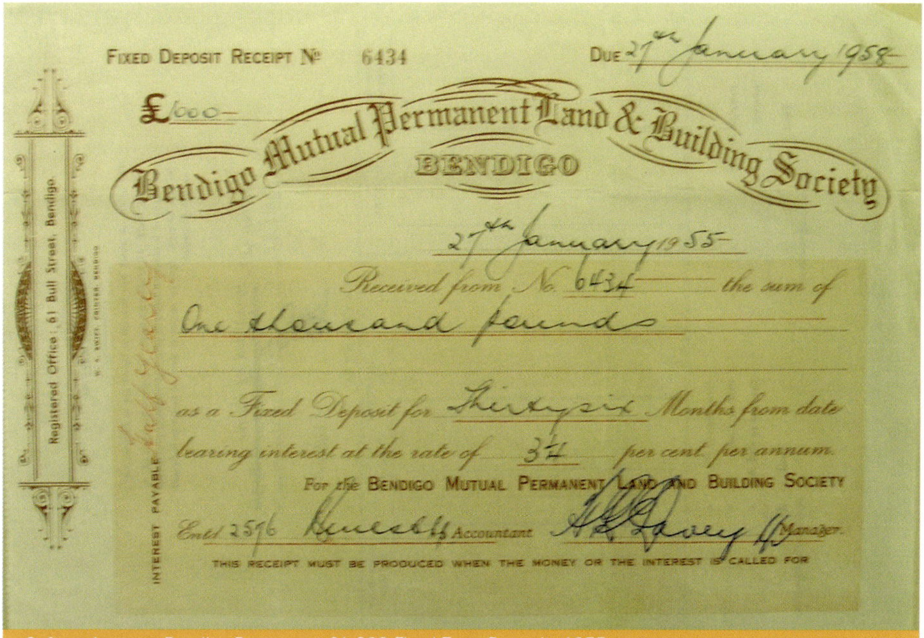
FIXED DEPOSIT RECEIPT № 6434 DUE 27th January 1958

£1000-

Bendigo Mutual Permanent Land & Building Society

BENDIGO

Registered Office: 61 Bull Street, Bendigo.

27th January 1955

Received from No. 6434 the sum of

One thousand pounds

as a Fixed Deposit for Thirtysix Months from date

bearing interest at the rate of 3¼ per cent per annum

For the Bendigo Mutual Permanent Land and Building Society

Entd 2576 Accountant Manager.

INTEREST PAYABLE Half Yearly

THIS RECEIPT MUST BE PRODUCED WHEN THE MONEY OR THE INTEREST IS CALLED FOR

Safe as houses: Bendigo Permanent £1,000 Fixed Term Deposit, 1955.

Building society managers had previously felt nervous about the volatility of short-term deposits. Speaking to shareholders at the Sandhurst's annual meeting in 1938, Garvin referred to the society's reserves (which were mostly invested in Commonwealth bonds) and conceded that although the 'interest return from this class of investment was not so great . . . it was safer to have convertible assets when handling monies at call'.[155] During the Sandhurst's liquidity crisis in the late 1950s, Harold Abbott likewise 'stress[ed] that a certain amount of money likely to prove dangerous was held at call'.[156] In 1936, however, Balsillie had engineered a significant change of direction at Bendigo Permanent, successfully recommending 'the advisability of encouraging Thrift Savings by issue of Contributing Deposits'. These new deposit accounts, with monthly contributions and high interest rates, were designed 'to encourage systematic Thrift Savings'.[157] Balsillie's initiative triggered an avalanche of deposits that left Bendigo's other societies far behind. By 1949, deposit accounts at Bendigo Permanent comprised 73 per cent of investment capital, compared to 65 per cent at the Star and some 62 per cent at the Sandhurst. Bendigo Permanent's deposit accounts accumulated over £500,000 by 1951 (73 per cent of the society's investment capital), compared to just £98,000 (57 per cent of investment income) at the Star. By 1957 Bendigo Permanent's deposit accounts contained over £1 million, compared to £270,000 at the Star.

This switch in emphasis from shares to deposit accounts reinforced the neighbourly associations of Bendigo's building societies with their local communities. Paradoxically it also began to redefine their essence. As the building society sector challenged the banks for depositors as well as home-loan borrowers during the 1960s and 1970s, building societies increasingly resembled savings banks themselves. So did the trading banks. The Bank of New South Wales and the ANZ Bank established savings bank arms in 1955, followed by the National and Commercial banks during 1961. However building societies, less constrained by government regulation, could better adjust to inflation by raising the interest rates they offered to depositors. In 1962, as the Sandhurst's deposit accounts mushroomed, Harold Abbott drew attention to 'the Society's increased activities in Banking, and offered a word of caution as to the possibilities of such activities becoming objectionable to the trading banks. It was decided, however, that no action could be taken in this matter'.[158]

Concerns that building societies were over-extending themselves by offering depositors excessively high rates of interest culminated in 1973 when Frank Crean, federal treasurer in the Whitlam Labor Government, expressed misgivings about the financial stability of some building societies. Crean's comments prompted many anxious depositors to withdraw their savings. Bendigo Permanent sought to reassure nervous investors, commenting that the 'recent publicity relating to Building Societies did not materially affect your Society as Members and Investors showed their confidence and trust in the Society's history of security and strength'.[159] In Adelaide, however, rumours during 1974 that the Hindmarsh Building Society was associated with the ailing property developers Mainline and Cambridge Credit led to chaotic scenes as depositors queued to close their accounts. South Australian Labor premier Don Dunstan fronted the crowd and appealed through a megaphone for calm.[160] In Queensland, 16 struggling building societies were rescued during 1975 through their amalgamation with Suncorp, the state government-owned former State Government Insurance Office. Both the South Australian and Queensland building society crises had a ripple effect on deposits in Bendigo. In 1976 in Victoria, the Hamer Coalition Government legislated to better control and protect the building society sector.

The sector's continuing success in attracting depositors at the expense of the savings banks led building society managers to believe that they could challenge the banks' position as savings institutions, and in 1979 that did not seem an unreasonable expectation. In just over 40 years Australia's largest building society, St George, had built up one billion dollars in assets, a network of 130 branches and a staff of 800 people. However, the optimists in the building society sector overlooked two things. Firstly, mergers between some of the old trading banks were renewing the banking industry (highlighted by the merger of the Bank of Australasia and the Union Bank of Australia in 1951 to form the ANZ, and by its subsequent absorption of the English, Scottish and Australian Bank in 1970). Secondly, in 1979 John Howard, then federal treasurer in the Fraser Coalition Government, appointed an inquiry headed by Keith Campbell, chair of Hooker Corporation, to overhaul the entire Australian financial system. As the *Age* noted in July 1980, Victorian building societies hoped that Campbell's recommendations would aid them in supplanting the savings banks as the major source of home finance.[161] The newspaper was unsympathetic to the building societies' position, accusing the largest, Statewide, and other Victorian societies of lifting interest rates to depositors at a time of already high inflation because of their selfish drive for 'excess growth . . . as quickly as they can get it'. The *Age* contended that building societies had yet to learn to take 'responsible action as corporate citizens in a much wider community' and it predicted that the Victorian societies' 'fat days' of lax state government oversight that had enabled them to steal deposits from the tightly regulated national banking system, were numbered.[162]

As we have already seen (in chapter one) the Campbell Report, tabled in 1981, delivered a comprehensive victory to the banks and destroyed the building societies' ambition to usurp their functions. In the resulting shake-up, the 1980s became a period of turmoil and readjustment for Australia's building societies, which now had to compete with an increasingly unregulated and globalised banking sector, and a proliferation of cash management trusts, while also absorbing the local shocks of retractions (evident first in the collapse of Victoria's Twentieth Century building society during 1981) in what was now becoming a grossly over-extended financial sector. A spate of building society mergers attempted to make the sector more secure and competitive. In South Australia, for example, the Hindmarsh Building Society merged with the Adelaide Permanent Building Society in 1985 to create the Hindmarsh Adelaide Building Society. In 1986 Victoria's two largest building societies, Statewide Building Society and RESI Permanent Building Society, merged to become RESI-Statewide Building Society, the second largest building society in Australia. From the middle of the 1980s a trickle of building societies also concluded that since they could not usurp the functions of banks, they should themselves join the banking sector. By 1989 what had been Victoria's four largest building societies in 1981 had all become banks.

These developments made Bendigo, in Australia's bicentenary year, the home of Victoria's largest building society. This was not entirely the result of external developments. The city's building society managers had made huge adjustments over the previous decade. Indeed, the local push for mergers had begun in Bendigo even before the appointment of the Campbell Inquiry. Allen Guy recalls that when Cohen left the Sandhurst to become chairman of Bendigo Permanent in 1970 'I think that in the back of his mind was [the thought] that one day they would merge as one'.[163] Exploratory talks during the early 1970s about a possible merger between the two societies stalled because of Perrow's lack of interest. His opinion moderated over the following years, but it was the Star, not the Sandhurst, which participated in the renewed merger talks. On 6 July 1977 a specially convened board meeting of the Star resolved—notwithstanding opposition from E.T. Thomas—that in the light of encouraging preliminary discussions with Bendigo Permanent, it was in the interests of both these 'friendly rivals' to explore further the possibility of amalgamation.[164] An agreement in principle was reached on 27 July to merge as the Bendigo Building Society, with Brian Thomas as manager, and a board made up of five directors from each society. The last official meeting of the Star took place on 10 August 1978, and the first meeting of the Bendigo Building Society's new board was held on 5 September. The enlarged society had some 60,000 clients, over 50 staff, and a chain of agencies in Bendigo and Melbourne. Its total funds rose from $81 million in 1977 to $128 million in 1979.

These were big numbers for a local institution, but Thomas knew they were dwarfed by St George and by the largest Victorian societies. He worried about Bendigo's 'in-between size'; it was too big a player for the Bendigo building market alone, but not big enough to survive in the broader arena.[165] In order to be able to compete with these giants, Thomas set about mobilising the combined resources of the merged Bendigo societies so as to capitalise on their long history of neighbourhood engagement in Bendigo and Melbourne. Given that building society deposit and lending growth increasingly resembled that of savings banks, Thomas went a logical step further. He jettisoned Perrow orthodoxy and, imitating the largest building societies, began to assemble a neighbourhood network of building society branches. His focus was on Melbourne. Thomas visited the society's metropolitan agencies as he began to familiarise himself with his new duties and, especially in conversations with Leon Bates, then operating out of his own home as the society's resident valuer, he was impressed both by the good reputation the society had built up in the western suburbs and by the missed opportunities of capitalising on this goodwill because it had no metropolitan branches. Whereas Perrow had stonewalled branch development as being too costly, Statewide and other building societies had established branch networks in order to 'swoop up' the deposits and investments of Bendigo's borrowers.[166] Bendigo Permanent's first Melbourne branch, at 227 Barkly Street in Footscray, was opened as a part-time branch during 1979 with Bates as manager, and was officially launched as a full-time branch in the following year. Bendigo's board was initially lukewarm about the initiative, and Thomas conceded that deposits at the

Pioneer branch in Melbourne: 227 Barkly Street, Footscray, c. 1980.

new branch had grown 'pretty slowly' in the beginning.[167] However, by 1981 Bendigo Building Society had seven branches (three of them in the Melbourne suburbs of Footscray, Sunshine, and Williamstown), 68 staff and 50 agencies. A year later it had 15 branches and 77 staff.

Neighbourhood branch building in Bendigo and Melbourne was overshadowed in mid 1981 by the broader restructuring of the Australian building society sector. Perth Building Society—the third largest in Australia, with one billion dollars in assets—proposed a merger with Bendigo Building Society. The Bendigo's directors and staff were in the main enthusiastic, and shareholders were receptive (Richard Guy, for example, welcomed the 'huge premium' that Perth had offered in order to buy Bendigo shares),[168] but many among the society's neighbourhood base were not. Speaking on behalf of the sceptics, a hostile *Bendigo Advertiser* questioned whether the offer was really 'a merger, an amalgamation or a takeover'. The newspaper objected that 'the society is part and parcel of Bendigo and it is to be hoped that this successful enterprise will retain its local identity'.[169] Surprised by the parochial hostility to their proposal, Perth Building Society withdrew its offer in November (merging instead with Victoria's third-largest building society, the Hotham Permanent Building Society). In Bendigo, continuing disagreements about the botched merger and its implications for the society's future direction were played out early in 1982 in the elections for Bendigo's board. The result was a landslide victory for Cohen and the old board, who were strengthened by the election of Thomas and Richard Guy.

While the Bendigo Building Society squabbled, the rival Sandhurst embarked on its own programme of bank-like branch openings, building up a network of 32 branches (and over 20 agencies in Melbourne) by early 1982. However, Guest bluntly warned his board in January that the cost of branch expansion meant that growth on paper had not translated into increased profits. Guest was acutely aware of the tough new operating climate being created nationally by the post-Campbell deregulation of banking, and within Victoria by the new Cain Labor Government's encouragement of building society amalgamations to help prop up the sector. He warned that 'With the continual squeeze on margins, the outlook for the Society is grim. A complete rationalisation is needed to put the Society on a profitable basis'.[170]

A complete rationalisation was indeed achieved during the following year, when the Sandhurst merged with the Bendigo. This time the *Advertiser* welcomed the merger, calling it a 'sensible marriage' between the 'progressive' Sandhurst and its 'more conservative' former rival.[171] Whereas Perrow had been hesitant about such a merger in the early 1970s, Thomas was enthusiastic. In his opinion Bendigo was 'over serviced' with two building societies, and a merger would create a larger society that could better service the local, regional, and metropolitan home-loan market.[172] The merger, effective from 1 May 1983, positioned Thomas as managing director, Guest and Rob Hunt (previously an assistant manager at the Bendigo) as deputy managing directors, and created an enlarged board of ten members. Funds in Bendigo Building Society (it was briefly renamed the Bendigo Sandhurst Building Society) rose from $177 million in 1982 to $264 million in 1983. It employed 127 staff, and its branch network swelled with the addition of the Sandhurst's branches in Werribee, Mount Waverley, and Box Hill, and in the Gippsland towns of Morwell and Sale. In 1984 the society bought the former Kodak House (which it renamed Bendigo House) at 252 Collins Street, in the city's financial district, as 'a prestige branch presence in the heart of Melbourne'.[173] In the following year the Bendigo merged again, this time with the Mildura-based Sunraysia Permanent Building Society with whom merger talks had begun in the early 1980s. This created a business with over 200 staff and funds of $390 million. Overseeing this was too big a responsibility for Cohen, now in poor health, and in 1986 he stood down as chairman in favour of Richard Guy. By then the society's neighbourhood network included almost 30 branches (eight of them in Bendigo) and some 200 local agencies.

Mergers, together with the geographical expansion of Bendigo Building Society's business and the establishment of a branch network in Melbourne, had transformed the business horizons set for the society by Frank Perrow after the Second World War. However, its expanding scope had not rewritten the society's fundamental purpose. Thomas was as proud as Perrow had been of the 'special connection with our clients' in Bendigo that characterised the history of Bendigo

Melbourne's 'Paris End': Bendigo Sandhurst Building Society, 252 Collins Street, c. 1984.

Permanent, the Sandhurst, and the Star, and was determined to ensure that 'we didn't lose that culture' as the amalgamated building society expanded across metropolitan Melbourne. He arranged for staff appointed to the new branches to be brought to Bendigo for training ('to indoctrinate them' as Thomas jokingly put it).[174] One of John Perrow's projects was to establish this staff training programme. He devoted the first morning session of each course to the history of Bendigo Building Society, and emphasised Bendigo's 'personal touch' throughout the programme with the intention that the new staff would 'create . . . their own little Bendigo Building Society . . . wherever they were'. In essence his father's vision had not been discarded but reformulated to suit a wider scale of operations. Thomas invited new branch managers to stay at his home, so that they could be 'brainwashed at breakfast, dinner, and tea'.[175]

The powerhouse Thomas retired in 1988 as managing director, although he remained on the board where he was joined in the same year by the energetic young lawyer and businessman Robert Johanson (son of Warwick Johanson, a director and future chairman of Sandhurst Trustees). Thomas' managerial role was taken over by Rob Hunt, who became chief executive officer. Hunt had joined the staff of Bendigo Permanent in 1973. His new responsibility was to lead a building society that now claimed to be the largest in Victoria and the oldest in Australia. It held funds of some $774 million and employed 332 full-time staff. Prime Minister Bob Hawke opened its new Fountain Court headquarters in Bendigo in 1989.

Hunt's responsibilities were further increased in 1991 with the consummation of the last of the Bendigo-based mergers. Bendigo Building Society and other large Victorian building societies had since 1982 been awarded trustee status in order to strengthen their position in the tumultuous Australian financial sector by allowing them to access the lucrative trust fund field. The long-term logical consequence of this reform was Bendigo Building Society's merger in 1991 with Sandhurst Trustees. This enabled the society to provide a full range of trustee services including the administration of wills, estates, personal, corporate and charitable trusts, and expanded investment and loan capabilities. The then

Bendigo
WAREHOUSE
WAREHOUSE

managing director of Sandhurst Trustees, Ian Mansbridge, recalled that the two companies shared directors and shareholders, and in the climate of uncertainty that followed the Pyramid collapse 'it made logical sense being in the same town for the two to get together'.[176] The Trustees had grown enormously as a funds manager during the 1980s—a period that Mansbridge called 'a golden era' for trustee companies[177]—and established branches in Melbourne, Ballarat, and Albury. Its Melbourne city branch in Collins Street competed successfully for large-scale corporate trust business, and its eastern suburban branch at Elsternwick captured a large slice of the trustee business of Melbourne's Jewish community. The Trustees' new energy was sustained by the 'expansive mood' of Allen Guy, who remained its chairman until 1989. Absorbing Sandhurst Trustees' seven branches and 56 staff gave the Bendigo 36 branches and over 350 full-time staff; in the wash-up after the merger, the society's funds climbed to over one billion dollars in 1992. The Trustees' revenue streams were especially welcome in the aftermath of the Pyramid collapse when Bendigo found its own 'margins a bit tight'.[178]

Now clearly the largest building society in Victoria and the third largest in Australia, Bendigo Building Society emphatically declared that its mission statement for the future was to provide 'an alternative to the major trading banks for the personal banking requirements of many Victorians. We remain committed to providing home finance as our principal activity but to also provide other forms of financial accommodation to our existing client base'.[179] Notwithstanding its transformation from tiny beginnings in 1858 into a large regional bank in all but name by 1991, the Bendigo's focus remained on neighbourly social benefit.

Opposite page: Opened by Prime Minister Bob Hawke in 1989, Bendigo's Fountain Court headquarters was obsolete within just over a decade, such was the pace of the company's growth.

chapter

3 Settlers

Inland hub: Echuca, c. 1900. A railway truck is heavily loaded with wool bales, each stamped 'Avoca'. PHOTOGRAPH COURTESY OF THE STATE LIBRARY OF SOUTH AUSTRALIA, PRG 1258/2/291.

A faded photograph, taken in 1887, hangs in the public gallery of the Mildura and District Historical Society in far north-western Victoria. It shows Sarah Ann Trevatt and her husband Charles, reputedly the first European settlers in the new Mildura Irrigation Colony. This audacious inland settlement was begun, with Alfred Deakin's encouragement, by the American irrigation experts George and William Chaffey. Some 8000 acres were under irrigation by 1893 and 3500 settlers had become pioneer fruit growers. Among them were the Trevatts. They bought the land for their farm in November 1890 with a loan from the Sandhurst building society. The Trevatts did business with this Bendigo building society because Mildura's first shire secretary, William Sheridan, was also the Sandhurst's local agent.

'First settlers': Sarah Ann and Charles Trevatt, Mildura, 1887. REPRODUCED WITH PERMISSION FROM THE MILDURA AND DISTRICT HISTORICAL SOCIETY.

The Chaffeys' ambitious experiment ran into financial trouble during the 1890s depression and the Trevatts, in common with many of the settlers, faced hard times. In January 1896, Charles Trevatt requested the Sandhurst that he 'be allowed to pay Interest only on his loan for Two Years', and the society agreed.[1] Two years later the society's new agent (Sheridan had lost heavily on property investments, and died in 1897) advised 'that no payment had been made & the property was not improving'. Asked to investigate further, the agent reported 'that Trevatt could not pay anything at present'.[2] Little had changed when, in October 1902, Trevatt requested another two years of reduced payments. The Sandhurst's agent 'recommended the application to be granted conditionally on Mr Trevatt undertaking to plant the property with vines which would enhance the value considerably'.[3] The Trevatts could not afford even these liberal terms, whereupon the Sandhurst paid for the vines in return for the Trevatts planting and tending them. In March 1905 the agent advised that 'Mr Trevatt had performed his part of the arrangement for re-planting & payment of water rates but owing to the heat wave Mr Trevatt's crops had been practically destroyed. He was therefore compelled to request a further exemption from payments until April 1906'.[4] This request, too, was granted, and when Trevatt advised in 1906 that he was still unable to resume repayments the society refinanced the consolidation of his block with an adjoining one less encumbered by debt that was held in Sarah's name. The Trevatts were further assisted in 1909 and 1913 when their harvests again failed due to drought.

The Trevatts continued to put on a brave front, however, as another photograph, taken in 1913 at the time of their daughter Elsie's marriage to George Scott, attests. Charles, approaching 70 years of age, has a patriarchal air, but Sarah, in her early fifties, shows in her careworn face the hardships of their life in Mildura over the last quarter of a century. She died in 1929, aged 68. Charles died in 1935, aged 91. A

'First Mildura Family': Elsie Trevatt's wedding to George Scott, 1913. Charles and Sarah are seated in the front row, right of centre. REPRODUCED WITH PERMISSION FROM THE MILDURA AND DISTRICT HISTORICAL SOCIETY.

staple apricot variety, Trevatt, and a present-day Mildura street name, commemorate the hard-won achievements of this settler couple.

As the Trevatts' experience suggests, Bendigo Bank's nineteenth-century origins and its character today rest as much in rural Australia as they do in the cities. Its origins are to be found not only in the building of cities, but also in the development of new regions of European settlement in inland Australia. Bendigo Building Society's merger in 1985 with the Mildura-based Sunraysia Permanent Building Society capped off associations between Bendigo's building societies and Mildura that date back to 1890. Indeed it can be argued that the first building society 'branch' to be opened outside Bendigo was not the Footscray branch that began in 1980 but the Sandhurst building society's Mildura agency, where in November 1890, Sheridan's nominal relationship to the society as an agent was upgraded by appointing him 'an officer of the Society at Mildura for the purpose of collecting the Fortnightly Subscriptions due by members there'.[5]

Bendigo Building Society's merger in 1991 with Sandhurst Trustees brought to the building society business relationships in northern rural Victoria that dated back to the late 1880s. Bendigo Permanent had made loans on country properties since the 1860s. Regional lending played an important role in the building societies' development by providing a greatly enlarged market for capital supply. As Richard Abbott pointed out to members of the Sandhurst in 1928, 'It was important that a city like Bendigo should have financial institutions that were able to find money for the development of the north'.[6] Abbott had in mind the closer settlement of Victoria's northern agricultural regions. However, Bendigo Bank's rural pedigree was highlighted in 2000 by its partnership with the Australia-wide rural service provider, Elders Australia Limited, to launch Elders Rural Bank.

Bendigo's engagement in rural settlement, regional township development, and agribusiness financing can be divided into three periods: the establishment phase of intensive rural settlement in Victoria from 1879 to 1914; the inter-war period of rural consolidation across northern Victoria, during which time rural lending overshadowed lending both in Bendigo itself and in the developing markets of metropolitan Melbourne; and the joint venture with Elders, the first stage of which began in 1997, which entrenched Bendigo Bank's links with rural communities in South Australia and Western Australia, and provided a toehold for developing business with rural clients around Australia.

Funding Early Settlement

The first sustained rural lending by Bendigo's building societies was made by Bendigo Permanent during the late 1870s. The society had been financially challenged by the collapse in property values and the building industry in Bendigo between 1875 and 1878, and 'with the experience born of adversity . . . they wisely determined to extend the scope of the society's operations'.[7] In June 1879 the directors ordered Herman to obtain a buggy and spend half a day per week inspecting country properties. By the early to mid 1880s, Vahland and other directors were regularly travelling with Herman to Mooroopna and Shepparton north-east of Bendigo, and through Boort and Charlton to the north-west, to 'visit the various country districts in which the society's securities are'.[8] These visits were initially planned in response to applications received and letters of inquiry. However, the society moved quickly to appoint local agents in the surrounding districts to initiate business and value properties.

At Vahland's suggestion in March 1879, the society's first agent was appointed at Mooroopna, and was paid survey fees and a commission on loans. In August it was decided to appoint another agent at the bustling northern Victorian Murray River town of Echuca, terminus of the Melbourne railway and hub of the river-boat trade, to handle business in northern Victoria and (in the first venture by Bendigo building societies beyond Victoria) across the New South Wales border in the district around Moama. By October 1881, New South Wales business had become sufficiently brisk for the society to consider appointing an agent in Deniliquin, which, like Echuca in northern Victoria, functioned as a hub for wheat growing and the stock industry in southern New South Wales. The society's agents were local businessmen: stock and station agents, real estate agents, solicitors, architects and timber merchants. During the second half of 1881, Bendigo Permanent began to advertise in local newspapers in Mooroopna and Shepparton to the north-east,

First rural agency: Mooroopna, postcard, c. 1906. LA TROBE PICTURE COLLECTION, STATE LIBRARY OF VICTORIA.

Heathcote to the south-east, and Donald and St Arnaud in the north-west. In August 1881 it donated a prize at the Boort Agricultural Show. The directors resolved in June 1882 to open an account with the Commercial Bank at Echuca, and in August 1883 the secretary 'was instructed to open a/cs with some Bank in each agency district to enable the clients to make their payments there'.[9] By that time agents had also been appointed to the north-west of Bendigo at Inglewood, St Arnaud, Donald, Charlton, and Boort, and to the north-east at Shepparton.

These were new regions of intensive European settlement, and Bendigo Permanent and the newly established Sandhurst were understandably tentative about investing significantly in the frontier lands. When a hotelier from Wycheproof in north-west Victoria wrote to the Sandhurst in 1882 asking for a loan, the directors resolved to inform him that 'the Society does not propose at present to extend its operations so far beyond Sandhurst'.[10] In 1894 the insularity of the Sandhurst's directors was still evident when they requested the manager to contact the society's agent at Swan Hill about arrears by borrowers 'up there'.[11] Nevertheless, by the end of the nineteenth century, the two societies had built up a wide spread of investment activity—and a corresponding network of local agencies—across northern Victoria. This network included the northern towns of Echuca, Kerang, Swan Hill and Mildura. It extended north-west through Inglewood, St Arnaud, Wedderburn, Charlton, and Wycheproof. It also ran through north-eastern Victoria: to Shepparton, north along the Goulburn Valley, and through Benalla to Yarrawonga, Numurkah, Nathalia, and Cobram. And it reached across the border to the Deniliquin district of New South Wales.

The two Bendigo building societies were quick to realise that investment in regional development was another profitable outlet for the excess capital that they were unable to use in Bendigo. At its Diamond Jubilee celebrations in 1925, Bendigo Permanent recognised the late 1870s and early 1880s as a crucial threshold in the society's overall development, when

> the popularity of the Institution reached the younger towns opening up north of Bendigo, where its funds were readily made available to assist those brave and hardy pioneers who cleared and opened up the Mallee, which is rapidly becoming the 'Granary of Victoria', and many of which towns have to thank the Society for housing the early settlers.[12]

'A Stump Jump Plough in the Mallee Victoria', postcard, c. 1906. LA TROBE PICTURE COLLECTION, STATE LIBRARY OF VICTORIA.

'Reclaiming the Mallee Scrub', wood engraving in the *Illustrated Australian News*, 1 June 1892.
LA TROBE PICTURE COLLECTION, STATE LIBRARY OF VICTORIA.

In 1940, celebrating what they called three-quarters of a century of progress, the society's board compared Bendigo Permanent's small beginnings in 1858 with its achievements by 1886, at which time 'the Society was . . . assisting in housing those brave and hardy pioneers who cleared and opened up the Mallee and built the Northern Towns of Victoria'.[13]

The Bendigo building societies' expansion into regional Victoria and southern New South Wales coincided with a surge in rural settlement as a result of James Grant's 1869 Victorian Land Act, which introduced free selection before survey and deferred repayments on 320-acre blocks. The 1865, and especially the 1869, Land Acts generated a wave of rural settlement and township formation throughout inland Victoria during the 1870s and 1880s. Regional settlement and agricultural production were assisted by the proliferation of water networks and water trusts from the 1880s onwards into the twentieth century, and by the tapping of underground water reserves. For example in the district around Nhill in western Victoria,

Watering the inland: a water bore, 1900–1940. RURAL WATER CORPORATION COLLECTION, STATE LIBRARY OF VICTORIA.

Water tower, Kerang, postcard, c. 1908. LA TROBE PICTURE COLLECTION, STATE LIBRARY OF VICTORIA.

the first land selections took place in 1877, the town was established in 1880, and artesian drilling began in 1886. Rural settlement and the harnessing of inland water resources were reflected in a surge in Victorian wheat production from the 1870s into the early twentieth century. Although banks were the major financiers of this rural expansion, building societies also played a significant role. The *Advertiser* noted during 1886 that Bendigo Permanent's expansion into rural Victoria was helping farmers to take up new land, and the society's records confirm the granting of loans for the purchase of 320-acre free selection blocks.[14]

Notwithstanding the tapping of groundwater and artesian reserves during the late nineteenth century, drought burned the fingers of pioneer farmers and their financiers. Widespread crop failures during the early 1880s led Bendigo Permanent to change its rules in 1882 to enable it to take crops and even farm equipment as security from farmers in lieu of regular loan repayments. At Mildura likewise, the Sandhurst later accepted the projected future value of irrigation farmers' fruit crops in lieu of regular cash repayments. With the onset of the prolonged Federation Drought from 1895, Vahland acknowledged during the late 1890s that 'the continued bad seasons [had] greatly affected country securities', and loans on country properties were 'considerably written down'.[15] Chairing Bendigo Permanent's 34th annual meeting of shareholders in November 1899, Jacob Cohn reassured investors that 'The pruning knife had been used by the company with discretion, particularly with regard to country properties'.[16] Although the Federation Drought continued to impact on profit levels until early in the new century, Vahland expressed guarded hope late in 1904 that 'the troubles of the drought period were now almost overcome'. Nevertheless, on the eve of the First World War he conceded that rural Victoria had again been 'plunged into one of the greatest drought periods experienced for some years and he hoped the effects would not be as bad as predicted'. Sandhurst called its effects 'disastrous'.[17]

Such setbacks blunted the early enthusiasm of Bendigo's building societies for investing in rural settlement. In 1883, for example, Herman privately noted 'the evident disinclination on the part of the Board to extend operations in the country districts, and especially as far as regards [farm] lands'.[18] The Sandhurst had resolved by the mid 1880s to limit country lending

> to town freehold properties, and not [lend] on country lands held under leasehold, or even on freeholds. The board of management at present do not consider the latter class of properties as sufficiently safe investments for their capital, owing to the large advances required by their occupiers, the uncertainty of the seasons, and probable consequent failure of stock and crops to come up to expectation, besides the difficulty and expense connected with the collection of periodical payments.[19]

Rejecting a loan application in 1901 from the Nathalia district in northern Victoria, the board explained that the proposed security, land, 'is not a desirable one for the society to advance upon'.[20]

Whereas the Sandhurst quickly became unenthusiastic about investing in farm property, it imitated Bendigo Permanent in considering 'advances upon country town properties [as] excellent risks'.[21] The spread of rural settlement during the late nineteenth century was underpinned by what Weston Bate called the 'urban sprinkle': an emerging network of country towns that formed the spine of the inland growth corridors of regional Victoria.[22] Both societies invested in early township business development, with mixed results. In 1875, for example, Bendigo Permanent financed the building of a post and telegraph office at Kerang, and provided loans during the 1880s for a scattering of country hotels. The Sandhurst invested unhappily in a brewery and flour mill at Koondrook, near Kerang, during the 1890s, and in 1900 invested with even less success in a chain of hotels across northern Victoria. Both societies invested with more success in township house-building and land subdivision. During the late 1870s and early 1880s, for example, Bendigo Permanent instructed its agent at Mooroopna to send township plans and lists of unsold allotments. The opportunities and risks of investment in township development are highlighted by the Sandhurst's lending in Mildura.

When the society was first approached for a loan in Mildura in July 1890, the board was perplexed and instructed North to contact the Union Bank in Mildura and obtain 'any information that may be available' about properties in the new town.[23] Two of Sandhurst's directors subsequently visited Mildura and in September 1890 they submitted a 'very painstaking & exhaustive Report' that favourably assessed business opportunities in the town and surrounding district.[24]

Irrigation colony: Mildura, 1892. PHOTOGRAPH COURTESY OF THE STATE LIBRARY OF SOUTH AUSTRALIA. PRG 1258/2/1162.

Cautiously seeking to tap into the local knowledge of the district, the Sandhurst appointed shire secretary William Sheridan as its local surveyor. He was to receive fees for preparing 'a private report on each application as to the means, intention & bona fides of the applicant, so as to prevent the society granting money for speculative purposes'.[25] This arrangement was extended in November, after Sandhurst's solicitor advised that the handling of subscriptions, repayments, and members' passbooks could only be undertaken by officers of the society. Sheridan was therefore 'appointed an officer of the Society at Mildura for the purpose of collecting the Fortnightly Subscriptions due by members there, at a salary of . . . £1 per annum'.[26]

So many loans were generated by Sheridan that the board resolved in 1891 'That the Mildura Applications be not entertained at present & that the Manager inform Mr. Sheridan that the Board deems the amount already granted viz about £6000, sufficient until the District is further developed'.[27] The directors realised too late that they had over-extended themselves. The unwelcome news in 1895 'From Mr Sheridan re effect of winding up of Chaffey Bros Ltd on Mildura' was accompanied by a flood of letters from Mildura borrowers 'stating their inability to pay off arrears at present'.[28] The letters continued for the remainder of the century. In

Orange growing, Mildura, postcard, early 1900s. LA TROBE PICTURE COLLECTION, STATE LIBRARY OF VICTORIA.

1896, as the newly formed Mildura Mortgagors Defence League lobbied the society for assistance, Sheridan himself appealed for a suspension of his own repayments. The Sandhurst's new Mildura agent was urged 'to apply pressure upon those members whom he considers are in a position to pay'.[29] The properties of those who gave up the struggle were rented out by the society while the agent attempted forlornly to find buyers. When the Sandhurst was approached during 1909 for a new loan in Mildura, North was instructed to reply that 'the Board was not prepared to make advances there'.[30]

Notwithstanding the early disappointments of the Sandhurst's participation in the establishment of Mildura, the growth of country towns opened up significant new business opportunities for Bendigo's building societies. The movement of people, stock, equipment, supplies, and capital connected these rural towns into one vast inland corridor of regional settlement and development. Bendigo Permanent in particular was quick to engage with this corridor, and to embrace the new communication technologies that facilitated movement and exchange along it. By 1861, all Australia's capital cities were linked by telegraph, but it was during the 1870s and 1880s that the telegraph networks extended throughout the township network of regional Australia. Bendigo Permanent took advantage of the telegraph to expedite the handling of loan applications. It especially exploited the railway corridors that were being built to connect the country towns.

The key development that facilitated the growth of the rural economy and the diffusion of Bendigo investment capital throughout regional Victoria was the expansion of the railways. In 1864, a decade after the opening of Victoria's first railway line in Melbourne and two years after Bendigo was linked to the capital by rail, the opening of the Bendigo–Echuca line completed the colony's north-south railway corridor. A decade later, a branch line from Castlemaine (on the main Melbourne–Bendigo trunk line) to Maryborough and on to Dunolly was opened, beginning the expansion of the railway system and of more intensive European settlement into the central-west and north-west. In 1872 a new trunk line opened from Melbourne to Seymour and, in the following year, it was extended to Benalla. This likewise underpinned rural settlement in central-eastern Victoria. Then, in

The key to expansion: Bendigo railway station, c.1880. REPRODUCED WITH THE PERMISSION OF THE KEEPER OF PUBLIC RECORDS, PUBLIC RECORD OFFICE VICTORIA, AUSTRALIA. PROV, VPRS 12800/P1 H3444.

Deniliquin's first railway station, 1876. REPRODUCED WITH THE PERMISSION OF THE KEEPER OF PUBLIC RECORDS, PUBLIC RECORD OFFICE VICTORIA, AUSTRALIA. PROV, VPRS 12800/P1 H4418.

Bash in the bush: opening the Deniliquin and Moama railway, wood engraving, 5 August 1876.
LA TROBE PICTURE COLLECTION, STATE LIBRARY OF VICTORIA.

1884, the northern line from Bendigo to Kerang was opened and, in 1890, it was extended to Swan Hill. Further west, railway lines reached Donald in 1882 and Wycheproof in 1883, extending to Mildura by 1903. In the north-east the railway was continued from Benalla to St James and Tungamah in 1883–1884, to Yarrawonga in 1886 and Cobram in 1888.

In the midst of this regional railway expansion, Herman advised Bendigo Permanent in 1882 'to have advertising posters on the Country Railway stations'.[31] His advice was well heeded. The new railways were crucial for expanding the business range of the Bendigo building societies. The railways brought borrowers to Bendigo. And they facilitated distant property inspections and the establishment of a wide network of agencies. The building societies sometimes supported local lobbying for railway extension. In 1882, for example, Bendigo Permanent gave a donation to the Heathcote and Seymour Railway League. Sometimes the societies suspended regional investment until the routes of proposed lines were confirmed or if railway construction was delayed. Thus in 1895 a loan application

'Advance the Wimmera District!': celebrating the opening of the Horsham railway, engraving in the *Illustrated Australian News*, 21 February 1879. LA TROBE PICTURE COLLECTION, STATE LIBRARY OF VICTORIA.

from Mildura was deferred 'owing to the unsettled state of affairs with regard to [the proposed] Railway to Mildura', and in 1900 another Mildura loan application was declined because the 'Society [is] not making any further loans at present pending the passing of the Railway by Parliament'.[32]

The opening of railway stations often corresponded with the first stirrings of interest in the surrounding district by the Bendigo societies. In March 1882, for example, the board of Bendigo Permanent decided that the next inspection tour by several of the directors should be to Donald, where the railway station was due to open in the following month. In April 1883 the society's board resolved 'That Messrs. the Chairman [William Vahland] & [fellow director Darnton] Watson visit Charlton [in north-west Victoria] on the day of opening the railway & report upon applications & existing loans'.[33] At a special meeting of the Sandhurst board in November 1903 'It was resolved that Mr Abbott be asked to visit Mildura in connection with the opening of the Railway and inspect the various properties held by the Society'.[34] The Sandhurst had, however, been slower to adjust to the possibilities offered by rail. In 1890 the board had deferred consideration of advertising at railway stations with the comment that this was 'Not considered necessary at the present time'.[35] Their initial indifference quickly changed. The opening of Cohuna's railway station and the start of irrigation farming in the surrounding district prompted Richard Abbott in 1915 to 'submit . . . a report on the

Auspicious day: a large crowd at the opening of the Mildura railway station, 1903. PHOTOGRAPH COURTESY OF THE STATE LIBRARY OF SOUTH AUSTRALIA, PRG 1258/2/1174.

Crowds await the first train into Mildura, 1903. PHOTOGRAPH COURTESY OF THE STATE LIBRARY OF SOUTH AUSTRALIA. PRG 1258/2/1175.

Cohuna District consequent on the opening of the Elmore-Cohuna Railway'.[36]

A snapshot from Herman's field trips early in 1891 highlights the wide spread of business opportunities that the railways made possible. In February he reported to the Bendigo Permanent board that during the previous fortnight he had spent from Tuesday till Thursday of the first week visiting Dunolly, St Arnaud, and Donald, and that in the second week he had left Bendigo on the Monday and travelled via Melbourne to the Goulburn Valley and Yarrawonga, returning to Bendigo via Echuca on the Friday night. Over seven days he had travelled through much of the heartland of regional Victoria and had used seven different railway lines to do so.

The Bendigo building societies' country dealings in Victoria and southern New South Wales grew further during the early twentieth century, stimulated in part by the interventions of a new competitor, the Bendigo and Eaglehawk Starr-Bowkett Building Society (or the Star, as it became known from 1911). Between the turn of the century and the First World War, the Star developed a rural client base in Kerang to the north, Kyabram, Rochester, and Echuca to the north-east, Charlton and the Boort-Korong Vale district to the north-west, and Mandurang to the south. The Sandhurst responded by expanding its own network of agents to consolidate its lending activities in northern Victoria and southern New South Wales. Richard Abbott led this expansionist drive, assisted by a newly appointed director, the

A boom in irrigation farming: fruit pickers at Mildura, c. 1910. PHOTOGRAPH COURTESY OF THE STATE LIBRARY OF SOUTH AUSTRALIA. PRG 1258/2/1246.

architect William Beebe. Early in 1901 'Mr Abbott reported that he had visited Shepparton & Nagambie on his trip to Nathalia and considered there was a good opening there for safe business on behalf of the Society'.[37] Later in the year he visited and prepared reports on Swan Hill, Echuca, and Deniliquin. By 1910, the Sandhurst had established agencies at Shepparton, Rochester, Echuca, Kerang, and Swan Hill in the north, and at Castlemaine and Kyneton in central Victoria.

Agents continued to be appointed from among local businessmen. In 1906, for example, Beebe recommended the saddler at Korong Vale as agent for the district, having recently met him during an inspection of the area. Agents juggled multiple activities and sometimes multiple agencies. The Star's Kerang agent also became an agent in 1906 for the Sandhurst, which judged this service town for irrigation farming, wheat growing and cattle raising 'to be in a very prosperous state' and thus 'a suitable place for making advances'. By contrast, Charlton, on the eastern fringe of the Wimmera wheat belt, was deemed to be already 'a settled place with apparently little prospect of improvement [and therefore] it [was] unlikely the society would reap much benefit from an Agency there'.[38] The Sandhurst's chairman, William Neill, reported to shareholders late in 1909 that 'During the past year a fair share of business has emanated from the principal well-established and rising

Expanding the wheat lands: horses ploughing in the Mallee, 1901–1940. LA TROBE PICTURE COLLECTION, STATE LIBRARY OF VICTORIA.

country centres, and the Board intend further extending operations in this direction as the opportunity occurs'.[39] Early in 1911 the Sandhurst drew up a comprehensive list of country towns in which it calculated agencies could be successfully established, and Beebe was asked 'to map out a motor tour & cost of same'.[40] New agencies were subsequently established at Deniliquin, and at Nagambie and Euroa in central Victoria. Lending also began in the New South Wales border town of Tocumwal. The society reported to shareholders in 1913 that 'The further extension of operations has engaged the consideration of the Board, and the rapid development of the rich agricultural northern areas has opened a new field for investment'.[41]

Notwithstanding the expansion of regional business by the Star and the Sandhurst before 1914, their activities continued to be dwarfed by Bendigo Permanent. The latter increasingly focused on northern Victoria which, as intensive farming became consolidated, looked to Bendigo as its regional centre. Bendigo Permanent's directors astutely recognised that 'With the northern Mallee opened up almost to Mildura, Bendigo, apart from its mining wealth, was becoming the distributing centre of the north'. The society boasted in 1916 that 'the name of the society is a household word right through the northern district'.[42]

Supporting Regional Expansion

The 1920s and 1930s constitute the high point of the Bendigo building societies' twentieth-century engagement with country Australians, during which time rural lending became a cornerstone of the societies' business growth. This surge in country financing took place alongside government soldier settlement and closer settlement schemes that greatly increased the number of people on the land, although depressed world prices for food and wool meant slim profits for most farmers, and bare subsistence for many. The Bendigo societies established extensive networks of agencies and borrowers throughout the country towns and farming districts of Victoria and southern New South Wales. Bendigo Permanent led the way, reporting in 1919 that 'With the cessation of the war the Society can now adopt a more progressive policy and is extending its operations into all the important inland towns, opening new agencies with every indication of successful business resulting from such efforts'.[43] The society's expansionist drive was especially evident in the north. The 1924 annual meeting of shareholders was told that 'the society now ranks as the most popular Institution in Northern Victoria', and in 1928 its directors added to the society's advertisements the words 'Advance Bendigo in the North'.[44]

This growth surge was led by Andrew Balsillie, Bendigo Permanent's secretary between 1916 and 1945. Balsillie was an energetic man, aged in his early forties when he was appointed secretary. He was Bendigo born, the son of Scottish immigrants, but he had close links with the countryside. In 1903 he married Helen Calder, from Dunolly to the west of Bendigo, and in the early 1920s he bought a dairy farm at Grassy Flat on the outskirts of Bendigo. Balsillie was a hobby farmer, with most of the work being undertaken by his son. Balsillie senior commuted to his Bendigo office by horse and gig until the farm 'went bad during the Depression'.[45]

Balsillie was intent not only on expanding the geographical range of Bendigo Permanent's activities, but also on ensuring that 'our country clients . . . have their transactions dealt with as promptly as though they were residing in Bendigo, which is much appreciated by them'.[46] Achieving that goal had 'Mr. Balsillie . . .

soon travelling the length and breadth of Victoria, and even into New South Wales towns'.[47] In addition to maintaining its dominance in northern Victoria, Bendigo Permanent had by 1925 consolidated its presence in the central-east by opening agencies in Euroa and Mansfield, and had moved into three new regions: the south-east and south-west (with agencies in Leongatha and Colac), and the west (with agencies in Ararat, Stawell, Hamilton, Horsham, Warracknabeal, and Jeparit). It had also opened another agency in southern New South Wales, at Balranald, north of Swan Hill. By 1940, the society was operating in 100 Victorian towns, and had clients across the state and also in New South Wales.

Building society pioneer: Andrew Balsillie, 1925. Balsillie joined Bendigo Permanent in 1896 and was its secretary-manager from 1916 to 1945.

The Star and the Sandhurst building societies echoed Bendigo Permanent's activities, concentrating on strengthening their business profile across northern and central Victoria. The Sandhurst especially looked to build upon the foundations that it had established in the north before the First World War. Richard Abbott remarked in 1924 that 'Bendigo was becoming a big financial centre. The society's business extended as far abroad as the Goulburn Valley and along the Murray to Mildura. In all these important northern towns the society was trying to assist in settlement, and it was receiving applications from all over these country centres'.[48] Frank Cohen, the Sandhurst's solicitor, echoed his words in 1926, pointing out 'that Bendigo was prospering by reason of the fact that the country was prospering, and the country was as yet purely in its infancy. In carrying on the policy of extension the directors could not fail. Country towns were increasing in size, the value of buildings was increasing, and land values had improved enormously in the last few years'.[49] Township growth and rural industries offered opportunities for expansion well beyond the horizons within which Bendigo's building societies had previously operated. Abbott calculated that 'Fully two-thirds of the society's business came from outside Bendigo. The society was helping to develop the towns in Northern Victoria. They were becoming very prosperous, and provided a safe and solid business for the society'.[50] It is probable that as a result of rural expansion during the 1920s and 1930s, at least a third and perhaps half of the loans generated by Bendigo building societies went to rural clients.

Imitating Bendigo Permanent, the Sandhurst exploited the railway system to extend its business reach in country Australia. The society's chairman, William Neill, remarked in 1923 that 'The directors intended to extend their business to the north and the extension of the railways into New South Wales would considerably help with the expansion of the business'.[51] The Sandhurst launched a rural publicity campaign during the early to mid 1920s, with 'pictorial posters' in country railway stations[52] and advertisements in regional newspapers. By the 1940s it had turned as well to advertising in cinemas in country towns.

George Garvin, 1938: driving Sandhurst Building Society's rural expansion.

George Garvin, who had joined the Sandhurst board on Beebe's death in 1920, gradually took over from an ageing Abbott as the driving force behind the society's expansion of rural lending. Late in 1926 he 'submitted [a] proposal for visiting the chief country towns in the Northern and Goulburn Valley areas, and it was resolved that Mr. Garvin be authorised to make a preliminary inspection of the towns mentioned, and report as to the advisability of extending the Society's business in those districts'. There was an undercurrent of hesitation, however, in the board's decision. The phrases 'make a preliminary inspection' and 'report as to the advisability of extending the

Society's business' had been substituted for Garvin's original proposal that he 'be authorised to carry out the scheme outlined by him'.[53] The board was loth to commit itself unreservedly beyond the neighbourly bounds of Bendigo. Even Abbott, who initiated the Sandhurst's expansion into rural Victoria, would have raised eyebrows beyond Bendigo when in 1924 he referred to the communities dotted along the Goulburn and Murray valleys as being 'far abroad'.[54] In 1927 the Sandhurst rejected several loan applications received from Narrandera (to the north-west of Wagga Wagga in New South Wales), explaining that 'owing to [its] distance from Bendigo, and high costs of inspection, we were not extending to that district at present'. In the following year the board instructed the society's manager that an applicant from Albury 'be informed the Directors are not advancing money in that district on account of distance from Bendigo'.[55]

Notwithstanding the amber light that he had been given by his co-directors, Garvin set off through the Goulburn Valley early in 1927, then travelled north into New South Wales, looping through Tocumwal, Finley, and Deniliquin before returned to Bendigo via Echuca. At his recommendation, new agencies were established at Rochester, Tocumwal, and Finley. He made further tours through the north-east and north-west during 1928 and 1929. In 1936 Garvin (who during the year replaced Abbott as chairman of the Sandhurst) turned his attention to the mid-west, hitherto the preserve of Bendigo Permanent, advising that 'he would be making a trip of inspection through the Ararat, Stawell & Donald districts with a view to opening up the District for new business for the Society'.[56] In a subsequent trip he extended his inspections through St Arnaud, Horsham, and Warracknabeal, and Sandhurst agencies were quickly set up at Maryborough, Ararat, Stawell, St Arnaud, Horsham, and Warracknabeal. Garvin told shareholders at the end of the year that 'The society had opened business in several new towns in the Wimmera, such as St Arnaud, Warracknabeal, Ararat, Stawell, and Maryborough; and there were prospects of business being obtained in other country towns also. It had done a good deal of business in Mildura (nearly all on new properties) and also in Shepparton and Swan Hill. There were applications coming in for about as much as the society could handle'.[57] In 1937 Garvin reported that 'The area covered by the Sandhurst Building Society covered Bendigo, the north of the State, the Wimmera, the Goulburn Valley, and across to Wangaratta'.[58] The Sandhurst's loans were modest but extensive. The society noted in 1939 that 'Most of the loans now being made are in amounts not exceeding £500, and are located in practically every town of importance in the northern and midland districts'.[59]

Inter-war lending by the Bendigo building societies was directed in the main to the booming country towns, supporting both home-building and business expansion. Abbott remarked in 1928 that 'in addition to assisting people to provide homes for themselves, [the Sandhurst] was helping in some towns in the north in regard to business premises'.[60] Residential lending went mostly to home-owners, although the societies also dabbled in speculative housing projects. In 1922 for example, a real-estate business in Shepparton informed the Sandhurst that 'they were holding a large sub-divisional sale in Shepparton, and were desiring to know whether the society would advance money for building purposes'.[61] In 1926 the society flirted with another housing subdivision at Shepparton, but decided that the building blocks were too distant from the town centre. Bendigo Permanent participated in township development at Horsham, although Balsillie was disappointed in the results, noting after an inspection of the town in 1929 that 'Crop prospects

Inter-war township growth: Shepparton fruit cannery, 1923.

are poor & residential allotments of the several subdivisions are not maintaining values'.[62] Business loans were mostly on a small scale. In 1933, for example, a loan of £650 was advanced on a town block in Mildura for the building of a shop and dwelling. Larger business loans were however occasionally granted by the building societies. In the same year the Hepburn Chalet resort at Hepburn Springs was advanced £1000 by the Sandhurst.

The building societies also expanded their lending to farmers, despite their earlier misadventures and the continuing vulnerability of rural production to drought. Garvin was forthright in his support for the farming sector, declaring in 1932 'that the man on the land, who was producing a vast proportion of the country's wealth, should be assisted to the fullest possible extent. Unless the primary producer were supported, he would have to cease operations, and the country would go to the wall. Australia's prosperity was wrapped up in that of the farmer'.[63] Farm loans on acreages of from 300 to over 1000 acres were advanced during the inter-war period, loans as large as £8000 being considered. The borrowers were Murray River irrigators and wheat-sheep farmers. It was not unusual for the societies to receive the proceeds from the sale of a farm's entire wheat harvest in lieu of regular cash repayments.

The second half of the twentieth century, unlike the inter-war years, was a period of rural consolidation—and in some regards even retreat—by the Bendigo building societies rather than continuing expansion. Paradoxically this hiatus coincided with a long period, from the end of the Second World War to about 1980, of rural affluence as world commodity prices strengthened and moister weather conditions set in. As Blainey put it, during these years 'the big country towns oozed prosperity'.[64] Although rural borrowers now represented a substantial fraction of the building societies' clients, the interface between these clients and the societies' offices in Bendigo was poor. Balsillie's goal to provide a level of service on a par with that offered to clients in Bendigo had been overtaken by the sheer pace of growth. A better rural presence was required than could be delivered by part-time agents and periodic inspection tours from Bendigo. Rural customers wanted easy points of contact, and uniform standards and procedures. The Bendigo building societies,

Post-war agricultural boom: wheat farming, 1948. FROM THE COLLECTION OF THE NATIONAL ARCHIVES OF AUSTRALIA, A1200, L9600.

their strategic thinking veering back towards insularity, were slow to provide them.

The necessary adjustments were especially slow in coming at Bendigo Permanent, where the momentum of state-wide growth that had been begun by Balsillie stalled during the post-war years. During the immediate post-war period, Lansell reported that loan applications to Bendigo Permanent 'continued to come from all towns throughout Victoria', and his colleague Dr Albert Beischer calculated that the society 'had 1500 clients throughout Victoria in 95 country towns and 60 Melbourne suburbs'.[65] Bendigo Permanent could claim at its 1965 centenary celebrations that there was scarcely a city or town in Victoria where a borrower or an investor had not benefited from association with Bendigo Permanent. However, its inter-war vision of spreading into new regions and across state boundaries had dimmed. Although by 1965 directors were congratulating themselves upon new business growth in the Western District and—boosted by expanded electricity production—the Latrobe Valley, their attitude to rural business had become timid. Their main focus had contracted to Greater Bendigo. The board had instructed Perrow in 1953 that the 'Society [should] proceed with caution in future advances to some country towns. All future advances in the areas visited to be on conservative basis'.[66] Brian Thomas sought to turn things around when he became manager of Bendigo Permanent in 1978. It seemed obvious to him that local demand could not sustain the growth of three building societies, and he resolved to again 'put our foot in the water' of a bigger pond.[67] Thomas was eager to expand the society's rural loan book, looking especially to Shepparton, but his energies were directed mainly to building up business in metropolitan Melbourne. At Sandhurst Trustees, Allen Guy used his business connections to establish trustee work with agribusinesses in the Shepparton district and recruited Peter Ross-Edwards, the former state leader of the rural-oriented National Party, to the Trustees' board. Like Thomas, however, he looked mainly to Melbourne to stretch his growth targets.

Expanding irrigation farming: Mildura vineyard, postcard, c. 1950. LA TROBE PICTURE COLLECTION, STATE LIBRARY OF VICTORIA.

Whereas Bendigo Permanent and the Trustees trod water during most of this period, and the Star focused its energies on Bendigo and Melbourne rather than rural Victoria, the Sandhurst pursued a different course. At first its activities seemed undifferentiated from those of Bendigo Permanent. The society initially focused, like Bendigo Permanent, on consolidating its existing country operations. It therefore concentrated on the Goulburn and Murray valleys, the north-east and the west, and built up its lending in Kyabram as irrigation farming in the

VIC
GJZ·923

district expanded. Its largest regional client bases in 1954 were Mildura, Stawell, Ararat, Benalla, Echuca, Horsham, and Shepparton. These seven centres continued to dominate rural lending into the 1960s, although the relative positions of each were changing. By 1961, Shepparton had become the largest regional market, followed by Stawell, Mildura, Benalla, Horsham, Ararat, Swan Hill, and Echuca. However, the old agency network could not sustain the substantial volume of business that these centres were now generating. In 1961, in a sign of things to come, the Sandhurst closed down its agency at Horsham, which had emerged as the hub of the Wimmera farming belt, and in its place opened an account at the ANZ Bank 'for the convenience of clients in the district for the payment of subscriptions'.[68]

The logical next step was to imitate the banks and establish branches of its own. After Brian Guest was appointed Sandhurst's manager in 1965, he set about building up a network of Sandhurst branches. By 1982 there were 32 branches, with supporting country agencies scattered across Inglewood, Maryborough, Maldon, Castlemaine, Kyneton, Daylesford, Woodend, Gisborne, Sunbury, Romsey, Seymour, Euroa, Nagambie, and Heathcote in central Victoria; Stanhope, Kyabram, Tatura, Shepparton, Benalla, Wangaratta, Yarrawonga, Cobram, and Numurkah in the north-east; Rochester, Echuca, Cohuna, and Kerang to the north; Swan Hill, Sea Lake, and Mildura in the north-west; and Wedderburn, Boort, Charlton, Wycheproof, Birchip, Donald, St Arnaud, Minyip, and Horsham to the west. Country loans accounted for approximately 62 per cent of the Sandhurst's total loans in October 1954, as against some 26 per cent in Bendigo and 12 per cent in Melbourne. The countryside's relative position eroded thereafter as home-lending boomed across greater Melbourne. By October 1960, country loans had slipped to 45 per cent of the total, Bendigo comprising 29 per cent and Melbourne 31 per cent. In October 1961, country loans represented about 40 per cent of the total, Bendigo 32 per cent, and Melbourne 28 per cent.

After its merger with the Star in 1978 and the Sandhurst in 1983, and influenced also by Brian Thomas' new management style, Bendigo Building society not only

Opposite page: Harvest time in the Wimmera, 1957. RURAL WATER CORPORATION COLLECTION, STATE LIBRARY OF VICTORIA.

'Make Dough out of your Wheat Harvest Dollars', Bendigo Sandhurst Building Society advertisement, 15 January 1985.

set up branches across Melbourne, but sought to consolidate its presence in the larger country towns, as the Sandhurst had done, by upgrading key agencies to branches. Thomas' goal was to establish a branch network throughout Victoria. It was a radical shift for, as John Perrow recalls, in the early 1980s the great majority of the society's loans were allocated across Melbourne, followed by Bendigo.[69] During the mid 1980s, branches were opened in Morwell, Traralgon, and Sale in the south-east, Cobram, Benalla, and Shepparton in the central-north, Echuca, Kerang, Swan Hill, and Mildura in the north and north-west, and Castlemaine in central Victoria. The society also lifted its advertising profile in the rural press. At the end of harvest time in 1985, for example, an advertisement in the *Donald Birchip Times* urged farmers to invest their harvest profits in Bendigo Building Society and thereby 'make Dough out of your Wheat Harvest Dollars'.[70] The society's profile was much lower in the south-east and south-west, where other building societies, among them Pyramid and Capital, were already well established.

Bendigo's merger with the Sunraysia Permanent Building Society in 1985 led it to establish a Mildura Regional Advisory Board (comprising members of the former Sunraysia board) to oversee operations in the district, and a Gippsland Regional Board was created in the following year. For the first time, regional engagement was matched explicitly by tailored administrative processes. By 1988 the building society controlled 35 branches and maintained 240 agencies. Bendigo's takeover of the Capital and Compass building societies in 1992 meant more branches in the Geelong district and to the south-east of Melbourne, further consolidating its state-wide presence. The takeovers also triggered another internal management overhaul, with the reorganisation of the society's activities into four regional divisions: central, Melbourne and the south-east, Geelong and the south-west, and 'Country and Provincial'. Although this divisional structure did not survive Bendigo's transformation into a bank, the new business's regional orientation was clear. In 1995 the newly established Bendigo Bank comprised 74 branches and over 400 agencies in Victoria and southern New South Wales.

It seemed to the new bank's managers that here was the beginning of something tangible by which to distinguish themselves from their well-established banking competitors. Whereas banking deregulation had encouraged the major Australian banks to reposition themselves as global players, Bendigo Bank occupied 'a unique position as the only regionally-based Australian bank' and was thus the bank best placed to meet the needs of rural Australians.[71] Chairman Richard Guy commented in 1998 that 140 years of history had shown that 'We are . . . close to the communities we serve'.[72] Although that history was best known for the neighbourhood relationships that had been developed in the cities of Bendigo and Melbourne, Guy was also conscious of Bendigo Building Society's long engagement with regional communities, and knew from his father Allen of the business connections that Sandhurst building society and Sandhurst Trustees had also built up in rural Victoria. Guy was keen for the new bank to extend those relationships. He knew from running the Guy family's successful Bendigo-based businesses across northern and central Victoria just how vast the market for rural financial services had become, and his family's long established roots in the region gave him an affinity with the people, the activities and the values that were encapsulated in the proud phrase 'that's country!'[73]

'The Next Step'—The Elders Alliance

Bendigo Bank's 1998 annual report carried the subtitle 'Taking the next step'. Guy explained that the step the bank had in mind was to become a national bank for regional and rural Australians. There were two apparent shortcomings in Bendigo Bank's thinking. Firstly, its regional coverage was limited to Victoria and southern New South Wales. Secondly, even in these regions its business was largely confined to country towns rather than the surrounding farming communities.

The new bank's difficulties finding traction within those farming communities was underlined in the Victorian Wimmera where, despite a history of engagement in the region dating back to the mid 1920s, a Bendigo Bank branch was not established in the regional hub of Horsham until 1999. Bendigo's managing director Rob Hunt was well aware of these shortcomings, and had devised a solution for them. In August 1998 the bank announced an agreement with Elders Australia Limited 'to form a joint venture company to deliver more effective banking services to rural Australia'. The joint venture company would be established as a separate rural bank, operating through Bendigo Bank's 78 branches and Elders' broader national network of 220 outlets. It would accept rural deposits, expand farming loans, and provide a wide range of financial products right across Australia that were 'tailored for the needs of primary producers'.[74] Bendigo Bank called the alliance 'extremely complementary to Bendigo given the Bank's stated commitment to regional and rural areas'.[75]

The announcement came like a bombshell. Australia's newest and smallest bank was to be an equal partner with one of Australia's oldest and largest agribusinesses. The alliance would give it a springboard for servicing the banking needs of rural customers across Australia. Elders was many times the size of Bendigo Bank in 1998. Its business empire had originated in South Australia in 1839 and expanded around Australia, handling wool broking, livestock, farm management, stock and station merchandising, insurance, and real estate. It had merged in 1962 with its New South Wales equivalent Goldsbrough Mort, making it the master of rural services in Australia's 'brown country' beyond the coastal plains, and a rival to the other national agribusiness juggernaut Wesfarmers, which in 1993 took over the Victorian-based Dalgety Farmers Limited. The *Financial Review* summarised news of the Elders-Bendigo joint venture with the headline 'Bendigo to go even more rural', and the *Weekly Times* noted approvingly that the deal would 'offer farmers an alternative to the big-four banks'.[76] The *Business Review Weekly* predicted that the joint venture, by combining 'the skills of Bendigo Bank (particularly the financial, technology, risk and banking framework) with Elders' capacity to service the rural community . . . across the country will produce a new "bank" to service rural

Australia'.[77] In Adelaide, the joint venture was applauded because it gave Elders an entry point into rural banking, the *Adelaide Advertiser* announcing 'Elders leaps into banking'.[78] In Bendigo the alliance was hailed because of the vastly expanded banking horizons which the alliance with Elders promised. The *Bendigo Advertiser* called the joint venture with the Elders 'farm services conglomerate' an 'inspired' move. It was an 'exercise in lateral thinking' because it enabled Bendigo Bank 'to build on its already giant-slaying reputation as a bank which cares about the bush'.[79]

Bendigo Bank's concept for the alliance was masterminded by Hunt and Johanson. Hunt saw in the joint venture an opportunity for 'adding one and one and trying to make three'. The joint venture would 'use the front office' of Elders' rural branch network to supply banking products, and 'the back office of Bendigo' to generate those products, ensure regulatory compliance, and maintain the systems technology. It would thereby create 'a virtual bank' in between the rural operations of Elders and Bendigo Bank, achieving collaboratively what neither of the two participants could attain on their own.[80] Bendigo had what Elders wanted most—a banking licence—together with the systems and the knowledge to make it work. Elders was confident that by acquiring these things it would succeed in rural banking where others could not, because it already had a large national rural branch network and the brand recognition that came from a long history of servicing primary production around Australia. Elders' key assets were what Bendigo Bank enjoyed in Victoria's towns and cities: local credibility and neighbourhood knowledge. Bendigo needed these assets if it was to develop a national presence in Australian banking. They were personified by Elders' local branch managers, 'the local bloke type fellow as they call them'.[81] Not only did they have the farmers' confidence; they were a well of local intelligence that could be harnessed in order to wind back the risk factor that constrained rural banking. As Johanson remarked, 'Elders deals with virtually every farmer in the country. They know—the people from Elders who are driving around every day, they're selling them fertiliser, they're buying the cattle from them—they know who the good farmers are, they know who they want to lend to'.[82]

The 'local bloke type fellow': cattle sale at Coolah, New South Wales. PHILIP QUIRK (AAP IMAGE/WILDLIGHT).

Johanson and Hunt acknowledged that it would take decades of hard work and expense for Bendigo Bank to build up a credible rural network on its own. No bank could compete with Elders' experience in providing seasonal finance to farmers. Assessing Bendigo Bank's competency in farm lending, Ian Mansbridge (a senior Bendigo executive, formerly the managing director of Sandhurst Trustees, and the first managing director of the joint venture project with Elders) conceded that 'we wouldn't have a clue'.[83] Neither did Bendigo have banking products tailored to farmers' needs. It did not understand farming. In order to build national scale and quickly roll out rural products, Johanson and Hunt were prepared to develop 'a radical approach to franchising banking business'.[84]

Bendigo Bank did not initially fully appreciate the thinking that had shaped Elders' endorsement of their alliance. Since 1996 Elders had been controlled by the Western Australia-based Futuris Corporation, and its strategy for the Bendigo joint venture was driven by Alan Newman, Futuris' chief executive officer. Newman's goal was to add value to Elders' rural branch network by joining banking to the activities that their 'local bloke' could undertake at the branch level. As Hunt put it, they wanted 'to get more through that . . . shop'.[85] Elders did have long experience in arranging seasonal finance for farmers through the branch network, but because of federal regulatory controls, this was necessarily ancillary to its bread-and-butter stock and station activities. Its rural loans book could be counted in the billions of dollars by the 1980s but the demand for rural lending was many billions more, which Elders—without a bank's ability to accept deposits—could not supply. One option was for Elders to become a rural bank itself. Another option was to form an alliance with an existing bank in order to tap fully into the huge rural finance market.

Elders had attempted to become a bank during the 1980s and again in the mid 1990s. The first attempt was part and parcel of the company's soaring though rocky ride into the corporate stratosphere of Australian business operations during the 1980s. In 1981 the company had been merged with jam maker Henry Jones IXL to become Elders IXL, with John Elliott its managing director. Elliott built up a big rural financial services arm within Elders IXL, and unsuccessfully sought a full banking licence from the Australian Reserve Bank in order to expand it further. Elliott's business interest, however, was more in brewing than in rural financial services. In 1983 he took over Carlton and United Breweries, the first in a series of takeovers that made Elders IXL one of the largest brewers in the world. But in doing so Elliott overextended himself, and during the economic downturn of the late 1980s he lost control of Elders IXL. He left its Elders arm in crisis, bled dry to finance company takeovers, its loans book shrunk from billions to millions of dollars, saddled with bad debts, and savaged by staff cuts and branch closures. In a rescue mission, Max Ormsby was recruited from the NAB in 1990 to become general manager of Elders' rural finance division in Adelaide. His task was to shore up the rural loans book and create a secure basis for re-establishing the rural finance business.

Although Elders was hived off from the parent company in 1993, with the Farmers' Federation and Futuris becoming major shareholders, Futuris' boss Alan Newman supported Ormsby's efforts to revive the company's rural finance arm. Newman understood banking (he was on the board of Challenge Bank, created in 1987 through the merger of the Perth and Hotham building societies, until its takeover by Westpac in 1995). Newman and Ormsby recognised that Elders needed better access to rural deposits in order to rebuild and expand its loans book. When Futuris won control of Elders in 1996, Futuris executive David Hills was appointed to run the company in Adelaide, and Ormsby was confirmed as manager of rural finance. Elders again lobbied the Reserve Bank for a banking licence, but the existing regulatory framework still barred it from achieving that goal.

The federal government's Wallis Review in 1996 provided another opportunity for Elders to put its case for specialist rural banking status. In several confidential submissions, Elders argued that it was manifestly 'in the bush for the long term' whereas the major banks were not, and that it had multiple and well-established business connections with rural Australia (in wool, livestock, merchandise, insurance, rural finance, real estate) whereas the banks' already tenuous relationship with the bush was being rapidly eroded by their closure of country bank branches. Elders asked Wallis for greater regulatory flexibility to enable it to offer a full range of financial services to rural Australia. Encouraged by Wallis's 1997 report, which recommended regulatory flexibility to accommodate 'niche players', Elders renewed its bid for a banking licence. It put its case directly to the Australian Prudential Regulation Authority (APRA), the new banking regulatory authority, and simultaneously lobbied Treasury for approval.[86] Bendigo Bank was sanguine about the rumours it had heard about these manoeuvres. Even if a rural banking licence was granted, Hunt thought, the result would be 'a tiny bank'.[87] But Elders had another option. Mindful of its disappointments in the past, and worried that the Wallis report foreshadowed tighter regulatory control of their 'local blokes' in the stock and station agencies, Elders also began talks with Westpac and NAB with the object of forming an alliance with an existing major bank. Elders knew that its rural loans book was a carrot for any bank partner. By 1998 the loans book had been built up again to some $600 million, about 60 per cent of it in seasonal loans.

The idea of an alliance between Elders and Bendigo Bank did not come from Hunt and Johanson, nor even from Hills at Elders or his boss Newman at Futuris. It was suggested by the chairman of Futuris, William Beischer. Bill Beischer was a Bendigo boy, and the son of a former chairman of Bendigo Permanent. He had forged a successful career as a senior executive in Pacific Dunlop, and he became chairman of Futuris after his retirement. He also took on other company directorships, among them Elders and Sandhurst Trustees. And after the Trustees' merger with Bendigo Building Society in 1991, Beischer was invited onto the latter's board late in 1993. The invitation was recognition of both business talent and history. Bill's father, Dr Albert Beischer, had been appointed a director of Bendigo

Joint venture advocate: William (Bill) Beischer, chairman of Futuris and a director of Bendigo Building Society and Bendigo Bank, 1993–2001.

Permanent in 1936 and became its chairman in 1959, shortly before his death in 1961. Bill's uncle, Dr William Beischer, was also a director of Bendigo Permanent (from 1965 until 1980). Upon joining Bendigo's board, Bill Beischer became privy to its discussions about repositioning itself as a bank, developing farm products, and also about community banking (see chapter four). He was aware as well, from Futuris, of its attempts to expand the financial services function of Elders to a new level. He grasped the synergy as Bendigo moved to reposition itself as a bank, and suggested an alliance to both boards.

Neither board was initially convinced. Futuris was pursuing its own banking option for Elders, and was discussing joint ventures with the major banks. Beischer countered that Bendigo Bank was rural-based like themselves, and that because it was small it was not in a position to dominate the alliance as a larger bank would seek to do. Bendigo Bank was preoccupied with bedding down its new operating systems as a bank, and was cautious about Elders' own turbulent recent years in rural services. By 1997 however, with Elders' branch network and rural loans book stabilised, Bendigo was ready to begin negotiations. As Hunt noted cautiously at mid year, 'certainly [a] franchising or agency [agreement] is a possibility—but first we must demonstrate some advantage for [Elders]'.[88] For its part, Elders-Futuris was prepared to talk to Bendigo as it was already doing with other potential bank partners.

It was a complicated process. Bendigo was not prepared simply to provide its banking product to a new Elders-owned rural bank. Elders was not prepared to see its financial arm subsumed under Bendigo's banking licence. Initial talks were held during mid 1997 between Hunt and Newman, with follow-up discussions involving Johanson, Beischer, Hills, and Ormsby. Futuris's scepticism about dealing with so small and recently established a bank was turned on its head by Beischer's argument that a smaller bank would be easier to deal with, and by Bendigo's pragmatic proposition that because it had recently successfully gone through the licensing process with the regulatory authorities it had the expertise and the documentation on file to do it again, and expeditiously, for a joint-venture rural bank. Late in 1997 detailed negotiations began between Johanson and Newman's financial adviser Les Wozniczka, who 'fought like cat and dog' on behalf of their companies' interests as they drafted a workable financial structure for the joint venture.[89] Grant Samuel and Associates were engaged by Bendigo midway through 1998 to fine tune the financial framework that had been hammered out, and a 'Heads of Agreement' between Bendigo and Elders was announced in August. A Bendigo negotiating team of Hunt, Richard Guy, Johanson, and Mansbridge undertook the final round of discussions with Elders-Futuris, and an agreement was signed in December. The formal launch of the joint venture company, Elders Rural Services Ltd, which was to operate initially under Bendigo's banking licence, took place on 4 January 1999. Bendigo Bank's Mansbridge had been appointed as the new company's managing director before its public launch, and moved to Adelaide on Grand Final day in 1998 (auspiciously won by the Adelaide Crows) to oversee the company's establishment and the application process for its separate licensing as a bank. It was a difficult assignment. Although Futuris withdrew its banking application to APRA, and Elders Rural Services immediately began to prepare a new one, there was initially little trust on either side.

The tensions were generated in part by putting together two different business management styles. Many Elders staff were suspicious of city-based bankers who knew little about farming operations. They were loth to adopt different procedures dictated by a 'pure bank guy', whether from Bendigo or from APRA, which was scrutinising the bank application process.[90] However, Bendigo staff found that their Elders colleagues were not as ready as they thought they were for full-blown rural lending. Mansbridge, who knew many of the

Farmer-banker: Ian Mansbridge, formerly the managing director of Sandhurst Trustees, and inaugural managing director of Elders Rural Bank, 2000.

APRA staff from their recent Reserve Bank days when they had processed Bendigo's banking licence, quickly detected APRA's concern that Elders' stock and station network would not adjust to the strict compliance standards that were the condition for issuing a banking licence. Mansbridge's task was to reassure APRA and to re-educate the Elders branch managers without destroying the 'stockie' culture on which Elders' credibility rested in rural communities. The challenge facing Mansbridge was lessened because, given the fierce competition with Wesfarmers for stock and station business, most Elders stockies wanted to become local bank managers. Creating a new rural banking culture was nonetheless a harrowing experience for Mansbridge. He pulled it off because, in addition to being a banker, he was a third-generation farmer himself. When visiting farms with the Elders 'local blokes', 'I'd do something deliberately . . . We'd go into a shearing shed [and] (because, you know, I'm also a wool classer) I'd go up and pick up a fleece, throw it on the table . . . I wouldn't say anything, I'd do it quietly and see the guys look and they'd talk about it and say "Ah, this bloke *does* know something about farming, he's not just a pure banker." And I think that . . . helped our relationship'.[91] The banking application submission was completed late in 1999 and a banking authority was granted in June 2000. Elders Rural Services, renamed

Launching Elders Rural Bank, Canberra, 27 June 2000. Left to right: Ian Mansbridge, Rob Hunt, John Dawkins (chairman, ERB), Joe Hockey (Federal Financial Services and Regulation Minister), and David Hills (managing director, Elders Limited).

Elders Rural Bank (ERB), was launched on 28 August 2000. The bank's chairman, John Dawkins (a former treasurer of Australia, and an acquaintance of Newman), hailed it as 'the first bank of the new millennium', which gave rural Australia a unique combination of personal service and leading edge technology.[92]

Beneath the surface, however, tensions between Bendigo and Elders were sustained by competing strategies. Although Hunt advised the Bendigo board in May 1999 of 'continued improvement in the understanding, by Elders/Futuris of Bendigo's objectives and the benefits that the Bank can bring to the venture', he privately worried that Futuris was 'much more in tune with taking over businesses than running them'.[93] Futuris was very proprietary about the new bank; it was to be called Elders and no Bendigo Bank logos were to appear on its advertisements. Hunt did not mind these conditions because his goal was quickly to develop new rural banking products that could be accessed through the branches of both ERB and Bendigo Bank. Futuris, which in 2000 was a much larger company than Bendigo Bank, resisted that thinking and initially treated Bendigo as a late inclusion in an undertaking that had originated in Perth and Adelaide. There was another more fundamental strategic tension. As Beischer concedes, Futuris initially 'flirted with the idea' of taking over Bendigo Bank, and Bendigo was aware of this thinking.[94] Under the joint venture agreement, Futuris rolled its business from Elders Finance into Elders Rural Services but, in return, Bendigo was obligated to make a multi-million dollar goodwill payment, in addition to raising 50 per cent of the new company's operating capital through an issue of Bendigo shares. Futuris 'bought a swag' of that share issue,[95] in part to protect Bendigo's share price at a time when capital mobilisation for the joint venture was essential, but also to exert pressure on the Bendigo board. Bendigo responded in 2001 by formally reviewing its relationship with Futuris, and seeking legal advice. Beischer reaffirmed that Futuris 'was committed to [the] building of a first-class relationship with Bendigo' and would cap its shareholding in the bank.[96] Guy, Johanson, and Hunt met with Newman and his senior executives early in 2002 to ease the crisis, but rumours reached Bendigo that Futuris had approached APRA about the ramifications of Futuris, already Bendigo Bank's biggest shareholder, further increasing its stake in the bank. After Beischer retired from Bendigo Bank late in 2001, Futuris unsuccessfully sought to have its own nominee appointed to replace him.

By 2002 the heat was switching from Bendigo Bank to Futuris. Indeed, by August 2002 the board of Bendigo Bank 'noted the change in circumstances for Futuris Corporation and possible implications for the joint venture, Elders Rural Bank'.[97] Elders was losing market share in the bush. The privatised Australian Wheat Board (AWB) monopoly, which made its profits less by exporting Australian wheat than by lending to farmers against the AWB's future distribution of profits from its sale of their crops, competed aggressively with other rural service providers for merchandising business, for livestock, fertiliser, and real-estate sales, and for rural financing and insurance. AWB launched share raids on its two largest competitors, Elders and Wesfarmers Landmark. In 2003 it bought the Landmark rural business from Wesfarmers, and turned its attention to gaining a majority shareholding in Elders. The ensuing tussle for control was 'nasty and bitter', with Futuris ultimately fending off the AWB takeover.[98] Bendigo Bank had by then overtaken Futuris in size, and the hypothetical of taking over the bank was replaced by the pragmatic reality of maximising the profitable return from a successful partnership with a booming collaborator.

ERB had to ride out one other tension. In addition to the tensions over management and strategic direction which impinged upon its supply of rural products, the new rural bank had to overcome a residual demand antipathy to Elders in the bush. This created headaches both for Elders and for Bendigo Bank. As Ormsby realised, the crash of the Elliott empire in the late 1980s left many country Australians—farmers and retrenched Elders employees—with their fingers burned and 'the Elders brand was tarnished in a big way'.[99] As Hunt tactfully put it, the 'past behaviours of Elders had left some scarring'.[100] Anti-Elders sentiment was especially strong in Western Australia, Queensland, and Victoria, in some communities as a result of deep-seated antipathy to Elliott (Mansbridge remembers people saying to him 'Elders? Oh, that's John Elliott!')[101] and in others from the continuation of the historical split in loyalties between Elders and Dalgetys-Wesfarmers-Landmark.

Anti-Elders sentiment caused unexpected problems for Bendigo Bank as it rolled out its ground-breaking Community Bank initiative (*see* chapter four) across country Australia simultaneously with the launch of ERB. Key rural interest groups in the Wimmera, where the Community Bank programme began, conceded that they were 'a bit taken aback' by the Elders joint venture announcement in August 1998.[102] Reaction was more robust at a Country Fire Authority forum at Fiskville, near Bacchus Marsh in south-west Victoria, in September. A scribbled note from one Bendigo Bank executive recorded the meeting's sentiment: 'Elders bad name. Take hard line with Cockies. Kick them off the land—a lot of farmers would lynch them'.[103] Hunt was acutely discomfited by the 'enormous resistance' of the new Community Bank branches in the Western Australian wheatbelt to Elders and to the joint venture.[104]

That resistance came to a head in June 2000 when an injudiciously worded Bendigo Bank press release about the granting of a banking licence to ERB caused widespread offence within the Community Bank movement. The press release distinguished between the new rural bank, 'tailored to meet primary producers'

Western Australian wheatbelt near Kulin, 2005. PHOTOGRAPH BY ALAN MAYNE.

needs', and Community Bank 'with its emphasis on consumer and small business banking'.[105] The phone of Bendigo Bank's Western Australian Community Bank coordinator, Simon Cornwell, was soon 'running hot' with calls from staff and customers 'feeling somewhat deceived' that 'a news article can be originated from within the bank that downgrades our business in the eyes of the farming community'.[106] As one local Community Bank chairman from the wheatbelt explained to Cornwell:

> 90% of my business is large rural clients as you well know. I have a large Elders branch at Northam (43 kms away), Wongan (48 kms) and Dowerin (23 kms). These branches have a 60 year head start in their dealings with local farmers, and have a data base that would include 95% of the local farming community. They also have a raft of products that we don't have such as stock accounts, crop liens and cashflow lending facilities with no fees. A pretty good platform from which to compete on potential and existing business. The bottom line is that we knew we had to deal with competition but we did not know that it would come from within.[107]

Hunt issued a personal statement to explain the complementary role of ERB to Community Bank, and to locate both initiatives within Bendigo Bank's broader commitment to 'securing banking for communities in the longer term'.[108] Even Hunt's renowned patience snapped, however, when the south-central New South Wales branch at Coleambally—which, with Wentworth in the south-west of the state, had been a hotspot for anti-Elders feeling within Community Bank since the late 1990s—demanded to know 'have we been taken for suckers? Has Bendigo joined the ranks of the BIG banks? . . . What ethics at Bendigo now?'[109] Hunt replied tersely that 'I can never remember in my career receiving a letter which questions so directly my own and Bendigo Bank's motive and integrity'. Apologising for causing offence, the Coleambally branch explained that 'The announcement of Elders Rural Bank opening and the extensive media coverage conveying the perception of another "community bank" in our rural town came as somewhat of a surprise'.[110]

Beischer characterised the establishment of ERB as a 'rocky road' and maintains that without Hunt's continuing guidance the bank would not have survived.[111] Hunt himself concedes that even today not everyone in Bendigo Bank is as proud of the joint venture as they should be. By contrast Hunt relishes the convergent histories of Elders and Bendigo in rural Australia. He respects the 'local bloke' culture at Elders to 'do whatever is necessary for his local farmers, whatever he can get through head office', and seeks through ERB to 'weld . . . that to good skills and competencies'.[112] That combination has delivered impressive results for ERB and its customers. The bank's profitability grew by over 25 per cent per annum in its early years because its co-partners were already shouldering the infrastructure costs of rural lending, and because the bank inherited Elders' existing loans book. ERB's quickly expanding depositor base thereafter covered the bank's operating costs. Notwithstanding drought, ERB's after-tax profit had increased to over $36 million in the year to 30 June 2007, its rural loans book had grown to over $3.2 billion, and another $3.2 billion was held in deposits. Through ERB, Bendigo Bank has intensified its long history of engagement with rural communities, and broadened that engagement across regional Australia.

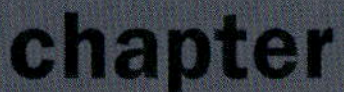

chapter 4

A typical scene at a Community Bank branch opening. Here, scores of school children join in celebrations in November 1999 at the opening of the Cranbrook site of the Tambellup Cranbrook franchise in Western Australia.

Communi

cies

Bendigo Bank announced two startling initiatives during 1998 that transformed the local Australian banking environment. One of them, its joint venture with Elders Australia Limited to establish a bank for rural Australians, was announced in August (*see* chapter three). The other, the launching of a Community Bank for all Australians, had been flagged late in the previous year and was implemented in June 1998. It was enthusiastically endorsed by communities around Australia as a bold experiment in 'people's banking',[1] and resonated especially well in small-town Australia. Chairman Richard Guy emphasised at the Bank's annual meeting of shareholders in October 1998 that the Community Bank and Elders joint venture were key elements in the new bank's emerging strategic direction. Both initiatives expressed Bendigo Bank's 'clear vision of our identity as a regional community bank'.[2] As such they consolidated community-focused activities that had always characterised the bank and its antecedents.

The Community Bank concept was initially firmly anchored in the bush. The changing economics and practices of Australian farming, and its fuller integration into the global commodity trading system, had halved the number of Australian farmers over the previous decade and triggered a slump in the populations of many country towns. These changes were accompanied by the winding back of government services, further job losses and widespread bank closures, creating the gloomy vista of boarded-up shopfronts along the main street of towns throughout rural Australia. It was in response to these events that the Community Bank project was foreshadowed by Hunt in October 1997, during a much-anticipated and widely publicised speech that he gave at Horsham in the Victorian Wimmera. The project was confirmed in March 1998 at a joint announcement by Bendigo Bank and community representatives of a pilot Community Bank for Rupanyup

The first of the first. A large crowd – and many media – gathered on 26 June 1998 outside Australia's first locally owned bank branch, the Minyip office of Rupanyup Minyip Community Bank in Victoria's Wimmera.

and Minyip, two tiny wheat-belt communities near Horsham. It was realised with the launching of the first Community Bank branches in these two towns in June 1998. A decade later, over 200 Community Banks were in operation in every state and territory of the nation.

The *Age* called the new Community Bank the start of 'a banking revolution'. Country towns such as Rupanyup and Minyip had been 'blighted' during the 1990s, the newspaper suggested, as a consequence of the withdrawal of government services and especially of branch closures by the major banks. If towns had no face-to-face banking facilities, their financial transactions, and then shopping and other services were transferred to the nearest regional hub. Local capital was siphoned off from the region, and the business underpinnings, the physical fabric, and the social sustainability of its local communities were eroded. However, at Rupanyup and Minyip, the local community had 'decided to fight back and establish their own bank' as the first step in reasserting the social sustainability of their towns. The *Age* concluded that perhaps, after years of neglect, country people were seizing control of their own finances and their own destinies.[3]

Residents of the two Wimmera communities—besieged by national television and radio—confirmed the *Age*'s assessment. Minyip, 40 kilometres north of Horsham, was a typical Wimmera town of some 550 residents. Its hospital had closed, as had its newsagent, stock and station agent, and garages. Even its football

Wimmera stalwart: Stewart Petering, 1998. *AGE*, 28 MARCH 1998, HEATH MISSEN/FAIRFAXPHOTOS.

club had merged with former rivals in order to survive. Nearby Rupanyup, a township of about 450 people, was 'little more than a main street with a pub, a couple of shops and a primary school'.[4] Even its railway siding and grain elevator had closed down. Both towns had supported three banks in the early 1990s, but early in 1997 the last branch had shut its doors. Stewart Petering, an energetic man in his mid 60s, was a third-generation grain farmer and chairman of Minyip's progress association. He explained at the March announcement that 'At the time we lost our banks there was a lot of anger and resentment', but that local reaction was now being mobilised 'into a positive force to secure the long-term viability of our towns'.[5] David Matthews, spokesman for the people of Rupanyup, was a charismatic local businessman who had just turned 40. He too was a third-generation Wimmera farmer, and the co-owner of a local grain export business. He had thought that when Rupanyup's last bank branch closed it had sounded the town's 'death knell' (his own export business thereafter had to bank three times a week at Horsham), but instead some 500 people from town and district came together at an emergency meeting to discuss their future. A community consultative committee was established with Matthews as its chairman.[6]

Bendigo Bank offered these towns a lifeline. It promised to give them back a measure of local control. As Matthews remarked after Minyip-Rupanyup's first successful year of operation, 'The important lesson is that you don't have to accept decline. People here tend to get a mindset that decline is inevitable, we don't have any power. This demonstrates clearly that people, if they work together, can have some control and make changes that will be for their own good'.[7] One local farmer predicted that the success of the Community Bank at Minyip and Rupanyup would mean the creation of 'a network of community banks across the state, pulling in a significant amount of business from farmers and small-town residents who want the convenience and virtue of a locally owned and operated bank'.[8]

Rob Hunt was the 'architect of the "Community Bank branch" model'.[9] His interest was simultaneously local and universal. He returned one early Bendigo Bank planning document that described the goal of Community Bank as being

People power: David Matthews, 1999. *AGE*, 12 APRIL 1999. FAIRFAXPHOTOS.

'to extend community banking across Victoria' with the last word crossed out, and a cryptic note added: 'nowhere else?'[10] But his broad strategic vision of Community Bank as a regional banking solution that would work across Australia was grounded in his direct knowledge of the external pressures that were undercutting the well-being of rural Victorians. Hunt contended that whereas the major banks had lost touch with their grassroots, Bendigo Bank felt the pain of bank closures 'Because we're country-based, [and therefore] we recognise the plight of country people and what was actually happening when they lost their last bank'.[11] Speaking at the opening of the twin branches in the Wimmera in June 1998, he emphasised the impacts of bank closures and the flow of capital from the country to the city, and asserted the potential of community banking to rekindle local capacity building. Hunt argued that 'Bendigo, being country-based, [has] used its skill and knowledge to think laterally about the problem, but *success is totally dependent upon community* leadership and the community uniting behind the project'.[12] In doing so, Hunt articulated the accumulated historical relationship of Bendigo's building societies with neighbours and settlers, and translated this into a banking model that would empower local communities on the cusp of a new century.

The Community Bank model that Bendigo Bank developed comprised two elements. The first was its franchise-style system of operation. Other banks, such as the Bank of Queensland and Colonial State Bank, had experimented with branch franchising. The new twist in Bendigo Bank's franchise model, or 'the cornerstone' as Hunt had described it in his Horsham speech, was its approximate 50:50 revenue share agreement between the bank and local communities.[13] This formed the second and core element of Community Bank, and distinguished it from all other experiments in community banking. This new approach was a risk and reward sharing model, and did not embody the weaknesses associated with the sales model that is incorporated into many franchise structures.

The first important element of Community Bank was its operating system. Hunt's concept was 'to run a local franchise-style branch of Bendigo Bank' in order to offer a full range of across-the-counter banking services for small communities that had no proprietary bank branches. As Russell Jenkins, the energetic and charismatic head of project design, explained, 'the way Rob had been thinking of doing this was through some sort of franchise structure. So in essence what we are doing with Community Banking is not terribly different to McDonald's or Bakers Delight or any other franchise networks'.[14] What could be done with bread and hamburgers could also be done with banking. Under a banking franchise, 'the community owns the bank, the infrastructure and pays the employees' wages and uses Bendigo's services to do the backroom banking'. In each participating community, a local public company is established and 'purchases from Bendigo Bank the right to run a franchise-style banking branch'. Under the terms of this franchise agreement, which runs for five-year periods, the community-based company receives 'a "turnkey" banking operation from Bendigo Bank', complete with banking logo, systems, marketing and products.[15] Hunt explained to the Australian Prudential Regulation Authority, the government regulator, that each community bank operates under the licence and through the protocols of Bendigo Bank. Thus, he said, the '"franchise" is not a true franchise as that term is commonly used. Rather, it is an agreement whereby the community company . . . agrees to provide premises for the branch and services such as office equipment, staff and a branch manager. [However] banking business carried on at such a branch is the banking business of Bendigo Bank', and could not be accessed by the directors of the local franchise company.[16] Bank staff are employed by the community company but are trained by Bendigo Bank and follow its manuals of banking procedure.

Bendigo Bank insisted that each new branch be commercially viable. Every potential community partner was carefully surveyed and required to develop a comprehensive business plan. The next step was for the community company to raise sufficient local capital through the sale of company shares to cover the bank's establishment and initial operating costs. Bendigo Bank initially set this community buy-in at some $250,000, though by 2003 this had risen to approximately $500,000. As Matthews explained when the first Community Bank was opened at Minyip and Rupanyup, 'the aim [of the share float] was . . . to have the ownership as widespread as possible and so have total community involvement'.[17] As a result, a majority of the customers of every community bank were also part owners.

The second and most important element of Community Bank is its risk and reward sharing structure (in effect, sharing the profit from banking activities). The model gives local communities control over the distribution of profits from their half share in the bank's revenue. This distinguished the project from community banking in the United States, which Hunt had carefully studied and which, he concluded, differed fundamentally from Bendigo Bank in terms of 'empowerment and involvement of local participants'.[18] The project was developed by Bendigo Bank with the intention of making a solid commercial gain (and indeed, Community Bank quickly contributed significantly to overall bank profits). As Hunt regularly emphasised, 'We're not philanthropic; we're a commercial organisation. This is unashamedly a commercial operation—for the Bank and for the community'.[19] Hunt was a professional banker, and knew that he had to prove to Bendigo Bank that communities could be profitable partners, but his real passion was to deliver substantial financial returns and generate sustained social and economic improvements for those communities. By June 2007, Bendigo Bank had paid $340 million to Community Bank boards as their share of the banking revenue that had been generated by the network. That translated locally into dividends for shareholders, and funding for community clubs and services.

Guy had remarked during 1998 that the launch of Community Bank 'would go a long way to position Bendigo Bank as the "bank of the country"'.[20] The approaches to Bendigo Bank from rural communities across Australia over subsequent years quickly confirmed Guy's prediction. The *Herald Sun* commented early in 2000 that 'The more branches the big banks close, the more community banks open'. Despite the major banks deriding Bendigo's strategy as 'naive and untenable', the *Herald Sun* concluded that 'Bendigo's scheme is roaring ahead' with inquiries received from 600 communities across Australia and from others overseas.[21] The first interstate Community Bank opened at Henty in New South Wales in November 1998 and others opened at Coleambally and Wentworth during March 1999. All three towns are in southern New South Wales, a region that had for many years been part of the client base of Bendigo's building societies. However, in July 1999, the first interstate Community Bank outside Bendigo's

Dragons welcomed South Australia's Community Bank pioneer, Virginia.

traditional areas of operation opened at Virginia in South Australia, and later that year, the first Western Australian Community Banks opened their doors.

As the result of the expansion of the Community Bank network, by 2004 half of Bendigo Bank's branch network was located outside Victoria. When the bank was formed in 1995 it had only two interstate branches. There was, however, an unexpected twist to the national growth of Community Bank. As the *Herald Sun* noted in 2000, although 'Community banking was initially aimed at rural towns, [the] suburbs are also clamouring to replace lost services'.[22] By 2004, Community Bank branches made up half of Bendigo Bank's branch network, and half of these were in the cities and suburbs. In Community Bank, the bank's foundation stories of neighbours and settlers converge. There were over 200 Community Bank branches in 2008, Bendigo Bank's sesquicentennial year. This chapter will firstly explore the considerations that shaped Bendigo Bank's decision to launch the Community Bank project. It will secondly examine the beginnings of Community Bank in Victoria, New South Wales, and Western Australia between 1997 and 1999. It will conclude by discussing the consolidation of Community Bank across the nation between 2000 and 2008.

Why Community Bank?

A senior Bendigo Bank insider predicted early in 2000, as the first Community Banks consolidated themselves and other communities queued to join the programme, that 'in the not too distant future, Community Bank will become the primary face of Bendigo Bank—that we will be perceived Australia-wide as "*The* Community Bank"'.[23] However at that time many people were uncertain about what the concept really meant. Its essentials had been clear to Hunt since the lead up to the launch of Bendigo Bank, but he had initially hesitated to reveal all of the reform agenda that he had in mind. It was so large, he decided, that 'it was impossible to put all of those issues out as a challenge to everyone, including in my own organisation. So it was really important that we broke it down into small do-able tasks'. His goal was radical: to 'build . . . a completely new business model between the neo classical shareholder model and the traditional community model, which was effectively co-ops and mutuals (not for profit type organisations)'. Hunt needed a new model because he wanted to go 'right out to the tentacles' and partner with communities in order to build up their capacities.[24] The prevailing supply-side banking model could never deliver this. He wanted to prove that the Community Bank model could.

The conceptualisation behind this model can be divided into four main propositions. Hunt's first proposition was that Community Bank, because it was a joint venture with each community partner, would provide a better mechanism than traditional proprietary bank branches for delivering banking services at the neighbourhood level. Hunt argued that 'A new model was clearly needed as the old branch model was failing the banks and the communities'.[25] Hunt's argument went beyond sniping at the major banks for closing branches; he recognised that the traditional branch model was suiting neither customers nor banks, and that branches were closing because many customers had already deserted them. His criticism of the old branch model was in one sense a policy reversal for Bendigo Bank, because its progenitors, the Bendigo and Sandhurst building societies, had embraced the bank branch model since the late 1970s (*see* chapter two). But in a more important sense, Hunt was informed by the neighbourly face-to-face relationships between

Bendigo's building societies and their clients, and by their pre-branch model of country town agencies (*see* chapter three). Agencies continued to play an important role after the establishment of Bendigo Bank, and by 2008 held well over one billion dollars in deposits. Hunt had emphasised the relevance of the new bank's extensive agency network during early planning meetings for Community Bank in 1997. He later explained to then Victorian Premier Jeff Kennett and to David Hawker's House of Representatives 1998 review of rural banking that 'In devising its Community Bank concept, Bendigo Bank drew upon its extensive knowledge and experience of running small branches and agencies in country areas' in order to 'take the uncertainty out of access to banking services for many towns where there is still substantial community support and focus'.[26]

In criticising the proprietary bank branch model and acknowledging the local community aspirations which agencies partially expressed, Hunt explicitly linked his thinking about Community Bank to the historical origins of building societies in Bendigo. In 1998, the year in which the first Community Bank was established, Hunt and Guy compared the spirit behind Community Bank to that which had animated the founders of the Bendigo Land and Building Society in 1858. The latter 'began the philosophy of community obligation' which still underpinned the operations of Bendigo Bank in the present day. As Guy contended, 'Our service culture did not happen by accident, it grew out of our origins as a community bank'.[27] Hunt sought to harness Community Bank to this history, and thus to the tradition of neighbourly service and accountability that had been built up not only in Bendigo, but also in country town agencies throughout Victoria and southern New South Wales. He argued that 'Bendigo's knowledge of country people, of running smaller branches, its expert technology and its ability to partner, empower, unite and involve community in the solution are the key ingredients that enable the building of this new approach'.[28]

Hunt's second proposition (which few others initially grasped) was that neighbourhood banking was merely a starting point from which to connect clients to a full range of hitherto undreamed of financial services and products. As he told a group of senior managers in November 1998,

> While we [can] put back a basic banking shop, the future says there will be less and less overall savings in the banking system. Therefore the shop will be a shrinking business—so we would not want to rest the whole future on it. The shop must become a window to the finance system—capturing other money moving to centralised structures (stock exchange, superannuation, etc).[29]

Hunt explained to the Hawker Inquiry that using Community Bank to return basic banking services was only a short-term objective: 'Longer-term, the branch might change to become more of a finance and investment shop, rather than being cash and transaction-based. This will also assist in managing local capital'.[30]

Hunt's third proposition was that Community Bank would shore up capital investment in regional communities. He recognised the inherent strength of rural Australia as 'the food belt resource and commodity supplier' of the nation, but worried that the centralisation of banking decision-making and superannuation funds management was draining capital away from regional Australia in order to support development elsewhere. 'Take away the mechanism for [a] community to control capital', he warned, 'and you sign its death certificate'. As regional communities 'lost control of their destiny', he predicted, they became locked into a self-fulfilling belief in their own marginalisation and powerlessness.[31]

Hunt speculated that 'Much of the problem of rural decline is caused by capital drain. It's pulling people and capital away from communities. Everything that used to bring communities together is being diminished. We have all seen this. [But the problem] is not necessarily population, and it's certainly not economics in terms of production over consumption. We probably have more efficient farms now than ever before'.[32] This disjunction sometimes perplexed him. He insisted that

> Country people are tremendously innovative. They have to be, simply to get by. Many of Australia's greatest minds and most brilliant ideas have come from country towns.
>
> Even today, innovation is part of the country culture. But we risk losing this productive capacity if we continue to withdraw support for regional Australia in pursuit of an immediate rationalisation of cost rather than consider the long-term impact on towns.[33]

Drawing upon his own experiences when growing up in country Victoria, he recalled, 'I heard all of my life about regional and rural decline, yet the people I knew didn't see themselves as being in decline. They saw themselves as being deprived of some of the things that were essential to regenerate'.[34] Sometimes he exclaimed, exasperated, 'Decline? I hear it everywhere I go in regional Australia. Yet when I look around at the natural resources, the skills, and the capacity that is there, I can't help but ask—WHY?' Answering his own question, he concluded that 'The real issue is the decline in the number of ways the community is engaged in a common objective'.[35]

Hunt's final proposition was that Community Bank should be used to help mobilise the full social capital of each community. This was his key purpose in debunking the supply-side banking model, and this was his point of difference with other banking experiments such as co-operative banking in Europe and community banking in the United States, because as he pointed out, 'We are empowering and involving rather than just returning basic banking'.[36] During the 1994 reappraisal of Bendigo Bank's future direction, Hunt had identified a set of conditioning factors as the building blocks for sustainable communities. These included social inclusion, engagement, access to information, technological innovation, environmental sustainability, and lifelong learning. He insisted that 'Community is much more than a population base', and that it was possible to mobilise 'our entire resource base . . . (intellectual, productive, human and financial)'.[37] That was the ultimate objective of his alternative demand-side model. Guy argued in 1998 that almost a third of Bendigo Bank's shares were owned by people in the Bendigo district, which equated to almost three million dollars in dividends directed back into the local economy. There was an historical message here, he said, concerning neighbourhood decision-making that should be heeded by their new partners in community banking.[38] Hunt agreed, but in his thinking local capital mobilisation and control was only one part of the equation. He argued that Community Banking 'provides community with the capacity to change things and injects a "can do" attitude. [It helps] local business . . . investment . . . It also assists innovation and creativity'.[39]

Like Guy, Hunt pointed to history in order to underline his message. He argued

> that these communities need to recreate themselves. By this I mean that these communities were once vibrant, creative, innovative communities—full of people who combined their resources to create 'community' in the first place.
>
> The Bendigo Bank sprang from community—from people needing housing . . . The Bendigo was established when people decided to join together and pool some money—so that every now and then they could allocate a housing loan for someone to build a house.[40]

As he declared at a public meeting in Rupanyup in February 1998, 'Community Banking can be likened to our history as a building society—[it's] not a new idea that the community helps itself'. And as Bendigo Bank's 1998 annual report put it, 'Just as Bendigonians [in 1858] came together to develop their city, we are helping other communities to do the same'.[41]

Hunt's intent was informed by history, but he also energetically looked forward, seeking to replace conventional supply-side banking logic, whereby banks generated products and services that they sold to clients, with a demand-side imperative that enabled customers to voice their needs and participate in shaping solutions for them. In doing this, Community Bank would incubate the potential within every community to mobilise not only financial capital, but all the human resources that sustained healthy communities. Hunt had never thought of Community Bank only in terms of financial capital, but 'was thinking about productive capital, human capital, intellectual capital, and if you think about and co-ordinate those issues they can clearly add up to much improved social capital!'[42]

Hunt first showcased the basic building blocks of his Community Bank concept when he gave a dinner speech for the Wimmera 2020 forum at Horsham on 31 October 1997. However, he had revealed his thinking to senior bank executives a year earlier, triggering their enthusiasm by emphasising strategies such as 'wealth creation', 'quality service to our client base', and 'franchise operations' that could mobilise local participation in order to expand the client base and cut back on bank branch costs. Recognising that they were embarking upon a high-risk strategy, Hunt and his colleagues decided to establish 'a formal project team to work on this proposal'.[43] The project could therefore be designated as experimental work rather than core business. In April 1997, Hunt selected Russell Jenkins, a young and energetic engineer who headed the bank's strategic planning section, to lead what first became known as the 'remote banking team'.[44] The phrase implied that Jenkins' team would weigh up the options for delivering banking services to distant places, but the wording also hinted that the team was testing the margins of conventional banking and seeking to extend beyond its accepted limits. Hunt's speech at Horsham in October 1997 described the community banking concept that Jenkins' team had developed from a more traditional franchise model over the preceding 12 months.

The choice of venue was strategic: Horsham was the hub of Victoria's productive Wimmera agricultural region, and Wimmera 2020 was an influential forum that brought together its leading agribusinesses to stimulate economic growth and champion sustainable development in the region up to and beyond 2020. Wimmera 2020 was a perfect ally for Community Bank. Horsham was especially important because Bendigo Bank's initial talks with potential community partners about pilot sites for Community Bank had been most productive in the Wimmera.

Harvest near Horsham, 2004. PHOTOGRAPH BY ALAN MAYNE.

Some 120 guests packed into the Wimmera 2020 Dinner forum in Horsham on Friday 31 October 1997. As savouries were served, they listened to a welcome speech by the chairman of Wimmera 2020, John Millington, who was an award-winning regional businessman based at Nhill. The guests then settled down to entrees of soup or yabby salad, followed by guinea fowl or Wimmera roast beef with Yorkshire pudding, and finally dessert. Then, amid sudden silence, Hunt began to speak about 'Banking in the Bush'. His initial theme was stark and compelling: 'Our sense of community is under threat'. Hunt pointed out that on average two bank branches a week had closed in country Australia during the three years to June 1996. The decisions to close those branches had been made in the capital cities where the banks were headquartered, without reference to the affected communities. Decision-making was being taken away from rural communities, and simultaneously the capital generated by those communities was being exported to the capital cities.[45]

Hunt had got a quarter of the way through his prepared speech when, galvanising his audience, he 'threw the notes away and let the passion takeover'.[46] He postulated that community spirit was still strong in the bush, and asserted that by partnering with Bendigo Bank to establish their own Community Bank, local communities could take control of their banking services and plough back profits to support local business growth and community capacity building.

Hunt put it to his audience that Bendigo Bank '*alone is a voice for the country in the banking sector*'. Pointing to his bank's own history, he argued that:

> In a very real sense, Bendigo Bank itself is a *community* bank.
>
> It is *one of Australia's oldest financial institutions*, starting as a building society on the Bendigo goldfield in 1858.
>
> Ironically, it started for the very same reasons I have outlined tonight—*to give local people the chance to support their own community.*
>
> Local depositors effectively financed local borrowers to build their homes and so *develop their town.*

His conclusion was clear: 'Community Bank puts you back in control of your destiny'.[47] To applause, he added that Bendigo Bank was already talking with community representatives in Nhill and several other Wimmera towns, and would soon announce pilot branches for the new Community Bank.

Notwithstanding the spontaneity of Hunt's delivery, his Horsham announcement had been carefully orchestrated by Bendigo Bank and masterminded by Owen Davies, its manager of communications. The bank ensured that the invitation list for the dinner included local federal and state parliamentarians (for as Davies noted, there was 'Potential for Government support for [the] concept'), the Victorian municipal association, farmers' organisations, and regional development bodies.[48] Copies of the speech had been prepared for distribution during the evening. Journalists from the local newspapers, the *Wimmera Mail Times* and the *Nhill Free Press,* had been briefed, and reports were ready to roll in the next day's Bendigo *Advertiser* and in Melbourne's *Herald Sun.* State government politicians had been confidentially briefed earlier in the month.

Davies had rolled out a media campaign during October to maximise the impact of Hunt's speech. He faced the challenge that 'Bendigo Bank was virtually unknown interstate, so as well as explaining the Community Bank concept . . . we also had to explain who the heck Bendigo Bank was'.[49] He also wanted to get across the message that there was money and energy in country towns, but that city-based banks were letting down the country towns. As he remarked to the *Weekly Times*, 'It wouldn't be out of order for a medium sized wheat belt town to have $40 million to $50 million in funds. There's a lot of old money in some of those areas'.[50] Davies' first media statement, released in early October, was captioned 'Country towns losing control of their destinies' and featured Hunt's warning that the erosion of services and closure of bank branches in country towns was undermining the 'innovation [that] is part of the country culture'.[51] Davies advised Hunt shortly afterwards that 'We got a good run in regional media with the "destiny" press release'. The *Wimmera Mail Times* drew extensively from the release for its front-page announcement that Bendigo Bank 'plans to expand into the Wimmera', and the Bendigo *Advertiser* announced that 'a new concept in country banking' was about to be unveiled by Bendigo Bank.[52] Davies' last media release, 'Bendigo looking to pilot Community Bank concept', was timed to coincide with Hunt's 2020 speech, and likened his announcement of Community Bank to the throwing of 'a lifeline to communities which are willing to work together to stop the downward spiral of services disappearing from their towns'.[53] Davies' strategy also included a two-page mission statement, 'Community Bank . . . "Our bank"', which was widely circulated.[54] He prompted Hunt before an interview by Channel 7's *Today Tonight* programme, 'We also need to try to mention "Bendigo Bank" in every answer. The more we can mention it, the more exposure we get'.[55]

Behind this public relations positioning, it is possible to identify three considerations that influenced Bendigo Bank to proceed with Community Bank. Firstly, the new bank's profit margins, which—built up as they were from the practices of building societies—relied heavily on home loans, had slumped by a third during 1997 as the result of substantial cuts in bank interest rates. Senior Bendigo Bank executives worried that key metropolitan branches were losing money on their operations, and outside 'critics were laying bets on how long [the bank] would survive'. Hunt responded by adjusting 'the bank's strategy to reduce its dependence on home lending and strengthen its position in regional and community markets'.[56] The new Community Bank model scaled back the costs of proprietary branch operations. The onus lay with local communities to mobilise volunteers, pay for the feasibility study, raise share capital, provide banking premises, and cover operating costs. Greg Gillett, Bendigo Bank's General Manager Retail and an early adopter of community banking, reported to Hunt late in 1997 that rigorous statistical testing of the model had revealed that the 'return to the Bank in all this is extremely healthy, given that we have only the costs of providing franchise support'.[57]

Secondly, Bendigo Bank was anxious to pre-empt its competitors or claim back rural banking business from them. When the Australian Bankers Association sought information about Community Bank in November 1997, Hunt cautioned his senior executives to speak only about principles and not to reveal the core formula. Bendigo Bank kept a watch on Westpac's 1997 scheme to develop a rural sub-branch network through 'newsagents in the bush', which some observers characterised as a credible alternative to Community Bank.[58] Bendigo also monitored the

Colonial State Bank's project in 1997 to 'go . . . bush' with a rural franchise network in New South Wales, and its opening of a 'community bank' in the Queensland Gold Coast hinterland town of Yandina (which had also approached Jenkins' staff) during 1999.[59] Bendigo Bank also noted the Commonwealth Bank's plans in 1998 to establish bank franchises through local businesses, together with John McFarlane's announcement in 1998 that the ANZ would stop its rural bank closures, and the NAB's 1999 announcement that it would rebuild its rural banking presence.

Bendigo Bank also monitored the moves of alternative banking providers. It watched the progress of Australia Post's giroPost service (established in 1995 in collaboration with the Commonwealth Bank) and proposals that it be expanded to become a major provider of business banking services. Bendigo Bank looked with especially jaundiced eyes upon the activities of CreditCare, a federal government initiative that was designed 'to assist rural, remote, and indigenous communities gain access to basic financial services'.[60] Only days after Hunt's 2020 speech, the federal government announced funding for a pilot scheme in which credit unions would establish branches in country towns where the banks had closed. CreditCare's operations manager announced forthrightly after the 2020 speech that it was 'not appropriate' for the savings of small towns to be put at risk in order to aid a commercial bank's expansion, and protested directly to Hunt after the launch of the Rupanyup and Minyip Community Bank that it had already been facilitating the development of financial services for rural communities through partnerships with local credit unions, and that the new Community Bank was 'creating confusion and division within these communities'. However, some Bendigo Bank executives privately expressed satisfaction that CreditCare was 'far from happy with us' because CreditCare had spent many months negotiating with Matthews and his colleagues at Rupanyup only to have Bendigo Bank steal the prize.[61] Community Bank publicity emphasised the advantages of financial services that were provided 'Not [by] a credit union, but a fully-fledged bank which shared your commitment to your region'.[62] Jenkins' colleague, Robert Musgrove, reported in June 1999 that Queensland credit unions blocked the easy expansion of Community Bank into that state, and complained that the Heritage Building Society's recently launched community banking programme 'virtually mimics our structure'.[63]

Thirdly, Bendigo Bank sought to influence and second-guess government policy making and to win support from federal and Victorian politicians. The bank was well aware, as it began to assemble its Community Bank model during 1996, that the future shape of Australian banking hinged upon the as yet unknown recommendations of the Wallis Review, and in its submission to Wallis emphasised 'the leading role played by regional community banks in servicing regional communities and in providing competition and product innovation'.[64] Although full franchising of banking, they knew, was impossible under existing banking regulations, they tailored the Community Bank model to accommodate full franchising if this were to be allowed in the post-Wallis banking environment. They were, as well, acutely aware of the danger that other government policy initiatives might leave them flat-footed. As a Community Bank planning group noted in October 1997, their worst-case scenario would be for 'the government to hijack the concept at this stage'.[65] Bendigo Bank also keenly anticipated the recommendations of Hawker's House of Representatives 1998–1999 committee inquiry into 'bush banking'.[66] The bank prepared a submission for the inquiry and Hunt was twice interviewed by the committee and regularly briefed it on the early progress of Community Bank. Bendigo Bank welcomed Hawker's March 1999 report, which acknowledged that Bendigo's Community Bank programme 'has attracted strong interest around Australia', and which urged that the erosion of regional banking services be reversed.[67] Bendigo Bank also cultivated—with less success—Victorian Premier Jeff Kennett's interest in Community Bank, and invited—with greater success—the attention of Deputy Prime Minister (and National Party leader) John Anderson. Hunt briefed the Victorian National Party and simultaneously contacted John Brumby, the former MHR for Bendigo and now leader of the Victorian Labor opposition, and Senator Gareth Evans, who was then shadow federal treasurer.

Beginnings

The rollout of Community Bank began as Hunt's vision for sustainable communities combined with the independent efforts of local communities—in Victoria,

New South Wales, and Western Australia—to preserve local banking services. In August 1997 Phil King, the manager of Revell Seeds at Dimboola in the Victorian Wimmera, phoned Hunt and invited him to be the keynote speaker at the next dinner of Wimmera 2020. King had heard Hunt interviewed on regional radio and was impressed by his comments about capacity building in regional Australia. Hunt agreed, and suggested that he come to Horsham to find out more about the group and its aims. Hunt duly visited Horsham in early September and met King, 2020 chairman John Millington, and Ross Haby, the chief executive officer of the Wimmera Development Association. Hunt outlined his concept plan in a presentation that King described as 'very positive and enlightening'. Millington recalled that 'Everything just clicked like that'.[68]

Millington's reaction was not simply enthusiasm at Hunt's vision. His excitement resulted from the overlap between what Hunt was saying and what had already been attempted at Nhill. Millington and other Nhill businessmen had played a leading role in having small communities such as Nhill included in the Cain Labor Government's Rural Investment Fund, into which surplus funds from regional shires could be pooled to seed local business innovation, and Rural Enterprise Victoria, which appointed business facilitators to towns to assist local business growth. These initiatives were scaled back when the Kennett Coalition Government was elected in 1992. However, Millington remained secretary of Rural Investment Fund P/L and another Nhill businessman, the widely respected Bob Pola, was a director. It seemed to Millington as he listened to Hunt's presentation and then described Nhill's experiences with the Rural Investment Fund and Rural Enterprise Victoria that they all had 'basically the same philosophy'.[69]

Hunt had initially expected Community Bank to begin 'in some of the larger country centres' which combined 'strong local commitment and a reasonably-sized population base'.[70] He did not see its relevance to, or demand emanating from, the largest country hubs like Horsham or Ararat, which could support regular bank branches. He had in mind smaller centres, but he was open to suggestions as to what population range such towns might span. Millington and his colleagues set out to convince him that Nhill, a medium-sized town of some 1900 people (and some 2300 more living on nearby farms), fitted the bill as 'the pilot project' for Community Bank.[71] Ross Haby relayed Hunt's comments at the Horsham meeting to the Hindmarsh Shire Council based at Nhill, where rumour was rife that two of the three banks in the town were about to close their local branches. The councillors, 'all fired up' at the thought of establishing a Community Bank in their place, requested Hunt to meet councillors and local business leaders.[72] The meeting took place at Nhill in mid September. It was chaired by Mayor Darryl Argall, a farmer from Dimboola, and Millington and Pola also attended. It was agreed that Jenkins and Millington would meet again to 'talk through the numbers'.[73] Millington and Pola immediately briefed their friend Malcolm Anderson, the town's doctor, who was chairman of the Nhill Community Committee. They agreed that the Community Committee was the appropriate local body to develop the proposal further.

Rural landmark: Noske flour silos, Nhill, 2004. PHOTOGRAPH BY ALAN MAYNE.

Meanwhile, Hunt went on from Nhill to Horsham for a late afternoon follow-up meeting with Haby. Jennifer Todd, the chief executive officer of neighbouring Yarriambiack Shire, which includes the towns of Minyip and Rupanyup, also attended. She immediately briefed her shire councillors (one of whom was Petering) and then phoned Bendigo to request their own meeting with the bank. Todd advised that community groups led by Petering at Minyip and Matthews at Rupanyup (both of whom were involved with the Wimmera Development Association) had responded to the closure of their last bank branches by exploring the option of setting up credit union facilities in their towns. Hunt was informed that 'They are *very* keen to arrange for us to meet'.[74] Matthews' and Petering's enthusiasm was sparked in part from hearing of an alternative mindset that challenged the prevailing pessimism about the inevitable decline of rural communities, and which reasserted the grassroots energy that had built up these Wimmera communities in the first place. Matthews' grandparents and parents had belonged to the first generations of farmers who had settled and developed the Wimmera into a food bowl. He was well versed in the bittersweet story of how

> it's less than a hundred years ago when we were having such fantastic development through this region. We had the . . . channel system go through which took water right up through the north west of the state, which really allowed the communities to . . . flourish. We put through railway systems to start to handle the produce, the wheat and the wool. It's a relatively recent event . . . In the twenties and the thirties we were seeing all these silo systems built through the north west as well, all on the back of the commodities that Australia was growing at that stage, canola, wool and wheat. Now we are seeing that that commodity production is not even sustaining that infrastructure. The railway lines have been closing, the grain silos are closing.[75]

Matthews' and Petering's enthusiasm was reinforced by finding an ally who might aid their long-standing efforts to shore up their communities. They were seasoned activists, just as were Millington, Pola and Anderson at Nhill. Petering, for example, had been president of the Minyip football club and its hospital board, and had been a local government representative for the town since the mid 1980s.

Both men chaired their respective township associations: the Progress Association in Minyip and the Consultative Committee in Rupanyup.

Behind Davies' media campaign in late September and October to assert the apparently unstoppable flow of the community partnerships that Bendigo Bank was forming in rural Victoria, frantic efforts were being made by Jenkins' team to turn Community Bank from a concept into a working model, and to win acceptance for it from potential partners in time for Hunt to make a clear announcement in his Horsham speech. The obstacles were enormous. Some of these were deliberate. Hunt wanted a rigorous testing process in order to gauge the level of community commitment as much as the business case likelihood on paper of return on investment. There were unwanted obstacles as well. Scepticism and uncertainty within Bendigo Bank threatened to scuttle the experiment. Tensions surfaced between supply-side banking traditionalists and the remote banking team, whom Hunt was tutoring in demand-side thinking about building up social capital. Hunt sometimes worried that, even within the remote banking team, there persisted a gap in approach between the concept of Community Bank and the mechanics that they were putting together to realise it. At one planning meeting he remarked that the franchise model that the group had constructed 'Seems overly influenced by business developer type of people'. Hunt also expressed dissatisfaction at the tameness of some of the initial thinking about how profits might be returned to local community partners, insisting that the 'Distribution of profits should be done to enhance economic activity [and] not just to support local "nice to do" projects'.[76] However, Hunt's anxieties focused on his regular banking staff. On the day of his evening speech in Horsham, a confidential circular was sent to all staff alerting them to the pending announcement, and reassuring them that the Community Bank initiative was simply an extension of the relationship that Bendigo's building societies had always enjoyed with local communities. As the circular emphasised, 'We have confirmed this many times over in our own discrete community (i.e. Bendigo) during the past 139 years'.[77] A later circular to bank staff, supported by Retail chief Gillett, sought to stave off dissension by further explaining Community Bank and reaffirming that 'Branches should not see this as a threat. We will see whatever is done is complementary to the service we currently provide. We see these franchise-style branches will be very complementary and will assist us in developing a much better coverage for our client base in the country'.[78]

Just as delicate was the craftsmanship that was needed to win Reserve Bank of Australia approval for the proposed Horsham announcement. The key for success, it was decided, lay in emphasising to the Reserve Bank 'the possibility of a bank operating through subsidiaries' rather than—as they explained the concept more loosely to the general public—through franchisees.[79] Negotiating to secure a prime radio interview slot, Davies told one ABC journalist that a Community Bank was 'a bit like a McDonald's franchise'.[80] That analogy was often used by Jenkins' team, but the Reserve Bank expected a different rationale. Bendigo's lobbying of the Reserve Bank became increasingly urgent as the date for the 2020 speech drew near. Hunt explained to the Reserve Bank that they were attempting to provide banking services for rural communities 'which are being disenfranchised or under-serviced by the banking sector', and that by 'utilising our experience in running agencies, we have now developed a concept which might enable a community to own and operate a branch (thus securing local banking services)—with Bendigo Bank providing all of the implementation, training, and support necessary to facilitate that banking service for their district'. The community-owned bank would be bound by the rules of Bendigo Bank, and would operate under its banking licence. Hunt contended that although in its daily operations a Community Bank 'would be similar to an upgraded on-line agent', community shareholding and local oversight of each branch distinguished the new model and were essential for it to work: 'If the community were to own the *licensed branch*, we feel there would be a far greater loyalty and support derived—thus sustaining the likelihood of an economic operation'.[81] Bendigo Bank's own board of directors remained confused about the legal distinction between a franchise and a licence even after the first Community Bank branches had been launched. As Jenkins explained to them, 'If the Communities were granted a full franchise, they would, in effect, be delegated the Authority to Conduct Banking Business which is presently illegal'. The solution was therefore for 'The Communities [to] purchase management rights from the Bendigo Bank rather than a full franchise'.[82]

Winning the approval of the Reserve Bank and the confidence of their own staff were as nothing compared to the difficulties of confirming a community partner to pilot Community Bank. Hunt visited Nhill again in late September and addressed the Shire Council on the case for 'Regional Community Banking' in an effort to seal a deal.[83] He also visited Horsham and Dimboola. The first issue that had to be resolved was the minimum viable size for a community partner. Nhill put the case for a medium-sized town to be considered, and Hunt agreed with them. However, at Minyip and Rupanyup, anxiety grew that Bendigo Bank was discountenancing their smaller communities in favour of Nhill. Uncertain of their ability to sustain a community bank independently, the two towns proposed a Rupanyup and Minyip Community Bank with part-time branches in both towns. Bendigo Bank staffers were sceptical. Haby drove a 'posse' from the two towns to Bendigo in late October to attempt 'a direct farmer approach' with the bankers. As

A new school fence at Minyip – just one of hundreds of local projects funded by Community Banks throughout the nation.

Petering and Matthews recalled, the meeting did not initially go well until Hunt, arriving late, sensed the mood and took his delegates out for a private briefing. They returned saying that, upon reflection, a joint Community Bank could work well.[84] What neither negotiating side had initially realised was that Hunt knew and liked Rupanyup, having often passed through the town when he was a young banker working in the district.

Behind the issue of community size was a bigger challenge, the adaptation of a clinical model, developed by a banking team in Bendigo, so that it would work within the different realities of small country towns. Farmers around Minyip were doubtful that there was 'much difference between any of the banks', and they also doubted Bendigo Bank's depth of experience in servicing the special needs of farmers.[85] Negotiations between Nhill and Bendigo strengthened the town's concern that the proposed franchising model borrowed too much from a Bendigo perspective and would not work in smaller towns. A delegation from Nhill comprising Pola, Millington, and Argall travelled to Bendigo to voice their concerns. There was goodwill on both sides, but the stakes were high and the prospects for success were uncertain. The meeting stalled when the bank team, intent on pushing negotiations to the next level, pointed out that the model required an immediate up-front financial contribution from the community of $20,000. They explained that this was needed in part to commission a business feasibility assessment, but also as a demonstration of community commitment. Jenkins added bluntly 'that we can't afford to have a pilot fail'. Jean Wright, Hunt's senior assistant, recalled that the discussion 'was all very interesting—all very open, but everyone was afraid—and the discussion remained on a very clinical level'.[86] At Argall's request, Hunt and a bank delegation attended a public meeting in Nhill on 28 October to further explain the concept, the costs and purpose of the feasibility study, and the process for raising further local capital through shares in order to cover the bank's establishment costs. Hunt and his team continued on to Minyip and Rupanyup to present the same case there on the following day. Meanwhile King, impatient with the apparent procrastination at Nhill, advised Jenkins that Dimboola businesspeople were prepared to go ahead alone 'and set up their own franchise'.[87]

There were too many active strands in play, and insufficient time to reconcile them. Hunt was not in a position to formally announce the first pilot branch when he described the Community Bank concept at the Wimmera 2020 forum in Horsham on 31 October. But his speech gave momentum both to the broad Community Bank project and to the selection of the first pilot. Attention initially focused on Nhill. Argall was reported in the *Herald Sun*'s coverage of the event as saying that a feasibility study would definitely be undertaken for Nhill, and would be funded by the state government agency Business Victoria, the shire, and the local community. He told the Bendigo *Advertiser* that when they had asked for ten local businesspeople to put in $500 each to help fund a feasibility study, 30 had immediately put their hands up. The *Wimmera Mail Times* announced unequivocally in its coverage of Hunt's 2020 speech that Nhill had been chosen for the first Community Bank trial.[88] The Nhill Community Committee wrote formally to Hunt on 12 November to register interest in a branch being established at Nhill. However, a week later they were bypassed when a twin-town meeting authorised Minyip and Rupanyup to proceed immediately to the feasibility survey and business plan. Matthews had taken the initiative at the 2020 dinner and 'quizzed' Hunt further about a Community Bank for his district, and the Yarriambiack Shire immediately backed him by providing seed funding for the business plan to test the project's viability. As Rupanyup storekeeper Adrian Tyler explained, 'We did up a list of all the town people and district people. We just went around doorknocking with an explanation of how it was going to work'.[89]

The Community Bank organisers at Nhill faced a bigger challenge because their town, with multiple banking options still in place, did not face the same pressures that drove bankless Minyip and Rupanyup to mobilise support for a community bank. However, the biggest problem for the Community Committee at Nhill, whose negotiations with Bendigo Bank were more advanced than those with Minyip and Rupanyup, was less about fund-raising than convincing Bendigo Bank to fine-tune its model to ensure that it would work in country towns. The Nhill committee still did not think Bendigo understood how small communities worked. Anderson recalled that 'we drove them crazy' by altering Bendigo Bank's media releases so as to give them 'a small town type feel'. In Millington's opinion Bendigo had 'the wrong model' to deliver Hunt's vision in small country towns, and it was only through the bank's negotiations with the Nhill committee during late 1997 and into early 1998 that the model was sufficiently redesigned to make it work. Millington and Anderson did not go into the negotiations claiming to have all the answers, but they obstinately pointed out to Bendigo Bank the elements of its model that would not work in their community.[90] Bendigo Bank's senior management remained confident that the revenue-sharing model could satisfy a broad range of communities, and responsive to the wishes by particular communities to utilise the model in order to address specific needs and objectives.

Nhill's initial point of difference with Bendigo Bank before the Horsham speech had been over the population threshold that was needed for a community bank to succeed. After Horsham, disagreements centred on the best means of mobilising a community's participation. The Nhill negotiators were 'quite adamant' that it was essential to win 'the broadest possible base'.[91] However, Bendigo Bank negotiators suggested that the quickest strategy to get a community bank up and running was to mobilise the support and capital backing of half a dozen or so key participants. The Nhill committee acknowledged that this might raise the share capital that was needed to launch a bank, but countered that it would not win the project community support. As Millington put it, 'in a small community you'd get the "tall poppy" syndrome—"oh bugger them, it's just those rich bastards, it's their bank" . . . but if you make it so that everybody's got a chop at it then you've got support everywhere'.[92] Jenkins accepted this bluntly expressed logic, and in early December, at a public meeting in the Nhill Community Centre, the $20,000 set by Bendigo Bank to cover the cost of the feasibility study was oversubscribed, 80 people contributing $250 each towards the 'community buy in' and Hindmarsh Shire pledging another $5000.[93]

The principles thrashed out at Nhill were also applied at Rupanyup and Minyip. Rupanyup quickly oversubscribed its share of the survey costs, but Minyip struggled to raise its contribution to the required 'commitment fee'. Bendigo Bank negotiators conceded that 'it has become clear that we are unlikely to gain support from their larger farmers. Further to this, there is a mild but clear questioning of Bendigo's motives from elements of that community'. Jenkins warned that they might need to find another site, and Musgrove cautioned that 'it was still obvious in discussions at Minyip that there is some scepticism about the viability of the project'.[94]

Once funding for the feasibility study had been secured, the next stage was the community survey and business plan. Again Nhill forced important changes to the evolving model. The volunteers on the town committee spent many hours translating the wording of Bendigo Bank's draft survey and modifying its underlying assumptions, pointing out that the proposed income brackets and questions about internet and telephone banking were out of touch with the social realities of their town. Millington called the proposed survey document 'totally foreign; [there is] no point asking something if you know you're going to get 100 percent zero'.[95] The modified Nhill survey of local banking needs was finally distributed, along with a four-page explanatory newsletter, by the *Nhill Free Press* in mid January 1998.

Minyip: 'Heart of the Wheatbelt', 2005. PHOTOGRAPH BY ALAN MAYNE.

Bendigo Bank was disappointed with this delay, having hoped that the survey results would be available shortly after Christmas, and Jenkins' staff sought to identify 'back up sites should either Nhill and/or Rup/Minyip not proceed to pilot'.[96] However, the Nhill committee pointed out the unreality of the bank's assumption that a business survey could be completed in a wheat town in the middle of harvest. As Millington commented, 'In December it's all about harvest here . . . and the dollars in this community come from the farmers . . . And then in January it's the one time in the year where they take off, they've finished harvest, they pack up, and they go away down [to] the beach for two or three weeks'. Minyip and Rupanyup followed the same harvest cycle. Millington's message to Bendigo was clear: 'you can't drive communities', you had to fit in with '"the way it is" in small communities. If you want to . . . be able to tap in, this is the way it has to be'.[97]

Anderson regarded Nhill's remodelled survey form as successfully representing a 'total change from a country city type way of looking at it to [that of] a small town'.[98] Here at last was the basis for a feasibility study that Nhill's community committee and Jenkins' banking team agreed would work. The final challenge for Anderson's committee was to convince the whole community to throw their support behind the proposed bank. Another public meeting was held in early February, in the middle of the survey period, to reiterate the benefits of Community Bank and answer any lingering concerns. Even Hunt, who again travelled to Nhill to address the meeting, seemed 'a bit nervous', because this was the first time that an actual community was being directly asked to apply the model to their banking needs and assess its relevance. The Nhill Community Committee was still more apprehensive as the meeting began, because, as Millington put it, 'We didn't know what the hell was going to happen with questions'.[99] To their relief, the meeting again strongly endorsed the project. The case for community banking was advocated even from the pulpit, Millington recalling with amusement how the town's Roman Catholic priest 'gave his sermon one Sunday at church, [and] it was based around the bank. Talked about the bankers in the, you know . . . about Christ going into the temple, tipping over the money changers' tables. He turned the whole story around to reflect what the whole Community Bank was on about. About the community helping themselves. He did an excellent job'.[100]

Bendigo Bank supported the business surveys in all three towns. Davies prepared media releases and shopfront posters. However, Jenkins privately warned that although an overall positive response could be expected, he anticipated 'elements of cynicism' to express themselves in both Minyip and Rupanyup, and for apprehension to surface in Nhill that a Community Bank would guarantee the closure of the other bank branches in the town. There was also, he acknowledged, some scepticism about 'Bendigo's understanding/ability to support rural community'. Anderson tackled the first concern by pointing out that 'trends in surrounding towns suggested Nhill could also eventually face reduced or closed services'. He cautioned that 'country bank branches across Australia had closed at the rate of two a week and no town could be certain its banks would not be the next to go'. Argall countered the second concern by saying publicly that he was 'willing to put his money where his mouth [was]' and bank himself with Community Bank.[101]

The *Nhill Free Press* announced hopefully in its headline news during early February that, with the banking survey well underway, the 'Community Bank [is] a Step Closer for Nhill', and it reported in mid April that the survey results confirmed that the proposed pilot 'had won the backing of a majority of residents'.[102] But in reality, progress had stalled. Although the consultants' feasibility study was broadly positive, it identified significant concerns within the community that a Community Bank would accelerate the closure of existing banks and hence perhaps erode the delivery of financial services in the district. Local solicitors, who were significant lenders in the district, had also cautioned their customers against the proposal. Survey results indicated that an insufficient number of customers were likely to transfer their banking business for the Community Bank to succeed. Respondents expressed disappointment that Bendigo Bank 'wasn't offering any cut-price deals' and that therefore new customers would lose money by transferring their loans to the new bank.[103] Although the Community Committee and Bendigo Bank continued to work towards a positive resolution of these issues, Anderson and Millington reluctantly concluded that the branch would have to be postponed until estimates of likely business volumes unequivocally justified its establishment.

During further discussions between Millington and Jenkins in August, Jenkins suggested the possibility of a different franchise model in Nhill, with Bendigo Bank initially taking 'the lion's share' of the ownership of the Community Bank and the community buying back their 50 per cent share of the bank over time as business volumes grew.[104] The proposal languished. The Nhill Community Committee tried to revive it in 2000 when Westpac, one of the three remaining banks in the town, downgraded its operations from a full branch to an in-store agency. Jenkins advised Hunt in March that 'Apparently Nhill is firing up again', and Anderson prepared a circular letter (after running its draft wording past Davies) to local investors, urging that the Westpac downsizing should prompt the town to reconsider establishing a Community Bank.[105] It was not to be. In 2005, reflecting on what might have been and noting enviously the recent opening of a Community Bank at nearby Dimboola, Millington and Anderson concluded sadly that a Nhill Community Bank 'would have been a roaring success and the dollars would be all around this town instead of the dollars coming out of it. But the community wasn't ready for it at that stage'.[106]

By contrast, said Millington, the people of Minyip and Rupanyup 'picked up on what we did and took it from there'.[107] The unambiguously positive results of their business case study feasibility report were released in February 1998, endorsed by the local communities, and at a joint press conference with Bendigo Bank on 22 March it was announced that the two towns would pilot the first Community Bank. The timing could not have been better; anger was rippling across rural Victoria at ANZ's almost simultaneous announcement that it would cut 2000 jobs and close its branches in Ballarat and Bendigo. It was predicted that Wimmera branches especially were 'to be targeted', and the *Nhill Free Press* made the point—too late for Nhill itself—that if bank branches were to close even in regional cities such as Ballarat, Bendigo, Shepparton and Albury, the future was bleak indeed for bank branches in country towns.[108] In the midst of this angry reaction by rural community groups, local councils, and farmers' organisations, Hunt received further positive national coverage when a feature story in the *Weekend Australian* highlighted his undertaking—so different from the course of action being pursued by the major banks—that Bendigo Bank 'would pioneer its novel Community bank concept' at Rupanyup and Minyip in order to 'assist country towns to develop new initiatives to develop their long-term futures'.[109] As Minyip and Rupanyup set about raising local share capital to cover their bank's establishment and initial operating costs (almost $230,000 was quickly raised), the wider Community Bank project gained further momentum when, in late April, another major bank, the NAB, signalled more country bank closures and its managing director was widely reported as justifying the move by saying that 'the bank could not afford to keep unprofitable branches open for country people to enjoy as a "social experience"'.[110]

Whereas the NAB ridiculed country aspirations, Bendigo Bank began part-time banking services at Minyip and Rupanyup in early May, using temporary facilities, and a series of media briefing papers were released by Davies in the build-up to the Community Bank's formal launch in late June. Matthews, who had become the first chairman of the two towns' franchisee company, Rupanyup/Minyip Finance Group Ltd, announced on ABC talkback radio in the lead-up to the Community Bank launch that 'people in the bush . . . are taking action themselves'. He did not speak publicly about the 'rocky patches' that at times had threatened to derail the project.[111] Jenkins, too, was acutely sensitive to the likelihood that local opinion in these Wimmera communities might yet turn against the bank on the grounds that 'you don't really understand' and, on one occasion when a Bendigo Bank delegation arrived at Rupanyup, Davies worried that the 'invasion of the suits'

In the past four years in Australia, 284 country bank branches have closed.

Ours are about to reopen.

RUPANYUP, 32 Cromie St

MINYIP, 63 Main St

We'd love you to join us on 26 June and help us make history

RUPANYUP/MINYIP COMMUNITY COMMITTEE

'Help us make history': launching the Rupanyup-Minyip Community Bank, 26 June 1998.

might not go down well amongst the casually dressed locals who were waiting to greet them.[112] Jenkins later conceded that the legal nightmare of working through the fine print of the new banking model meant that both sides were forced to move ahead of their legal advisers and, in a 'leap of faith', commit themselves to a launch date even though it seemed that the legal contract might not be completed in time for the two parties to sign before the bank opened.[113] Then, almost unbelievably, the documents were cleared for signing on the evening before the launch, and just half an hour before the start of a party in Minyip for the negotiating teams and for the many local shareholders who had each invested between $100 and $5000 in this community banking experiment.

The two branches of the Rupanyup and Minyip Community Bank were formally launched on 26 June 1998. It was a cold winter's day, especially when Bendigo Bank chairman Richard Guy began proceedings in Minyip at 9:30 in the morning. Jenkins, an avid cyclist, drew cheers when he braved the chilly weather to ride from Minyip to Rupanyup just before formal proceedings began there in the early afternoon. Hundreds of people attended the festivities in the two towns,

'The bush fights back': Community Bank leaders outside the Rupanyup branch, 1998.
REPRODUCED WITH PERMISSION FROM THE *HERALD SUN SUNDAY*, 5 JULY 1998.

partaking of the public breakfast and lunch, and sampling the champagne. There were music and balloons. The children frolicked. Helicopters flew in and out, and city television crews roamed the streets. Petering joked that 'you couldn't have bought that sort of publicity'.[114] Journalists quoted Hunt's prediction that 'The local people will be the ones calling the shots about banking in their town, rather than Collins Street or Pitt Street bankers'. Applauding that sentiment, the *Herald Sun* announced forthrightly, 'We applaud their boldness'.[115] The day was mostly a blur for Hunt. He recalls, 'I remember a little bit about the speech at Rupanyup where I said if we could marshal this level of community spirit in other places around Australia what a tremendous country we'd be'.[116]

In the wash-up after the launch, Davies reported to the Bendigo Bank board that coverage of the Community Bank initiative by the regional press and by national television and radio had been extensive and 'overwhelmingly positive . . . From a public relations viewpoint, the launch could hardly have gone better. We have established ownership of the Community Bank concept, built awareness of Bendigo Bank and emphasised our bona fides as a champion of regional Victoria'.[117] The Community Bank's early business figures were icing on the cake. The *Australian* reported in early September that 'The first branches, at the Wimmera towns of Minyip and Rupanyup, surprised even the bank itself, meeting half of year-one budget targets in only eight weeks of operation'.[118] Media interest built up again as the new bank's first anniversary approached in 1999. Interviewed in April, Matthews announced that the Community Bank had met its $15 million business volume target for its first year in only seven months, and that the bank 'would've been cruising into profit by now' had not severe frosts wiped out much of the district's harvest. Matthews predicted that they would reach break-even point by the end of June, and that they were on track to repay all the initial investors within three years.[119] The June 1999 anniversary celebrations included a barbecue and birthday cake, and Davies' hard work to ensure good media coverage again paid off.

The Melbourne *Age* later interviewed Matthews and reported as follows:

'The financial spin-off for the towns has been considerable,' Mr Matthews said.

'We've basically retained shopping dollars in the towns. People used to travel to Horsham, which is a 100-kilometre round trip; now they're supporting the local supermarket again. The owner says his profits are up by some 25 per cent and he's recently renovated his store.'

The other benefit to the two towns has been a psychological one, according to Mr Matthews.

'We no longer have a bunker mentality. We are perceived to be an energetic community which has get up and go,' he said.[120]

In an editorial leader the *Age* had previously savaged the major banks for forgetting that their customer base had historically been 'built upon individual contact and personal service'. The newspaper commented that 'Banking is no longer like that. The banks, in the interests of commercial expediency and serving shareholders, have forsaken many of the traditions upon which the client-banker relationship was based'. It was in consequence of this abandonment, the *Age* maintained, that local communities were partnering with Bendigo Bank in order to develop financial services that suited local needs rather than those of the big banks.[121]

Expansion

During early 1998, even as they worked long hours at Minyip and Rupanyup to establish the first Community Bank, Jenkins' team began negotiations with other communities that had expressed interest in community banking. Gillett's strongly performing proprietary branch network provided Hunt with the financial muscle to accelerate his plans. Hunt suggested a target of six Community Banks to be in the advanced planning stage by the end of the year, and Jenkins was determined not to disappoint him.

Site visits were made to Dunolly and Avoca in central Victoria, Donald in the west of the state, and Toora and Lang Lang in Gippsland. Paradoxically, the second Community Bank to open was located on the fringe of metropolitan Melbourne, at Upwey in the Dandenong Ranges. The Bendigo *Advertiser* noted during August

Chairman Peter Marke at the opening of the second Community Bank franchise in the Melbourne fringe suburb of Upwey. The branch has been a tremendous success and has spread its wings into neighboring communities.

1998 that, amid the rush of country communities to enlist in the Community Bank programme, 'Perhaps the most surprising response has come from the outer Melbourne suburb of Upwey'. The Upwey bank was launched by Hunt in October 1998, the *Herald Sun* hailing it as 'the first of the Bendigo Community Bank branches within the boundaries of metropolitan Melbourne'.[122] Jenkins remembers with a smile that, with his 'country parochialism', he had quizzed Musgrove when they were first driving to Upwey on why they should be approaching a city-edge community. Jenkins recalls that 'I just didn't think that the spirit of community was alive and well' in such localities, and laughs that Upwey quickly established itself as the largest volume Community Bank in the entire national network.[123]

In the same month as the Upwey launch, the third Community Bank was opened at Lang Lang, near Phillip Island. The next Victorian launch took place in January 1999 in the historic farming town of Toora in South Gippsland. Further Community Banks began soon afterwards in Bendigo Bank's central-Victorian heartland, at Avoca in February 1999 and Maldon in April. Davies briefed one journalist that 'typically we get 200–300 people at these openings and there is plenty of movement and colour'.[124] The grass-roots messages that journalists picked up amid the movement and colour at all these launches was also very much the same, and it echoed the sentiment that journalists had previously encountered among the residents of Minyip and Rupanyup. As the *Gippsland Farmer* reported in its January 1999 issue,

> Banks, post offices, railway lines, and schools have all felt the fall of the knife, shires have been amalgamated, and hospitals have either been down graded or also closed—it's called rationalisation and many small Gippsland communities have felt its frightening sting.
>
> But several Gippsland towns have decided to 'dig in their heels' and call a halt to the slow death of their communities.
>
> With the assistance of Bendigo Bank the 600 residents of Toora are once again making history with their controversial stance against some of Australia's biggest institutions.[125]

'Let's Celebrate': opening the Lang Lang Community Bank, 29 October 1998.

The next bank to open marked a dramatic expansion of the Community Bank concept. Opened in July at Elwood, it was Bendigo Bank's first inner metropolitan Community Bank (a privately owned Bendigo Bank franchise had opened in Ringwood during June). Elwood, more so than Upwey, represented a significant shift in thinking by many at Bendigo Bank. Although Hunt had always believed that

Community Bank was designed with regional towns in mind and Bendigo's bankers were a little surprised to find equal demand from suburbs such as Elwood, in Melbourne, the first truly metropolitan site. Within a few years, the Community Bank network was evenly split between town and country.

the model could work in any market, he was initially cautious to apply it only in rural communities. When the Geelong Chamber of Commerce had approached Bendigo Bank in January 1998 about establishing a Community Bank in suburban Geelong, Hunt had responded that the programme was 'aimed at rural communities rather than suburban situations'.[126] In April Hunt responded similarly to an inquiry from Ivanhoe in suburban Melbourne, drawing attention to the expressions of interest already received 'from an enormous number of townships and districts in country regions—to whom we feel we must respond prior to moving to the metropolitan area'.[127] His priority list began to change as other proposals were received during 1998 from East Malvern, Burwood, Ashwood, St Kilda, Beaumaris, and Elwood. Jenkins and his colleagues found that, although the appearance of these city communities was very different, the mood was not. For example the beachside suburb of Elwood, just seven kilometres from the city centre, had been without a local bank after the last of its three major bank branches had closed late in the year. Jenkins was keen to respond to this unexpected need, but his staff found that branch development in city communities was difficult. As Musgrove explained, 'With larger population bases and less intimate and identifiable community support, the suburban committees find the fundraising process a lengthier task than regional communities'.[128]

Two milestones were passed in July 1999. Not only did the month mark the opening of the first metropolitan Community Bank, it also saw the start of the first Community Bank in South Australia, which constituted Bendigo Bank's first interstate community banking venture beyond its long-established client base in southern New South Wales. The South Australian branch opened at Virginia, a market garden district about 30 minutes' drive from Adelaide.

It was, however, at Henty in southern New South Wales that the Australia-wide expansion of Community Bank began. Henty was a good strategic choice by Bendigo Bank. It lies 70 kilometres north of Albury, in the heart of a wheat, canola, sheep, and beef farming region with which Bendigo's building societies had done business since the late nineteenth century. Henty has been well known since 1963 as the location of one of the biggest country show days in the world, the Henty

Machinery Field Days. The town had some 1000 residents in 1998, with another 2500 people living in the surrounding district. It had much the same size and character as Nhill, but it did not have its banks.

Milton Taylor was the driving force behind the Henty & District Community Bank and its Civic Centre project, the largest project undertaken by any locally owned branch.

Disengagement by the major banks, dating back to the first branch closure in 1972, had accelerated in recent years and sparked local interest in Community Bank. Its key proponent was Milton Taylor, a retired farmer, member of the Australian wheat and barley boards, and local councillor. Jenkins affectionately referred to him as 'the godfather of Henty'.[129] Taylor was fortuitously also a depositor at Bendigo Bank's Albury branch. Jenkins and his team held a series of meetings at Henty during May 1998. When in the following month the State Bank announced the closure of its Henty branch and the Commonwealth, the only bank remaining in Henty, declined to guarantee that it would not also close, the Community Bank option quickly gathered momentum. In mid June a delegation from the Henty Community Finance Committee, comprising Taylor, retired banker Keith Turnbull, and stock and station agent Max Davidson, joined representatives from Toora for a briefing in Bendigo, followed by visits to Matthews and Petering in the Wimmera. Davison later wrote to Hunt that the Henty delegation 'came away from Bendigo very impressed with the bank's philosophy, business ethics and enthusiasm for the community bank concept'.[130]

Over 300 enthusiastic residents attended a community meeting organised by the Henty committee in early July. They applauded Taylor when he called the meeting 'a turning point in Henty's history'. Nevertheless, Taylor privately warned Jenkins that 'our primary need is to overcome the impression held by some people that Bendigo does not have rural expertise', and to address this Jenkins agreed to arrange for David Matthews to address the next Henty public meeting.[131] In public, Taylor flamboyantly declared 'All out war with the big four', pointing to interest-rate inducements by the major banks to entice local customers to maintain their business with their regional bank centres, and complaining that 'The big banks weren't . . . satisfied just to pull out—they are now trying to make it impossible for others to re enter the market'. It was a pitch that the local *Border Mail* liked, and the newspaper slammed the big banks' rethink about country branch closures as being too little too late for country towns. Pointing to the public meetings at Henty, the newspaper predicted that 'the people of the bush' were turning to banks such as Bendigo Bank that 'are beginning to listen and grow a social conscience'.[132] In late July another community meeting at Henty oversubscribed the money needed for the feasibility study and business plan. These were successfully completed during August, and on 2 September Taylor wrote formally on behalf of the Henty Finance Committee to confirm the town's decision to establish a Community Bank.

Another successful public relations operation was devised by Davies in the lead-up to the launch at Henty, with Hunt interviewed in prime time by celebrity radio host Alan Jones, and *A Current Affair*'s report on Henty reaching a television audience of 2.3 million people across Australia. Taylor crowed at the Henty bank

A huge crowd turned out for the opening of the first interstate Community Bank branch, at Henty in southern New South Wales.

Coleambally Community Bank branch, one of more than 200 locally owned franchise branches across Australia by 2008.

opening on 6 November 1998 that 'We rattled the bowl and within 14 days we had $270,000' in local capital invested to establish their Community Bank.[133] As the local band played and the sausages sizzled, Jenkins introduced the speakers for the midday opening: Taylor, Hunt, Guy, and finally Tim Fisher—the local federal parliamentarian, leader of the National Party, and Deputy Prime Minister of Australia—who officially opened the branch.

There were two other Community Bank openings in southern New South Wales in March 1999. The first was at Coleambally, an agricultural town south of Griffith in the Murrumbidgee Irrigation Area. The next—and ninth—Community Bank was at Wentworth, on the junction of the Murray and Darling Rivers. Wentworth hosted a gala opening, the choreography for which was assisted as usual by Davies. The official party arrived mid morning by paddle steamer. By the time the speeches

TV host Ray Martin helped chairperson Cheryl Rix and Rob Hunt open the Wentworth & District Community Bank.

began in the early afternoon over 500 people had assembled. Wentworth Community Bank chairperson Cheryl Rix began proceedings, followed by Mayor Don McKinnon, Hunt, and special guest Ray Martin, the high-profile Channel Nine TV anchorman, whose brother-in-law was a member of the local Community Bank committee. Martin praised Bendigo Bank for being 'a good corporate citizen', acknowledged 'the tough times country towns were going through', and celebrated the 'community spirit' of the people of Wentworth in demonstrating that 'Aussies will always have a go and meet challenges'.[134]

Wentworth's original business plan had been completed at the same time as Henty's in August 1998, and the business consultant reported back enthusiastically to Bendigo Bank that 'It is the Nhill story without 3 banks'.[135] Indeed Wentworth had been without a bank for over two years. However, as in Nhill, the plan stalled, this time because its promoters' original model for a small consortium of 15 business-people to buy the franchise divided the community just as Millington and Anderson had predicted, 'and threatened to scuttle [the] whole project'.[136] Rix took over the leadership of the local planning group, and by December Wentworth resolved to go ahead with the Community Bank on the same broad-based community model that had been adopted by other communities.

The Henty Civic Centre was funded by the town's Community Bank profits and leveraged government funding. Hunt notes how communities have much more clout with government once they establish a sustainable flow of profits through their branch.

When the Henty Community Bank was launched in November 1998, the board of Bendigo Bank, enthusiastic at the pace with which the project was developing, set a target of two new branches added to the drawing-board per month, and 15 Community Banks open for business by the end of 1999. The opening of Wentworth and Coleambally in the New Year seemed to confirm the logic of this decision. However, with Jenkins' team members working at times to exhaustion, bank launches were already running at full capacity in Victoria and were only starting to gear up in South Australia. Expansion across New South Wales and in Queensland was blocked by competitors with strong existing community networks. After the Wentworth launch in March 1999, which brought the Community Bank network to three in New South Wales and six in Victoria, Musgrove therefore reported to the Bendigo Bank board that the priority recruitment area was switching to Western Australia, where Jenkins' staff were already at an advanced stage of discussions with nine communities and were investigating another ten sites.[137] Hunt had realised that the key to achieving the bank's growth target was indeed Western Australia.

The first inquiry from Western Australia about Community Bank had come in April 1998 from Graeme Campbell, the federal member for Kalgoorlie, who announced that 'I have seen something in the media about your bank's franchising proposal and feel that the idea has a lot of merit and could be applied very well in West Australia'. Campbell declared, 'I like the fact that your head office is not in a capital city and that your commitment seems to be to regional and rural Australia . . . The name Bendigo has good connotations in the Goldfields of West Australia'.[138]

The next serious contact came in September, when the National Party of Western Australia contacted Jenkins to request that a meeting be scheduled in Bendigo during November with Max Trenorden, the Nationals MLA for the state seat of Avon (the hub of which was the wheat-belt centre of Northam). Trenorden was secretary of the parliamentary National Party and chairman of the key parliamentary Public Accounts and Expenditure Review Committee. Hunt and Jenkins readily agreed, although as Jenkins reported to the board 'We are considering options and our ability to support such "remote" sites', and Hunt initially told Trenorden outright that Western Australia was 'not on our antenna'.[139] Hunt pointed out that the state would need to identify multiple sites in order for Community Bank to work in the West. It was nonetheless arranged for Trenorden to meet with Bendigo Bank executives during the morning of 20 November, and then be taken to Rupanyup. Trenorden was accompanied by a powerful delegation comprising Chris Fitzhardinge, executive director of the Department of Commerce and Trade, David Singe, head of the Wheatbelt Region Development Commission (based at Northam), and Greg Hadlow, chief executive of the Kulin Shire Council in the south-east wheat-belt region.

Hadlow had joined the delegation in large part because of the closure of Kulin's last bank at mid year, and, as Trenorden put it, he 'basically demanded to come with us'. Hadlow had been rocked when, at an emotional community meeting following the last bank's closure, 'someone stood up at the back of the room and screamed out, "What are the Council going to do about it?"'[140] Looking for options, the council were told by Trenorden about the launch of Community Bank in Victoria. Trenorden's interest in rural financial services was longstanding. Unlike many of his National Party colleagues, he refused to accept the banks' argument that branch closures were part of a natural cycle that could not be resisted. In April 1996 he had introduced a motion in the Western Australian parliament that deplored the withdrawal of rural banking services, and called for the 'creation of more competitive financial services in country towns'. Trenorden came from a farming family, and would not accept that the country towns he knew so well were doomed 'to go down'.[141] As a result of the success of his parliamentary motion, and the support he won for it from the leader of the Western Australian Nationals, Deputy Premier Hendy Cowan, a Regional Financial Services Taskforce was established in May 1996, chaired by Trenorden and staffed by Cowan's Department of Commerce and Trade and the Ministry of Fair Trading, to report on ways of minimising the impact of bank closures on rural communities. The taskforce report was presented in December 1997. It reviewed the winding back of banking services, assessed alternatives delivered through Australia Post, credit unions, electronic banking and automatic teller machines, and proposed a set of recommendations designed to shore up the provision of financial services in rural communities.

Trenorden became aware of Bendigo Bank as a result of the publicity that marked the launch of the Rupanyup and Minyip Community Bank in June 1998. Visiting the Rupanyup branch later in the year, he 'saw first hand what a difference it had made to the community'.[142] Trenorden understood and respected the angry mood amongst Western Australian rural communities when their banks closed. In March he had attended a community meeting at Goomalling, a wheat-belt town to the north of Northam, following the closure of its last branch, and copped 'a fair flogging' because of the government's inability to halt the closures.[143] Trenorden was not wedded to any specific banking solution; his interest lay more broadly in sustaining rural communities and maximising regional development. He therefore saw eye to eye with both Matthews and Hunt. Like Matthews he fumed that his wheat-belt electorate 'creates about three billion dollars of export income for the state, and gets virtually nothing back. And we have constant talk about crisis and dying rural communities and non-viable local governments. It's not because they're not earning the money, they're just not allowed to keep it'.[144] And like Hunt, he lauded the enterprise of rural Australians and espoused a vision of rural renewal. When he became leader of the Western Australian Nationals in 2001 he drew attention to the extreme hardship throughout the wheat belt that had been created by biblical-like scourges of frost, locusts, and drought, and declared that 'when faced with diversity, rural communities display the resilience, fortitude and character epitomised in our ANZAC spirit. This is the very reason the Bendigo Bank Community Banking concept is so successful'. Trenorden was determined to 'help people like Rob Hunt make it possible for people to use their own resources, generated by community banks, telcos, redistributed compulsory superannuation funds and a local knowledge to generate commercial and social activity'.[145]

In November 1998, immediately after the return of the Western Australian delegation from Victoria, Trenorden engineered the release of a Nationals media statement that declared that after enduring years of branch closures by the 'traditional banks', the people of the wheat belt at last had the option through Bendigo Bank to establish community banks and follow the successful lead of Minyip and Rupanyup.[146] Trenorden next contacted Hunt and invited the Community Bank planning team to visit Western Australia early in the New Year, saying that at least half a dozen communities were keen to talk and that the state government was likely to fund the community business plans and to waive stamp duty for customers transferring to community banks. Trenorden's initiative perfectly matched the target for Community Bank growth that had been set by Bendigo Bank's board in November, and Jenkins rushed to assemble a 'hit team' and head west.[147] It quickly became evident that with the resources of the state government being thrown behind the initiative, Bendigo Bank would have to radically increase the scale of the undertaking. Whereas Jenkins had initially planned to visit six communities, staff in deputy premier Cowan's Department of Commerce and Trade identified and contacted 21 potential rural communities for Jenkins (whose designation, significantly, was switched from being the head of remote banking to Community Banking) and project officer Simon Cornwell to visit during February 1999. State government support was crucial to the rapid success of Community Bank in Western Australia, and distinguished the West from other states and territories. As Trenorden recalled, many things became possible because the project 'had the State government tick'.[148]

Jenkins and Cornwell embarked on an extensive tour of regional communities, accompanied by Trenorden and his Nationals colleague and MLC member for the agricultural region, Dexter Davies. The tour was organised by the Department of Commerce and Trade, and used government-chartered aircraft 'so we were able to bounce all over the place'.[149] Jenkins' visit was planned to coincide with a conference on regional banking, arranged by the West Australian Municipal Association, at which Jenkins explained the Community Bank project and the steps required to establish a Community Bank. Cornwell described the response, especially from the wheat-belt shires, as 'enormous',[150] and Jenkins' speech received extensive coverage on state-wide radio and television and in regional newspapers. Keen to be seen to be addressing the erosion of country banking services, the state government announced a dollar-for-dollar programme to help up to ten communities to prepare business plans. Jenkins' staff were soon liaising with 20 Western Australian communities, from Tambellup and Cranbrook in the south to Meekatharra in the remote north.

The key site, however, was Kulin. The town—like Minyip and Rupanyup—had some 400 residents, plus a surrounding farmland community of another 600 people. Lying almost 300 kilometres south-east of Perth, it is the archetypal

Western Australian wheat-belt town. Its last bank branch had closed in March 1998. Kulin was the first community visited by Jenkins after the conference in Perth. Two hundred people crammed into the Kulin Recreation Centre to hear him speak. The meeting was chaired by Hadlow, now firmly a convert to Community Bank. During his visit with the Western Australian delegation to the Rupanyup Community Bank, he had been surprised that the town was smaller than Kulin, and found it 'heartening that it could be Kulin sitting over there in Victoria'. Hadlow told the Kulin meeting about his visit to Rupanyup and characterised the 'region [as being] very similar to the Wheatbelt of WA'.[151] When Jenkins addressed the meeting he also won the crucial support of local farmer Graeme Robertson, a municipal councillor and former shire president. Robertson got up to speak, and as Jenkins recalls he declared:

> As a farmer I don't need banking in town. I can do my banking by Internet, and that will suffice. I live . . . 25 k from town anyway . . . But I do need Kulin, to buy my goods and to service my tractor, and to do all the things I need to do to be a farmer, and for Kulin to survive we need a financial services centre, we need a bank in town.

Trenorden was also present, and remembers Robertson as saying simply 'I'm a farmer, I don't need a bank, but I need a community'.[152] Whatever the precise form of words, the message was the same and Robertson, a well-liked and respected man, exerted considerable influence.

A follow-up community meeting in March resolved to establish an interim Kulin Community Bank board chaired by Robertson, and to begin fund-raising. Jenkins enthusiastically characterised Kulin as 'the pioneers in WA with community banking', and scrawled a note to Hunt that the town had 'taken the same stature [as] Rup/Minyip, with all WA towns talking about Kulin, similarly as we saw in Victoria with Rup/Minyip'.[153] Privately, the Kulin committee sometimes despaired that they would reach their goal of becoming the first Community Bank in the West, but Robertson insisted that they would. A large thermometer was set up in the main street to highlight the rising level of money that had been pledged to establish the bank. Hadlow later chuckled that the committee 'did tell a couple of fibs now and then', holding back a little when fund-raising slowed and then updating the thermometer to show 'a big surge'.[154]

Sentiment at Kulin was strongly echoed by the twin towns of Tambellup and Cranbrook, located in the far south of the state in a district noted for its grain and wool production. The two towns, some 380 kilometres from Perth, each had fewer than 500 residents and, with the surrounding farming population, totalled about 1200 people. Goomalling, the town that had given Trenorden a verbal flogging when its last bank branch closed in March 1998, also responded enthusiastically to the Bendigo Bank road show. Goomalling is a grain town of 600 people in the central wheat-belt zone, some 130 kilometres north-east of Perth. The shire's chief executive officer, Clem Kerp, had visited Perth to attend the municipal association conference in February, and tapped Jenkins on the shoulder after his speech to ask that Goomalling be added to his list of potential partners. A community committee was immediately formed and began fund-raising.[155]

Jenkins and his team again visited Western Australia at the invitation of the state government in late April and early May, and followed another busy schedule around the state that had been organised by the Department of Commerce and Trade in collaboration with Cornwell. On this occasion it was Bendigo Bank's star recruit and fellow grain farmer David Matthews—with his message from Rupanyup that 'Our success shows that you don't have to accept decline'—that 'got the crowd's attention'. Davies aided Matthews' positive reception by issuing a media release showing Matthews besuited and drinking champagne at the Rupanyup launch, with the caption '12 months ago this man was a wheat farmer . . . Now he is chairman of Australia's first Community Bank'.[156] By the end of Jenkins' visit, 15 communities were linked into Cornwell's loop and seriously considering joining Community Bank, and nine of them were far advanced in fund-raising.

The leader was Kulin. Their business survey results, completed in June, were termed 'fantastic' by Jenkins,[157] and fund-raising netted over $320,000. The interim board, formalised as Kulin Community Financial Services Limited, launched a share issue in September (one-dollar shares in batches from 100 to a maximum of

Movement for change in Western Australia: opening the Kulin Community Bank, 15 October 1999. Left to right: Hendy Cowan (Regional Development Minister and Deputy Premier), Graeme Robertson (farmer and Kulin Community Bank Committee chairman), Rob Hunt, Russell Jenkins (Bendigo Bank head of Community Banking), Greg Hadlow (chief executive of Kulin Shire Council), Max Trenorden (MLA for Avon), and Ross Ainsworth (MLA for Roe). REPRODUCED WITH PERMISSION FROM THE PRIVATE COLLECTION OF MAX TRENORDEN.

5000) to convert these pledges into capital. Unable to afford the price tag for one of the former bank buildings in Kulin, the Community Bank instead opted to lease space in the new Wesfarmers agency. Even as the new building was being completed, Hadlow declared to the *Local Farm Weekly* that the prospectus had been oversubscribed and that 'We've got $3m on the books already, that is unbelievable, we haven't even opened yet'.[158] Cornwell moved from Bendigo to Perth in July to become Western Australian project manager. Shell-shocked by the positive reception he had received in Kulin and around the state, Cornwell confided to Wright that 'The Bendigo's profile over here is enormous. Everywhere you go they have heard of us. Even in Perth. Every time you hand . . . your Bendigo Bank Visa card over you get a compliment back'.[159]

Kulin's Community Bank opened on 15 October 1999, an early spring day, although the weather was already starting to warm up. Hunt was there, having 'indicated a very strong passion to attend the first WA opening'.[160] So too were

Trenorden, Deputy Premier Cowan, and key members of the National Party. In another public demonstration of their support, the Nationals transferred their parliamentary account to Kulin. Trenorden 'could barely contain his excitement at the opening of the bank', and in his speech declared that all of rural Western Australia was watching Kulin, 'the Capital of the Wheatbelt'. Kulin had shown, he said, that whereas 'the key banks in Australia believe that banking is about finance . . . in fact it is overwhelmingly about people'.[161]

The Goomalling Community Bank opened a week later, in the handsome, former NAB, 1930s art-deco bank. Capital raised by the community to establish the bank had been topped up by the shire, which bought the NAB building and leased it to the Community Bank. Local farmer John Bird, who was also a shire councillor (and later its president), became chairman of the new Community Bank board. Launch day was unseasonably hot for early spring, the temperature reaching the high 30s as the speeches began in the late afternoon and the audience sweating 'all dressed up in suits and that'. They nonetheless felt a 'tremendous vibe' at the occasion.[162] Jenkins formally opened the bank, and Trenorden also spoke, foreshadowing a development that they were all eagerly anticipating, the clawing back of some control over local capital flow. Trenorden recalled how his 'Taskforce[']s research shows that every time a person leaves a country town to bank elsewhere they take $200 spending money with them. They by-pass the machinery dealer, newsagent and local store. To most communities this represents a loss of over $500,000 per year'.[163]

The Tambellup and Cranbrook Community Bank was opened in November by Richard Guy, who good-humouredly talked about wresting back community destiny against a backdrop of frolicking kids and escaping balloons. Federal minister Wilson Tuckey and other key members of the federal National Party stood among the children and their balloons, and they heeded Guy's words. And Jenkins, returning to Perth from the launches, met the National's new federal leader (Fisher having resigned in July 1999) and Acting Prime Minister John Anderson. Jenkins pointed out to Anderson that 'Community Banking has certainly struck a chord with rural and regional communities across Australia. From a standing start less

Kicking up a storm: Tambellup and Cranbrook Community Bank opening, 5 November 1999.

than 18 months ago, Bendigo Bank has now launched 19 Community Banks with more scheduled in the New Year. Well in excess of 600 communities have expressed interest in the concept'. Clear benefits were already evident, he said, and 'All of the early sites are now producing profits which are being distributed back into the local communities. The pride these communities take in their achievements is tangible'.[164]

By the end of 1999, Western Australia, the fourth Australian state to establish a Community Bank, had three functioning branches and more in the pipeline. By contrast, as the *West Australian* scathingly said of the major banks in January 2000, 'WA has lost 120 bank branches and 245 bank agencies in three years, despite promises that rural communities would not be left without bank services'.[165]

With the completion of the first Western Australian launches, 19 Community Banks plus the private franchise in Ringwood, Victoria, were in operation at the end of 1999. Jenkins' staff had handsomely exceeded the target that had been set a year earlier. Moreover, the Community Bank network was already generating some $190 million in banking business, covering Bendigo Bank's operating costs for the network and contributing to the bank's overall profit margin. The Rupanyup and Minyip Community Bank had built up deposits and loans worth almost $13 million.

As the number and geographical spread of potential community partners grew, Jenkins had already visited New Zealand, and in November Hunt welcomed to Bendigo a delegation from Cairns in Queensland. There were already encouraging signs that the first steps were being taken to realise Hunt's vision of Community Bank as a hub for multiple community services. In April, Telstra began a partnership with Community Bank, offering some of its services through the bank branches. Unfortunately the offer and the commitment did not last, and this prompted Bendigo Bank to take up a franchise on behalf of Community Banks with Community Telco Australia. In May, an agreement was reached between Maldon Community Bank and Mount Alexander Shire to allow residents to pay rates and general registrations through the Bank, and for it to display council information sheets and set up a phone inquiry line to the shire offices.

At the beginning of the year the Melbourne *Age* had remarked that 'Since Bendigo Bank launched Community Bank in mid-1998, it has ridden a wave of popular enthusiasm for its plan to take banking back to the bush'.[166] However, during the course of 1999, tensions and anxieties also surfaced. In Western Australia, Trenorden marvelled that Bendigo Bank's public relations campaign had been 'able to extract tens of millions of dollars of free advertising', but Davies, the man behind that campaign, was already worrying by the start of the year that they could not count on this indefinitely. He warned in the lead-up to the Toora opening that the Community Bank story might be becoming stale and that 'by branch number six it is probably becoming a yawn'. By early 2000 Davies was definite that 'the first flush of publicity for Community Bank has finally dissipated'.[167] Another emerging source of disquiet was Bendigo Bank's new joint-venture rural bank with Elders (*see* chapter three). The new community banks at Coleambally, Wentworth, and Avoca voiced 'repeated concerns' to Bendigo that their viability was being threatened by the Elders joint venture, and Jenkins' team privately cautioned that 'our experience to date with Elders is anything but positive. They have actively campaigned against us in a number of sites both prior to and post launch'. Community banks reported back angrily to Bendigo that local Elders agents were telling customers 'that Elders are becoming a bank and will be providing products and full banking facilities'.[168] Community Bank's broadening relationship with city as well as rural communities was not all plain sailing either. Early in 2000 Jenkins cautioned that difficulties being experienced in Elwood could well lead some on the local board to 'expect Bendigo to come in as the white knight'.[169]

Another source of frustration for Bendigo Bank was its failure to win from the federal and other state governments the same level of commitment it received from the government of Western Australia. In Victoria, Premier Kennett, who had been lukewarm about the Community Bank project, lost office in October 1999 and Bendigo Bank scrambled to build contacts with the incoming Labor government, and especially with John Brumby, now the Minister for State and Regional Development. The federal government's announcement early in 1999 that it would establish a national network of 500 Rural Transaction Centres was initially welcomed by the bank as providing an opportunity for the joint development of service centres for rural communities. The government proposed that the new centres would provide banking, Medicare, and Centrelink services, as well as employment training and business development support. Hunt held inconclusive talks during the year with Senator Ian Macdonald, the Minister for Regional Services, Territories and Local Government, in an attempt to make clear to Canberra that 'One of our objectives in developing Community Bank was to use it as a vehicle to deliver non-bank services, and that the bank was eager to explore "a single solution" that combined the resources of Rural Transaction Centres and Community Banks'.[170] When Community Bank branches nonetheless found it difficult to be accepted into the government programme, Hunt briefed Jenkins to take up the matter with Deputy Prime Minister Anderson when they met in Perth after the launch of the Tambellup and Cranbrook Community Bank. Tuckey, another federal minister, was sent a letter thanking him for attending the Tambellup and Cranbrook launch, and pointing out that 'community banking structures would be very suitable partners with Government in providing services envisaged for regional transaction centres—as well as a number of other potential activities'.[171]

The most worrying development, however, was the mounting evidence of stress within Bendigo Bank itself and among its Community Bank partners. Jenkins warned that the pace and scale of growth 'has stretched internal support to the limit'.[172] Hunt was aware that on the community side as well, early experience indicated that 'Clearly the raising of substantial amounts of money can slow the implementation process and, in some cases, perhaps even make the task look too daunting for the local community'.[173] He was also alert to the need to sustain the enthusiasm of Community Bank boards once the excitement of launch day had passed. To help fund local marketing, Bendigo Bank offered each bank an incentive payment of $10,000 per annum on it generating its first ten million dollars of business, and a further $5000 per annum for every additional five million dollars of business. Jenkins nonetheless continued to worry about the mood he detected when he visited Community Bank board meetings. By mid 1999, he expressed concern that among the local boards 'the comfort level is under threat. In short, questions are being asked on the Group's performance levels and ability to deliver'.[174] When Cheryl Rix, chairperson of the Wentworth Community Bank, contacted Hunt to voice the concerns of her board he wrote back sympathetically and stressed that 'we . . . recognise the pressures and frustrations which inevitably occur in the early days of such a new and innovative venture'. By year's end, however, senior management acknowledged that more support and structure were needed at the local level to reduce 'the stress levels and pressures across the Community Bank Group'.[175]

In order to pull together the disparate groups that made up the Community Bank network, an inaugural Community Bank Conference was held in Bendigo in April 1999. It was attended by 17 managers and chairs from nine of the new branches. In the following month, the first issue of *Community Bank News*, an electronic newsletter, was distributed. However, Hunt was determined to delve deeper still to identify and resolve difficulties, and consolidate the emerging network. In January 1999 he decided to review the structure of Community Bank as it had evolved to date, and also to 'develop a plain English summary or addendum for easier understanding at a community level'.[176] A lengthy review was undertaken by legal firm Arthur Robinson & Hedderwicks, and its recommendations were built into the structures and processes of the maturing Community Bank network.

National Coverage

The spectacular growth of Community Bank between 2000 and 2008 suggested that the programme refinements that had begun in 1999 in response to the experiences of the first wave of community banks were having their desired effect. The 100th Community Bank opened in June 2003, and during the following year, with the launch at North Ryde in Sydney of the 150th branch, Community Bank equalled and soon exceeded the number of Bendigo Bank's conventional proprietary branches. The 200th Community Bank opened in June 2007. The network expanded into Queensland in 2001, Tasmania in 2002, the Australian Capital Territory in 2003, and the Northern Territory in 2006. During these years, Jenkins said with pride, there took place an 'amazing transformation of this business from 90 percent plus Victorian to true national coverage'.[177] In the process, city and suburban branches expanded to represent half the total network. And, as the network grew and changed in its nature, business volume soared, from $320 million in the 2000 financial year to one billion dollars by the end of the 2001 financial year, five billion by 2004, and some ten billion by 2008. Bendigo Bank's 2007 annual report estimated that Community Bank contributed approximately 15 per cent of the bank's overall profit before tax.

These successes were underpinned by many factors, but three were readily apparent. Firstly, the major banks continued to be pilloried for their unresponsiveness to community aspirations. Late in 2000 the head of the Australian Bankers' Association, when asked if banks had social obligations, replied 'No . . . Our position there is that banks are very good corporate citizens today. It's just that we don't see community service obligations are necessary, we think that it's better to be driven by the marketplace'. His comments 'caused an outcry'.[178] The anger over branch closures that had sustained the first wave of community banks gradually dissipated as the major banks tempered their rationalisation programmes, but as the anger diminished, the determination by local communities to build their village became more evident and their search for partners and advisers more urgent. Whereas the major banks were perceived as downplaying community service, Bendigo Bank defined itself by that concept and eagerly partnered community initiatives.

Community Bank, which in its early years of development had been kept separate from the bank's other activities, was progressively integrated into its overall structure and processes in accordance with Hunt's long-term plan. Russell Jenkins, having successfully implemented the Community Bank project, was redesignated to head the combined Retail and Alliance Banking structure in the Group. Gillett, having provided the financial bulwark and network support that gave Community Bank licence to grow, was entrusted by Hunt to create a new division charged with broadening Bendigo's community sustainability agenda.

The second factor underpinning its success was Bendigo Bank's commitment, learned during the establishment phase of Community Bank, to build genuine long-term relationships with its new community partners. This commitment was most clearly expressed in the annual Community Bank National Conference, the first of which was held in Bendigo in February 2000. About 100 people attended that event, and drew support and encouragement from one another as they compared their experiences in launching and running community banks. The national and state conferences brought together bankers and community representatives. They acted together 'like a family'.[179] Board members from newly established community banks thereby learned from the experiences of the pioneer branches and senior Bendigo Bank executives responded to questions, criticisms, and suggestions from their community partners. By listening to and heeding the voices of its partners at the national and state conferences, Bendigo Bank won the respect, commitment, and trust of its community network. Whereas the conferences showcased the forging and renewal of effective relationships, Bendigo Bank's recognition of, and support for, volunteer service was fundamental to sustaining those relationships as Community Bank became a national network and the scale of its operations increased. Each Community Bank was a locally owned public company which held a franchise agreement with Bendigo, and had its own locally elected board of directors who in effect were unpaid volunteers carrying the weight of community expectation on their shoulders. With each success recorded and each error rectified, Bendigo Bank strengthened its training and its protocols to guide the community volunteers who sustained the Community Bank network.

An early Community Bank, Lang Lang pioneered the formation of local branch clusters, boasting four branches by 2008.

The third factor was accumulating evidence of the tangible returns that were being delivered by these volunteers to the communities they served. This could be measured in part by branch expansion at the local level. Lang Lang Community Bank quickly became the hub for a district network of four branches, and other communities imitated their success. Community benefit was most evident, however, in the capital that began to be returned to communities, and the confidence that this brought with it. With returning confidence came new levels of collaboration, enterprise, and community commitment. Only six months after its opening, Western Australia's Goomalling Community Bank had generated millions of dollars in local residential and commercial construction, and Clem Kerp—who returned energised from the first Community Bank national conference—declared that the local bank had 'created a tremendous vibe and a feeling of increase[d] optimism and a positive outlook for the town and district'.[180] The first task for Community Banks was to recover their establishment costs and pay a dividend to local shareholders; only then could they begin to funnel profits back into their communities, and this did not become unambiguously evident until 2001. Jenkins reported in February of that year that 14 of the pioneer branches were returning a regular monthly operating surplus. A year later, 30 community banks were generating substantial surpluses.

The positive outcomes of these surpluses were highlighted by Upwey (which initiated a Community Support Grants programme, sponsored educational scholarships, and became a major investor in a new hospice) and Lang Lang (which supported the establishment of a local business centre) in Victoria, and by Henty in New South Wales. Henty, styled by the *Border Mail* as the 'town which refuses to die', quickly generated sufficient profits to buy the bank building from which it operated, and to act as a beacon for the renewal of other country towns. Its mayor declared in February 2001 that 'Henty is now riding on the crest of a wave, largely because of the success of the town's community bank'.[181] In 2002, the bank distributed $150,000 in grants to community organisations. Local community champion and the local bank's chairman, Milton Taylor, was already planning to use bank profits to help build a new hospital, and to provide scholarships to encourage nurses to staff it. By 2004, the local bank was pouring resources into a community function centre.

Under the leadership of its chairman Mark Boyd-Graham Maldon Community Bank made driver training the centrepiece of a $500,000 grants programme funded from its first ten years of profits, thereby helping young drivers like James Gray (above) to gain invaluable experience.

In South Australia, Cummins Community Bank refurbished the town's swimming pool, and in Victoria, the Maldon and District Community Bank had by 2007 invested well over $500,000 to support defensive driving training for teenagers, upgrades to the local library and kindergarten, solar power for the football club, equipment for the Country Fire Association, and sponsorship for Castlemaine's innovative biennial State Festival. Such returns to the village were small if measured according to the marketplace criteria that drove conventional banking decision-making, but they were profound in their local effects.

Opposite page: The fire brigade in Gosnells, WA, with their share of the $40,000 contributed to community projects by the local Community Bank in 2007/08.

FESA
Bendigo Bank
Pay Gosnells Volunteer Fire Service
The Sum of five thousand dollars
Drawer
Gosnells Community Bank® Branch
Not Negotiable
$ 5000-00

Goomalling is a Western Australian wheat town of just 600 people, around half of whom turned out for the 1999 opening of their community branch in the handsome art deco building vacated by NAB.
PHOTOGRAPH BY ALAN MAYNE.

Bendigo Bank's 2007 annual report noted that community banks had contributed ten million dollars to local projects and seven million dollars in local shareholder dividends since Community Bank's inception. At Goomalling, a typical small town community bank, this translated into an annual profit of $100,000 per year, meaning regular dividends for local shareholders, and financial support for the St John's Ambulance service, child-care facilities and youth activities. Kerp estimated late in 2005 that 90 per cent of the town now banked with the Community Bank, as did 40 per cent of farmers in the district. The bank's accumulating reserves had enabled it earlier in the year to buy the premises that it had hitherto leased from the shire council. The 'vibe' in the town that Kerp had reported in 2000 was now strongly established in the community, and new businesses were opening. Volunteers like Kerp in country towns like Goomalling in Western Australia, or Maldon in Victoria, or Henty in New South Wales, and their urban counterparts in places such as Goodwood in suburban Adelaide or Cairns in north Queensland, all regarded Community Bank as more than a banking facility: it was a community benefit. It helped communities to build their village.

But some of the impediments that had hampered the consolidation of the first wave of community banks persisted. Bendigo Bank was disappointed in its attempts to engage with the federal government, and no other state government followed the lead of Western Australia in supporting the project. Community Bank boards expressed continuing frustration at their inability to capitalise upon the rhetoric of support for community sustainability initiatives that surrounded the launch of the Rural Transaction Centre programme. After further meetings between Bendigo Bank senior executives and the deputy prime minister during 2000, Hunt decided late in the year not to pursue the discussions further as 'it appears the Minister can't quite understand . . . our model'. Hunt concluded, 'I think programs like

Community Bank, Community Bank stage 2, Bendigo Stock Exchange, Regional Development Fund, our Telco Model and programs such as our Lead On activities clearly demonstrate that there are ways to involve, engage and unite a community to create better outcomes than any proposal from Canberra or our capital cities'.[182]

There were ongoing tensions as well during the early 2000s with some of the more traditional staffers in Bendigo Bank, who still doubted the logic of integrating Community Bank into the company network. Jean Wright, Hunt's personal assistant, noted perceptively early in 2000 that 'We have already witnessed a little of the *"where do I fit in all this"* syndrome from (in the main) the more senior managers out there in our regional network. In future I fear the separation between our traditional and Community Bank networks may widen—and that insecure "spoilers" could cause real conflict within our organisation'. She recommended that Bendigo Bank 'embrace some of [the] "feel" [of Community Bank] into our traditional branches'.[183] Hunt had always confided with Wright and Owen Davies the broader plan to integrate Community Bank into the overall company structure. Both had embraced this broader concept with vigour and became its champions within head office, while Russell Jenkins championed the field operations. It took some time, but with Gillett gradually converting his middle managers to the cause, the full integration of internal structures and processes was completed by 2006. But in the interim, in order to head off internal disaffection, Hunt sent a circular to all staff in March 2000, charting Community Bank's achievements to date and the plans for further expansion, but emphasising that it was just one cog within Bendigo Bank, which would continue to expand 'our "company" branch network'.[184]

Doubts and sometimes disappointment were also evident at a community level, notwithstanding—or perhaps partly because of—the enthusiasm that had been generated by the first wave of branch launches. Hunt, sympathetic, predicted to Jenkins in 2000 that they would soon 'start to see some battle fatigue in the boards'. As he conceded, 'These people went in to run a basic banking enterprise & now they find they are directing the community's future. Tall order I know—and won't be fixed in 10 minutes'.[185] But Hunt and Jenkins were determined to provide support where it was needed. As they had anticipated, generating business and returning a profit were nowhere easy in the new network, and at some branches progress was especially slow and difficult. The early years of the Tambellup and Cranbrook Community Bank were a struggle. At Kulin, although the bank generated sufficient business to return a small annual dividend to shareholders, Hadlow acknowledged in 2005 that business volumes had fallen short of expectations and that profits were still too slim to enable the branch to begin a community grants programme.[186] One disgruntled Western Australian shareholder complained to Trenorden in the same year that he had received no return on his investment, and called Community Bank 'the biggest con job since the banks started to pull out of the country'. He alleged that 'the Bendigo in Victoria has become just like all the banks, creaming more and more money from the business by increasing their charges all the time'.[187] Uncertainty, and diversity of approach, had characterised some of the discussions at the first national conference in 2000, prompting Wright to remark that 'they all seem to be doing whatever they like . . . They do it first . . . then tell us'. More structure and coordination was needed, she warned. Agreeing with her assessment, Hunt expressed alarm at 'the vulnerability of the loose alliance that appears to be in place'.[188]

These early frictions came to a head among rural communities with the formal launch of Elders Rural Bank in August 2000. The tensions arose in part because, in the 'brown lands' where Elders had traditionally operated, some Elders agents were perceived to be working on behalf of ERB against Community Bank. Jenkins concluded from the feedback he received from Community Bank boards 'that the messages delivered through these guys is somewhat unhelpful to our cause. Common comments seem to be along the line "you don't need a Community Bank[;] we will provide all your needs" and "Community Banks can't meet your farming needs—their focus is retail and small commercial"'.[189] In South Australia, where Elders began, the Community Bank planning committee at Cummins on the Eyre Peninsula considered shelving their bank project until the ramifications of the Elders joint venture became clearer. However, it was in Western Australia, the heartland of Elders' rival Wesfarmers, that the Elders alliance caused the greatest disquiet. The pioneering Kulin Community Bank, for example, operated out of the town's Wesfarmers agency building. Cornwell relayed to Bendigo the mood prevailing in Kulin and other wheat-belt communities, warning that 'all concerned are feeling somewhat deceived'.[190] Jenkins and Hunt concluded that 'a circuit breaker' was urgently needed,[191] and both booked flights to attend the first Western Australian state conference in July 2000 in order to explain the Bendigo Bank strategy and to talk through grassroots concerns. It was a gruelling experience. Hunt acknowledged that he got 'tackled . . . with real vigour' at the conference, and a year later Jenkins, preparing for the 2001 Western Australian conference, urged Hunt that it was 'important that we avoid a repeat of the last conference in WA and tensions that were created around that period'. Both men again attended the conference, and afterwards a relieved Jenkins noted the 'overwhelming feeling that Bendigo was taking WA seriously'.[192]

It was in the context of these events that Hunt in 2000 began to explain in public his full social vision for Community Bank. He had initially shared with Jenkins only his ideas—anchored in bankers' orthodoxies—for developing a franchise model and, in the first stage of Community Bank, Jenkins' team in turn dazzled local communities by returning banking services to their districts. The time was now ripe, Hunt decided, to broach with Jenkins his broader vision of Bendigo Bank's role in building sustainable communities. And Jenkins, he found, was ready for this new challenge. The next step was to engage the communities themselves. Hunt was encouraged by the positive messages coming out of communities such as Goomalling, but disappointed by the continuing criticisms and misreading of Bendigo Bank's motives. It was time, Hunt resolved, to 'lift debate'; it was time to introduce 'Community Bank Stage 2'.[193]

Hunt likened the full mobilisation of a community's social capital to climbing Mount Everest. The challenges involved in establishing and running a community bank were equivalent, he said, to asking community bank volunteers 'to climb very, very large mountains'. But he added that even these 'may not be the Everest that ultimately we want them to climb'. It was now time to explain that, for all the effort hitherto expended, Community Bank had barely reached base camp—the real climb had yet to begin. To stand atop Everest, he knew, 'is where you are addressing all of the issues of sustainability around a community. The first [step] is to capture . . . financial capital. The second one is to make sure you make use of all of the intellectual capabilities that your district has'.[194] In April 2000, he released a discussion paper, 'Helping to Create Sustainable Communities', which began the process of explaining the broader social goals and principles of Community Bank, and the Bendigo Bank vision of sustainable communities into which the Community Bank project fitted.[195]

Hunt's decision was influenced in part by what he felt was the unnecessarily carping nature of recent Community Bank publicity about the major banks. As he reminded his colleagues, 'For some time now I have been asking that we lift the sights and the debate about Community Banking away from sniping or slapping at the major banks'.[196] Hunt's decision was influenced also by the angry reaction of many community banks to the Elders joint venture. That reaction, he concluded, showed that 'we have not managed to lift their sights' regarding the ultimate target of Community Bank. It was, he said, 'essential that we move away from

San Remo launched Bendigo's 100th Community Bank branch on 27 June 2003 with a typical main street fanfare.

painting Community Banks as being a banking solution only'. As Hunt simultaneously explained to the chairman of the Coleambally Community Bank, which was a centre of anti-Elders sentiment, 'It is my view that Community Bank is much more than a banking solution, or a way to gain access to banking products. It is about choice, certainty, participation, and successfully demonstrating that we in the country are capable of forming and running a commercial enterprise'.[197]

Hunt began to explain to those who had passed the test of establishing a community bank that they had been serving an apprenticeship with an 'enhancement tool' whose function was 'to create a prosperous village'.[198] The tool, and the concept behind it, had been applied thus far in Community Bank to re-establish basic banking services, and it was now time to add value to that achievement. In Hunt's vision, Community Bank overlapped with other community enhancement projects such as the Regional Development Fund, Bendigo Community Telco, Bendigo Stock Exchange, Lead On, and the Community Enterprise Foundation. They all sought to partner with communities to mobilise the resources needed to sustain community wellbeing and future prosperity. In none of these cases, he insisted, was Bendigo Bank's purpose the old philanthropic one of 'going out there with a gifting model, it's about sharing responsibility and reward'.[199] In a public letter to the whole Community Bank network in January 2006, Hunt made explicit how these community projects fitted into the 'broader activities' of Community Bank that were designed to deliver social benefit and community sustainability.[200]

The Lead On youth and community development programme, which was designed to encourage youth participation and innovation in town activities and local businesses, was established in Bendigo in 1999, and subsequently expanded throughout Australia. By 2008 almost 5000 young people had participated in Lead On activities. Community Telco Australia, established in 2000 with Bendigo Bank as its major shareholder, aimed to boost rural and regional business competitiveness by assisting participating communities to install advanced telecommunications infrastructure. After being successfully tested with Bendigo Community Telco, it expanded into Queensland, Tasmania, and New South Wales. The Community

Telco volumes continue to increase, along with the range of services offered. Also, in recent years a franchise has been formed to serve all of the Community Banks, should they see advantage in turning an everyday activity and expense into a new source of local cash through their local enterprise. The Community Enterprise Foundation was announced at the 2004 Community Bank national conference and formally launched early in the following year. It functions in part as a philanthropic trust, providing emergency relief. Its first undertaking was a disaster appeal in the wake of the Boxing Day tsunami in Asia, followed by fund-raising to assist rebuilding on the Eyre Peninsula after the 2005 bushfires, and at Babinda in north Queensland after Cyclone Larry in 2006. It also mobilises volunteers to support projects that promote sustainable communities and social justice. Community Banks were quick to support these activities. By the 2005 national Community Bank conference, 21 Community Banks had already become foundation partners, and increasingly local bank boards have contributed donations and partnered in providing co-funding for local projects within the Community Bank network.

Retrospect

Owen Davies remarked to delegates at the 2005 Community Bank national conference that Bendigo Bank had been founded in 1858 'as a community bank'.[201] Its founders had sought to invest local capital where it had been generated and where it was most needed. It had been established to help build a village. Rob Hunt's vision during the 1990s and into the new century was to replicate that local achievement across Australia. His vision related only partially to the technicalities of developing a new banking model. It was also about using banking as an instrument to build up the capacities of communities. As his prompts in a well-thumbed early PowerPoint presentation declared, the core principles were 'Sustainable Communities', 'Utilise entire district's skill and resource base', 'History of our Building Society', and 'Back to the Future'.[202]

As Andrew Watts said excitedly after Hunt had given one such presentation to senior staff at Bendigo Bank in 1998:

I believe many of us at Bendigo Bank have been searching for identity over the last few years. We have gone through bank conversion, acquisitions, restructures and have had a large injection of new management personnel. In my area alone, we have many staff who have come from other banking organisations. Stamping the 'Bendigo' philosophy on these people has often been difficult because our identity and attitude had become somewhat clouded.

Rob's presentation today was passionate, motivating and real. It cemented the type of thinking that makes us proud to work for this organisation. It is our point of difference.[203]

And as Max Trenorden recalled during harvest time in December 2005 in the Western Australian wheat belt, encapsulating the grassroots enthusiasm for Community Bank in local communities around Australia:

I was born and bred east of Goomalling and used to go through it all the time to go to school, and go to Perth and those sorts of things . . . It was just one of those dying communities . . . Now Goomalling has been transformed. A big part of it is the Community Bank, but Community Bank does not only bring in money, it brings in enthusiasm, people see the success. So if you go to Goomalling now there's four or five at least new businesses in the community since those days, not just because there's a bank there but because there's a belief there, and that's because . . . people get back to believing in their own communities.[204]

But the last word belongs to Hunt. Thanking Rupanyup farmer Jim Starbuck as he stepped down from the Rupanyup and Minyip Community Bank board in October 1999, Hunt emphasised that 'Communities were never created by someone waving a magic wand. It was always about people with a dream, immense energy and commitment to their district. That's what created (and will sustain) communities'.[205] By assisting communities to assert greater control over their destinies, Hunt took pride in the fact that Bendigo Bank, 'a tiny speck in the financial world', had changed 'the whole language of the industry'.[206]

Conclusion

Fulsome celebratory histories are easily written, though few stand the test of time. Sustaining a business for over 150 years, as Bendigo Bank and its antecedents have done, while simultaneously winning plaudits as Australia's 'likeable bank',[1] is a much harder task.

The challenge when writing a sesquicentenary history book is to move beyond a shallow celebration of achievements in order to properly assess their historical significance and to commemorate them appropriately. In the case of Bendigo Bank that task is made still more difficult because banking is seemingly such an indeterminate subject. For most bankers, the goal is simply to maximise profits. For most consumers, banking has relevance simply as the means to achieve other ends. For neither bankers nor consumers does banking *per se* appear to be a subject from which engrossing histories can readily be drawn.

Although many fine institutional and economic histories of banks have been written in Australia, they occupy a specialist niche and do not attract the interest of general readers. The history of banking in Australia has, at first glance, neither close associations with momentous national events nor with social developments that are valued by most Australians. To the extent that banking practices today generate strong responses among Australians, these are likely to be triggered by the banks' retreat over the last 20 years from direct participation in the social life of the nation. The widespread branch closures of the 1990s have left deep scars and resentments in communities throughout Australia, in the suburbs as well as in the bush.

Bendigo Bank went dramatically against the trend towards social disengagement that was set by the sector's major players during the 1990s. The bank's managing director, Rob Hunt, believes

> it's unfortunate that people think ill of banks today, because we have one of the best banking systems in the world in terms of safety, security, access, utility. I am not saying the industry hasn't acted poorly or inappropriately, and at times made silly decisions. But this little tiny bank, Bendigo, has changed the behaviour of a whole industry . . . They've stopped closing branches, they're back doing work at a community level, they're back putting services . . . into their branches.[2]

Since its establishment in 1995, Bendigo Bank has introduced a social agenda into the thinking of Australian bankers, and has actively applied that agenda across the nation through its partnerships with local communities, consolidating their economic and social wellbeing. In doing so, the bank has drawn upon principles and practices that it has built up since 1858 as a local building society and trust funds manager. It is in tracing the development of this social agenda that a worthwhile banking history can be told. In those 150 years of development from a proto-bank into Australia's seventh largest bank there lies, as Hunt says, 'a grand history of service to the community as well as service to its shareholders'.[3] It is a history of building the village, begun on the Bendigo goldfields in 1858 and replicated in communities across the nation.

Bendigo Bank's operations continue to be informed by that history. This results in what its chairman Robert Johanson calls, with a twinkle in his eye, a forward-looking strategy that necessarily unfolds by 'backing into the future'.[4] This is an enormous strength. When in 1997 the bank purchased the Australian operations of the Banca Monte dei Paschi di Siena, Bendigo's historically informed sense of its strategic direction within Australia intersected with a much longer historical time-frame of banking operations that stretched back to the origins of modern European banking. Banca Monte dei Paschi di Siena, founded in 1472, is the world's oldest operating bank. In Johanson and Hunt's opinion, a large and ancient bank like Banca Monte dei Paschi di Siena and a small new bank like Bendigo Bank have shared antecedents. The history of modern European banking, and indeed of modern Islamic banking, share with Bendigo Bank an emphasis upon what Hunt characterises as 'effectively using capital and therefore building a prosperous village'.[5] This concept of banks playing a significant role in feeding into rather than feeding off community wellbeing was criticised, Hunt says, during the course of financial deregulation in late twentieth-century Australia as being old-fashioned banking. However, in the early twenty-first century, with the globalisation of banking and the universalisation of banking products, it is now acknowledged that Bendigo Bank, by continuing to emphasise community building, is uniquely positioned in Australia 'to create a bank that is connected to its customers and their aspirations. Banks, Hunt asserts, remain the most effective way to deliver capital into the real local economies that create and sustain national prosperity'.[6]

In allowing its business practices to be informed by history, Bendigo Bank places value on that often ignored and sometimes derided feature of social life: localism. The bank recognises the significance of local identities, aspirations, needs, and opportunities. Hunt emphasised in his Alfred Deakin Innovation Lecture in 2005 that 'As the world becomes global, people are inclined to act tribally—and in fact all early communities emerged out of local aspirations and endeavour'.[7] In its own home-place, Bendigo, the bank continues to support local cultural events such as the famous Bendigo Easter Fair, which Sandhurst Trustees (now incorporated into Bendigo Bank as the main arm of its wealth solutions division) had sponsored since the Trustees' establishment in 1888. The bank also assists with the publication of the *Annals of Bendigo*, now in its tenth volume, a compilation of news items gleaned from the *Bendigo Advertiser* since its commencement in 1851. The Sandhurst Building Society (which merged into Bendigo Building Society in 1983) published the *Annals*' coverage of the years between 1936 and 1950; Sandhurst Trustees published the next volume, covering the years 1951–1987; and Bendigo Bank has published subsequent volumes. The bank's respect for local opinion and its sensitivity to local needs and opportunities is highlighted by the manner in which its 2000 merger with Queensland's First Australian Building Society was gradually implemented at branch level over following years; by its willingness to listen to the viewpoints of rural communities in Western Australia during the early 2000s in order to reconcile the local priorities of its Community Bank partners in the West with Bendigo's national rural banking strategy; and by its undertaking to maintain and enhance South Australia's local branch network following its merger in 2007 with Adelaide Bank.

Respect for local aspirations is symptomatic of Bendigo Bank's deeply rooted identity as a community business. Hunt drew attention to this in his Deakin Lecture, saying 'We were well aware that our own organisation grew out of community need for housing—the Building Society being formed by locals to capture savings and provide loans to establish this housing'.[8] Bendigo Bank's origins lie in a network of neighbourhood self-help organisations, the scale and spread of whose operations were determined by the local communities they served. Together those businesses performed many of the functions of a community bank long before the business was formally declared a bank in name, and before its Community Bank project was launched in 1998. In common with micro-financiers such as Grameen Bank and the Bangladesh Rural Advancement Committee (BRAC) in Bangladesh today, 'What makes their programs so successful is that they come out of the communities

Moving with the customer. An expanding ATM network increases access and convenience.

that they service and address the needs of the people in those communities'.[9]

These characteristics are supported by a well-developed sense of public ethics and business social responsibility. Bendigo Bank's managers and staff care about the wellbeing of the communities with whom they work. Russell Jenkins, who oversaw the national expansion of the Community Bank network, recalls that the launching of that network, when he worked long hours with volunteers in communities throughout Australia, was 'all so personal for me'.[10] Notwithstanding a gruelling personal schedule and the national spread of banking operations, he did not miss any of the first 50 Community Bank opening celebrations. Hunt always insisted that the Community Bank model had to operate on sound commercial principles and that the bank's community service had to be balanced by its responsibility to its shareholders. However, he also contended that by getting the balance right Bendigo Bank could do more than 'be a bank like everybody else', because its history had given it the 'right value system' to accomplish a better mission.[11]

This 'service ethic', as Johanson calls it,[12] has been directed in part at delivering basic banking services to as wide a spread of rural and urban communities as possible, and more importantly at mobilising each community's full social capital. It is an approach that encourages grassroots participation and supports the harnessing of local energies. In the words of Community Bank pioneer David Matthews, the bank has helped communities such as his, the tiny Wimmera town of Rupanyup, to 'take some control ourselves'.[13] Bendigo Bank has often been applauded as a friend of the bush, and it has indeed worked hard to develop business and social infrastructure in regional Australia. However, the bank's service ethic is not limited to correcting regional disadvantage; it promotes still broader possibilities for all Australians in terms of community sustainability and social justice.

This is, as Hunt acknowledges, a 'very broad agenda'. He sees Community Bank as only 'the most visible community enhancement' project that the bank has embarked upon, and emphasises the bank's participation in the early stages of building a network of 'strong community enterprises . . . right across Australia' that will help to support engaged, well resourced, and resilient local communities. This, he says, is 'the Everest you've got to climb' when building an inclusive and sustainable society. Thinking back over Bendigo Bank's history, he declares, 'In my view we are still in the very early chapters of a book, and those early chapters are bringing immense pleasure and success in communities. But they don't address all of the issues that they need to address'.[14] The possibilities, however, and some of the opportunities for realising them, are now clear.

Bendigo Bank's style of community banking is not constrained by the precedents in its history, nor is the bank prescriptive in the possibilities for future development that it offers Australian communities. The bank's perspective in 2008, developed over 150 years of building the village, is clearly summed up by Hunt. Assessing the principles that underpin each branch in communities across Australia, he states on behalf of Bendigo Bank, 'I'm not trying to determine what this community will look like. I'm only wanting it to achieve whatever its potential is, and not wanting it to be blinkered by whatever happened in the past. It's as simple as that'.[15]

And as difficult. It is one thing for a bank to understand how a successful community is a great place in which to operate its business: quite another to make the leap and actively feed the community's prosperity. Yet Bendigo has taken this approach, and by so doing remains more relevant and better connected to community than its competitors. This has delivered Bendigo a valued position in both banking and community. Communities continue to seek to engage with Bendigo; customers who see the impact a local Bendigo branch can make on their community continue to bring more business to the Bank. 'Through ensuring we remain relevant, connected and valued, I think we will have a great chance to become Australia's leading customer-connected banking group,'[16] says Hunt.

One village at a time.

Notes

Unless otherwise stated, items referred to in endnotes were sourced from the Bendigo Bank Archive.

Abbreviations

BBS: Bendigo Building Society

SBS: Sandhurst Mutual Permanent Investment & Building Society

StarBS: Bendigo & Eaglehawk Star Permanent Building Society

Introduction

1 Rob Hunt, 'Creative Capital, Creative Strategies, Community-based Wealth Creation', Alfred Deakin Innovation Lectures, 6 May 2005, p. 1.

2 *Age*, 22 May 1979. At the time of its conversion into a bank, it was the oldest surviving building society in Australia.

3 Joseph Stiglitz, *Making Globalization Work.* Camberwell, Vic: Allen Lane/Penguin Group Australia, 2006, p. 198.

Chapter one Bankers

1 Richard Guy, recorded interview, 5 April 2005. I have carefully reconstructed the events described in this chapter, using archived documents and recorded interviews. Although I have done my utmost to verify the accuracy of my narrative, it is necessarily based upon subjective viewpoints that will not be shared by all of the participants in the events that I describe. I apologise for any unintended offence.

2 Rob Hunt, recorded interview, 5 May 2005. Rob Hunt will retire in July 2009.

3 In May 2008 a proposed merger between Westpac and St George was announced.

4 Robert Johanson, recorded interview, 15 April 2008.

5 Bendigo Bank, *Annual Report 2001*, p. 13.

6 Johanson, 15 April 2008.

7 Bendigo Bank, *Annual Report 2001*, p. 12.

8 Bendigo Bank, *Annual Report 2003*, p. 6; *Annual Report 2002*, p. 6.

9 Brian Thomas, recorded interview, 5 October 1995.
10 *Age,* 17 November 1981, in *Scrap Book Cuttings.*
11 Johanson, 15 April 2008.
12 Bendigo Building Society, *Annual Report 1981*; *Annual Report 1983.*
13 Bendigo Building Society, *Annual Report 1986.*
14 *Herald*, 27 August 1990, editorial leader, in *Newspaper Cuttings 1990–1991.*
15 Bendigo Bank, *Submission to Standard & Poor's for Credit Rating,* March 1996, p. 36, Bendigo Bank Boardroom.
16 Johanson, 15 April 2008.
17 Bendigo Building Society, *Annual Report 1982.*
18 Bendigo Building Society, *Annual Report 1991.*
19 Johanson, 15 April 2008.
20 Guy, 5 April 2005.
21 Bendigo Building Society, *Annual Report 1990.*
22 *Age*, 18 May 1990, 'Pyramid's Parent Seeks Partner to Stay on Winning Streak', Capital Building Society papers, unmarked archives box.
23 Guy, 5 April 2005.
24 Johanson, 15 April 2008.
25 Guy, 5 April 2005.
26 Bendigo Bank, *Submission to Standard & Poor's*, p. 1.
27 Johanson, 15 April 2008.
28 Notes from a meeting with Rob Hunt, 27 May 2008.
29 Reserve Bank of Australia Press Release, no. 90-16, 'Building Societies and the Reserve Bank', 2 July 1990.
30 Guy, 5 April 2005.
31 Bendigo Building Society, *Annual Report 1990.*
32 *Sun,* 2 July 1990, 'It's Business as Usual at "The Bendigo"'.
33 Rob Hunt to Alan Mayne, 5 June 2008.
34 *Age*, 31 August 1990, *newspaper cuttings 1990–1991.*
35 *Herald*, 31 August 1990, editorial leader, ibid.
36 *Geelong Advertiser*, 11 September 1990, ibid.
37 Hunt, 27 May 2008.
38 ibid.
39 *Herald Sun*, 9 November 1990, in *Newspaper Cuttings 1990–1991.*
40 Bendigo Building Society, *Annual Report 1992*; *Annual Report 1993.* After the Wallis Review in the late 1990s, regulation of banks and building societies was transferred to the new Australian Prudential Regulatory Authority.
41 Johanson, 15 April 2008.
42 Thomas, 5 October 1995.
43 Hunt to Mayne, 5 June 2008.

44 John Perrow, recorded interview, 30 November 1995.

45 Jim Kennan to Brian Thom, 11 June 1991, in Capital Building Society, archives box with caption 'Farrow June '90 onwards. Records of Historical Importance'.

46 Guy, 5 April 2005.

47 ibid.

48 Directors' Report, Capital Building Society, 1990 Annual General Meeting, manila folder in Capital Building Society papers, unmarked archives box.

49 'Notes for Chairman for annual meeting, 24/10/91', typescript, ibid.

50 *Geelong Advertiser*, 11 September 1990, in *Newspaper Cuttings 1990–1991.*

51 Minutes of Directors' Meeting, 5 June 1991, 29 May 1991, Capital Building Society, Capital Building Society papers, unmarked archives box.

52 Guy, 5 April 2005.

53 Brian Tom, 'Capital Building Society. Report to KPMG Peat Marwick', August 1991, in Capital Building Society, archives box 'Farrow June '90 onwards'.

54 Capital Building Society, Minutes of Twentieth Annual General Meeting, 24 October 1991, manila folder in Capital Building Society papers, unmarked archives box.

55 Jim Kennan to Brian Thom, 11 June 1991, in orange folder captioned 'Liquidity Support Scheme', in Capital Building Society, archives box 'Farrow June '90 onwards'.

56 Kevin Roache to Brian Thom and other managers, 20 November 1991, ibid.

57 Capital Building Society, 'Minutes of Meeting of Directors, 29 April 1992', in Capital Building Society papers, unmarked archives box. Hunt, 27 May 2008.

58 Perrow, 30 November 1995.

59 Compass Building Society, 1 September 1992, in *Directors' Minutes, 4 August 1992–29 September 1992.*

60 Guy, 5 April 2005; Johanson, 15 April 2008.

61 Guy, 5 April 2005.

62 Johanson, 15 April 2008.

63 Bendigo Building Society, *Annual Report 1994.*

64 Bendigo Building Society, *Annual Report 1992.*

65 Perrow, 30 November 1995.

66 ibid.

67 Thomas, 5 October 1995.

68 Bendigo Building Society, *Annual Report 1994.*

69 Guy, 5 April 2005.

70 Johanson, 15 April 2008.

71 Bendigo Bank, *Concise Annual Report, 2005*, p. 4.

72 Bendigo Bank, *Concise Annual Report, 2000*, p. 5.

73 Bendigo Bank, *News Archive*, 1 May 2007, 26 June 2007 <www.bendigobank.com.au/public/about_us/news/news_archive>. *Age*, 19 March 2007, 'Bendigo Bank Shares Soar on Takeover Talk'. In market capitalisation, both companies

were virtually equal pegging (Bank of Queensland $1.85 billion, Bendigo Bank $1.81 billion). The Bank of Queensland's annual profit to 31 August 2007 (after tax) was $130 million, and its total assets were valued at $20 billion. Bendigo Bank's after-tax profit to 30 June 2007 was $122 million, with assets of $17 billion.

74 Johanson, 15 April 2008.

75 Bendigo Bank, *Annual Report 1996.*

76 Johanson, 15 April 2008.

77 Bendigo Bank, *Annual Report 1996.*

78 Bendigo Bank, *Minutes of Directors' Meetings, July 1996–June 1997,* 24 February 1997.

79 Bendigo Bank, *Minutes of Directors' Meetings, July 1997–June 1998,* 28 July 1997. *Age,* 4 November 1998, 'For Decades a Solid Citizen', Community Bank File 3, Box 157.

80 Bendigo Bank, *Annual Report 1997.*

81 *Australian,* 9 October 1997, 'Bendigo Recovery', Owen Davies' newspaper cuttings, 1997–1998, Bendigo Bank.

82 *Bendigo Advertiser,* 15 July 1998, 'Bank Share Price Surge'; 'Bendigo Bank in Profit Rebound' (undated c. 11 August 1998 cutting), both ibid.

83 Bendigo Bank, *Concise Annual Report, 2004,* p. 4.

84 Bendigo Bank, *Concise Annual Report, 2005,* p. 13.

85 ibid., p. 4.

86 Bendigo Bank, *Annual Report 1998.*

87 Bendigo Bank, *Concise Annual Report, 2001,* p. 10.

88 Hunt, 5 May 2005.

89 Rob Hunt to John Anderson, 17 July 2000, Community Bank File, Box 156.

90 Bendigo Bank, *Concise Annual Report, 2003,* p. 4.

91 Hunt, 5 May 2005.

92 ibid.

Chapter two Neighbours

1 Bendigo Bank, *Annual Report 1998.*

2 *Bendigo Advertiser,* 10 July 1858, and republished September 1908; 'Building Society', clipping in front page of Bendigo Land and Building Society, Minute Book (contained within BBS, *Annual Minute Book, 1858–1942).*

3 Bendigo Bank, *Annual Report 1998.*

4 Seymour J. Price, *Building Societies: Their Origin and History.* London: Franey & Co, 1958, p. 566.

5 *Bendigo Advertiser,* 12 December 1933, 'Sandhurst Building Society's Successful Year', in SBS, *Minute Book 1933–1939,* 11 December 1933, p. 45.

6 Bendigo Mutual Permanent Land and Building Society, 'Diamond Jubilee 1865–1925. Sixtieth Annual Balance. October 17th, 1925', in BBS, *Balance Sheets 1925–1949.*

7 BBS, *Annual Minute Book 1858–1942,* 27 November 1914.

8 StarBS, *Loans Committee Minutes 1907–1925*, 1 November 1927, p. 99 (G.B. Jackson).

9 SBS, *Minute Book 1881–1897*, 8 December 1885; 7 September 1886 (Mrs Homan).

10 Bendigo Mutual Permanent Land and Building Society, '38th Annual Balance, October 17th, 1903', in BBS, *Balance Sheets 1886–1924*; see also Sandhurst Mutual Permanent Investment and Building Society, *22nd Yearly Balance*, 31st October, 1903, 'Directors Report', p. 5, insert in SBS, *Minute Book 1897–1908*, 21 December 1903, p. 216.

11 'The Bendigo And Eaglehawk Star Permanent Building Society. Annual Meeting', insert in StarBS, *Minute Book: General and Special General Meetings, 1901–1956*, 22 September 1915, pp. 65–66.

12 'Report and Balance Sheet', insert, ibid., 17 September 192, pp. 71–2.

13 BBS, *Annual Minute Book 1858–1942*, 4 December 1891.

14 BBS, *Secretary's Monthly Reports 1880–1889*, 17 April 1884.

15 Bendigo Land and Building Society, 'Minute Book', in BBS, *Annual Minute Book, 1858–1942*, 4 February 1861.

16 Historian Frank Cusack suggested that this society was first established as a terminating society in 1857, wound up in 1862, and then re-established in the same year. There is no evidence of this in the Bendigo Bank Archive. See Frank Cusack, *The Sandhurst Building Society: A History*, Bendigo: Sandhurst Building Society, 1981, pp. 4–5.

17 'Bendigo Mutual Permanent Society', ms insert: *Independent*, 21 November 1908, in BBS, *Newspaper Cuttings 1894–1921*, p. 158. See also the advertising feature, ibid., p.151: *Bendigo Advertiser*, 27 March 1886, 'Operations of Building Societies. The Bendigo Mutual Permanent Land & Building Society'.

18 Bendigo Mutual, 'Diamond Jubilee 1865–1925', in BBS, *Balance Sheets 1925–1949.*

19 'A Lively Meeting', ms insert: *Saturday Advertiser*, 27 November 1909 and 'Bendigo Mutual Building Society', ms insert: *Saturday Advertiser*, 8 January 1910, in BBS, *Newspaper Cuttings 1894–1921*, p.158.

20 Bendigo Mutual, 'Diamond Jubilee 1865–1925', in BBS, *Balance Sheets 1925–1949.*

21 Bendigo Permanent Land, Building and Investment Society, Directors Monthly Meetings, 13 April 1877, 25 March 1877, in BBS, *Directors Monthly Meetings 1860–1885*, pp. 240, 241–242.

22 BBS, *Secretary's Monthly Reports 1880–1889*, 22 April 1881.

23 Bendigo Permanent Land, Building and Investment Society, *Directors Monthly Meetings 1860–1885*, 25 October 1882, pp. 406–7.

24 Bendigo Mutual Permanent Land and Building Society, *Directors' Minute Book 1925–1940*, 26 April 1929, p. 227.

25 'The Bendigo Mutual Permanent Land and Building Society: Balance October 13th, 1891', in BBS, *Balance Sheets 1886–1924.*

26 'The Bendigo Mutual Permanent Land and Building Society: Balance October 13th, 1893', ibid., Report of Directors, p. 4.

27 BBS, *Annual Minute Book 1858–1942*, 27 November 1894.

28 *Independent,* ms insert: 6 December 1897, 'Bendigo Mutual Permanent Land and Building Society', in BBS, *Newspaper Cuttings 1894–1921*, p. 154. See also 'Mutual Permanent Building Society' ms insert: *Independent*, 23 November 1901, ibid., p.155.

29 'The Bendigo Mutual Permanent Land and Building Society. Bull Street, Bendigo. Fifty Ninth Annual Balance. October 17th, 1924', p. 2, in BBS, *Balance Sheets 1886–1924.*

30 Bendigo Mutual, *Diamond Jubilee 1865–1925.*

31 'Special meeting, 16 December 1895', in SBS, *Minute Book 1881–1897.*

32 ibid., 8 August 1882.

33 BBS, *Secretary's Monthly Reports 1880–1889*, 16 June 1881.

34 SBS, *Minute Book 1881–1897*, 18 May 1893.

35 'Memorandum by John Neeson', 7 December 1887, reproduced in Sandhurst Trustees Ltd, *100th Annual Report: 1888–1988*, p. 4.

36 Ian Mansbridge, recorded interview, 21 August 2006.

37 'Bendigo and Eaglehawk Starr Bowkett Society', ms insert: *Independent*, 30 September 1902, in BBS, *Newspaper Cuttings 1894–1921*, p. 156.

38 *Bendigo Advertiser*, 17 December 1910, 'Starr-Bowkett Society', insert in StarBS, *Minute Book: General and Special General Meetings, 1901–1956*, pp. 55–56.

39 ibid.

40 Bendigo and Eaglehawk Star Permanent Building Society, 'Annual Meeting', ibid., 29 September 1911, p. 62.

41 BBS, *Minute Book 1925–1940*, 4 May 1928, p. 174.

42 BBS, *Balance Sheets 1866–1885*, 7 November 1878. See also *Bendigo Advertiser*, 5 December 1894, 'Bendigo Mutual Permanent Land and Building Society', in BBS, *Newspaper Cuttings 1894–1921*, p. 152.

43 BBS, *Annual Minute Book 1858–1942*, 30 November 1893.

44 ibid., 27 November 1896.

45 ibid., 19 November 1928.

46 'Report and Balance Sheet', typed insert in StarBS, *Minute Book: General and Special General Meetings, 1901–1956*, 17 September 1920, pp. 71–72.

47 BBS, *Balance Sheets 1866–1885*, 17 November 1879.

48 'The Bendigo Mutual Permanent Land and Building Society: Balance October 11th, 1892', p. 12, in BBS, *Balance Sheets 1886–1924.*

49 'The Bendigo Mutual Permanent Land and Building Society, Bull Street. 51st Annual Balance, October 17, 1916', p. 12, ibid.

50 Unattributed newspaper cutting, 'Sandhurst Building Society. Another Very Good Year', insert in SBS, *Minute Book 1923–1933*, 15 December 1924.

51 '10th Yearly Balance of the Sandhurst Mutual Permanent Investment & Building Society. 31st October, 1891', p. 5, insert, SBS, *Minute Book 1881–1897*, 21 December 1891.

52 'A Live Building Society. Sandhurst's Progress. Another Profitable Year', unattributed newspaper cutting in SBS, *Minute Book 1923–1933*, 14 December 1925.

53 'Report of the Committee of Management of the Bendigo Permanent Land and Building Society for the year ending October 8th 1867', in BBS, *Balance Sheets, 1866–1885.*

54 'The Bendigo Permanent Land and Building Society. Sixth Annual Report, 6 November 1871', ibid.

55 BBS, *Secretary's Monthly Reports 1880–1889*, 17 June 1880.

56 Bendigo Mutual Permanent Land and Building Society, minutes of board meetings, 8 June 1883–17 April 1885, 12 September 1883, in Bendigo Permanent Land, Building and Investment Society, *Directors' Monthly Meetings 1860–1885*, pp. 471–2.

57 'Report of Directors, The Bendigo Mutual Permanent Land & Building Society: Balance October 11th 1892', p. 4, in BBS, *Balance Sheets 1886–1924.*

58 'Souvenir: 1865–1915 Jubilee', insert, 26 November 1915, in BBS, *Annual Minute Book 1858–1942.*

59 'Report of the Committee of Management of the Bendigo Permanent Land and Building Society for the year ending October 8th 1867', in BBS, *Balance Sheets, 1866–1885.* This is an earlier example than the one given in N.G. Butlin, *Investment in Australian Economic Development 1861–1900.* Cambridge: Cambridge University Press, 1964, p. 256.

60 BBS, *Secretary's Monthly Reports 1880–1889*, 28 January 1886. 'Report of Directors, The Bendigo Mutual Permanent Land & Building Society: Balance October 11th 1886', p. 5, in BBS, *Balance Sheets 1886–1924.*

61 'The Bendigo Mutual Permanent Land and Building Society, Bull Street. 46th Annual Balance, October 17th, 1911', p. 14, ibid.

62 SBS, *Minute Book 1897–1908*, 21 May 1908, p. 365. 'The Bendigo and Eaglehawk Starr-Bowkett Building Society. Annual Meeting', insert, StarBS, *Minute Book: General and Special General Meetings, 1901–1956*, 16 October 1908, p. 44.

63 'Bendigo and Eaglehawk Starr Bowkett Society', ms insert: *Independent*, 30 September 1902, in BBS, *Newspaper Cuttings 1894–1921*, p.156.

64 SBS, *Minute Book 1881–1897*, 20 December 1894.

65 'Report of Directors, The Bendigo Mutual Permanent Land And Building Society. Balance, October 15th, 1896', p. 4, in BBS, *Balance Sheets 1886–1924.*

66 BBS, *Secretary's Monthly Reports 1880–1889,* 17 May 1883.

67 BBS, *Annual Minute Book, 1858–1942,* 26 September 1884. 'Nineteenth Annual Report, 8 November 1884', in BBS, *Balance Sheets 1866–1885.*

68 BBS, *Secretary's Monthly Reports 1880–1889,* 15 December 1887, 13 January 1888.

69 *Bendigo Advertiser*, 29 November 1894, 'Bendigo Permanent Land and Building Society', in BBS, *Newspaper Cuttings 1894–1921,* p. 153.

70 BBS, *Annual Minute Book, 1858–1942,* 26 November 1925, 21 November 1927.

71 'Bendigo Mutual Permanent Land and Building Society. Bull Street, Bendigo. Sixty-Fifth Annual Balance. October 17th, 1930', in BBS, *Balance Sheets 1925–1949.*

72 *Bendigo Advertiser,* 'Gratifying Position. Sandhurst Building Society. The Annual Meeting', insert, SBS, *Minute Book 1923–1933*, 17 December 1928, p. 206.

73 Robert Murray and Kate White, *A Bank for the People: A History of the State Bank of Victoria.* North Melbourne: Hargreen Publishing, 1992, p. 44.

74 *Bendigo Advertiser*, 29 November 1894, 'Bendigo Permanent Land and Building Society', in BBS, *Newspaper Cuttings 1894–1921*, p. 153.

75 'Building Society', unattributed newspaper cutting, ibid., p. 11.

76 *Bendigo Advertiser*, 'Gratifying Position. Sandhurst Building Society. The Annual Meeting', insert, SBS, *Minute Book 1923–1933*, 17 December 1928, p. 206.

77 'Own Your Own Home. Stop Paying Rent', in fawn binder folder with caption 'Bendigo Building Society'.

78 Bendigo Mutual, 'Diamond Jubilee 1865–1925', in BBS, *Balance Sheets 1925–1949.*

79 'The Bendigo Mutual Permanent Land & Building Society: Balance October 13th, 1891', in BBS, *Balance Sheets 1886–1924*. 'The Bendigo Mutual Permanent Land and Building Society. 37th Annual Balance, October 17, 1902', p. 14, ibid.

80 'Bendigo Mutual Permanent Land & Building Society, Bull Street. 51st Annual Balance, October 17, 1916', p. 14, ibid. 'Bendigo Mutual Permanent Land and Building Society, Bull Street. 53rd Annual Balance, October 17, 1918', p. 14, ibid. Emphasis in the original.

81 'The Sandhurst Mutual Permanent Investment and Building Society. 23rd Yearly Balance, 31st October, 1904', insert, SBS, *Minute Book 1897–1908*, 19 December 1904.

82 'Bendigo Mutual Permanent Land and Building Society, Bull Street. 48th Annual Balance, October 17th, 1913', p. 15, in BBS, *Balance Sheets 1886–1924.*

83 '10th Yearly Balance of the Sandhurst Mutual Permanent Investment & Building Society. 31st October, 1891', p. 14, in SBS, *Minute Book 1881–1897.*

84 'Sandhurst Mutual Permanent Investment and Building Society. Annual Meeting', unattributed newspaper insert, SBS, *Minute Book 1908–1923*, 13 December 1920.

85 'Bendigo and Eaglehawk Starr Bowkett Society', ms insert: *Independent*, 30 September 1902, in BBS, *Newspaper Cuttings 1894–1921*, p. 156.

86 'The Bendigo and Eaglehawk Starr-Bowkett Building Society. Annual Meeting', insert, StarBS, *Minute Book: General and Special General Meetings, 1901–1956*, 5 November 1907, p. 41.

87 ibid., 25 September 1919, pp. 71–71.

88 BBS, *Secretary's Monthly Reports 1880–1889*, 17 July 1884. See also 17 May 1883, 12 June 1884.

89 'Nineteenth Annual Report, 8 November 1884', in BBS, *Balance Sheets 1866–1885.*

90 BBS, *Annual Minute Book 1858–1942*, 25 November 1898; and see 'Bendigo Mutual Permanent Land and Building Society', ms insert: *Bendigo Advertiser*, 18 November 1898, in BBS, *Newspaper Cuttings 1894–1921*, p. 154. BBS, *Annual Minute Book 1858–1942*, 28 November 1902.

91 'The Sandhurst Mutual Permanent Investment and Building Society. 15th Yearly Balance, 31st October, 1896', p. 5, insert, SBS, *Minute Book 1881–1897*, 21 December 1896. 'The Sandhurst Mutual Permanent Investment and Building Society. Sixth Annual Report', ibid., 19 December 1887.

92 'The Sandhurst Mutual Permanent Investment and Building Society. 23rd Yearly Balance, 31st October, 1904', p. 5, insert, SBS, *Minute Book 1897–1908,* 19 December 1904.

93 *Daily Telegraph,* 28 April 1886, 'Operations of Building Societies. No. XIII: Sandhurst Mutual Permanent', cutting pasted to inside back cover of SBS, *Minute Book 1881–1897.*

94 'The Sandhurst Mutual Permanent Investment and Building Society. 24th Yearly Balance, 31st October, 1905', p. 5, insert, SBS, *Minute Book 1897–1908.*

95 SBS, *Minute Book 1908–1923,* 16 December 1919, p. 441.

96 ibid., 29 April 1919, p. 419; see 16 May 1912, p. 152.

97 BBS, *Minute Book 1925–1940,* 17 May 1927, p. 119.

98 ibid., 27 June 1928, p. 188.

99 'Sandhurst Building. Expansion of Business', unattributed newspaper insert, SBS, *Minute Book 1933–1939,* 14 December 1936, p. 292.

100 'Sandhurst Building Society Reports Steady Progress', unattributed newspaper insert, ibid., 13 December 1937, p. 366.

101 *Bendigo Independent,* undated insert, 'Sandhurst Building Society has Highly Successful Year', ibid., 12 December 1938, p. 454.

102 Tim Hewat, *Banking on the Bendigo.* Brighton, Victoria: Wrightbooks, 1992, p. 67.

103 John Balsillie, recorded interview, 14 December 2004.

104 John Perrow, recorded interview, 30 November 1995.

105 ibid.

106 'The Bendigo and Eaglehawk Star Permanent Building Society. Thirteenth Annual Report and Balance Sheet', insert, StarBS, *Minute Book: General and Special General Meetings, 1901–1956,* 10 September 1931, pp. 85–86.

107 BBS, *Minute Book 1925–1940,* 1 November 1935, p. 590.

108 *Bendigo Advertiser,* 4 December 1953, 11 December 1959, BBS, *Newspaper Cuttings 1948–1967.*

109 BBS, 'Annual Report & Balance Sheet. 100 Years, 1865–1965', BBS, *Balance Sheets 1950–1979.*

110 Perrow, 30 November 1995.

111 Brian Thomas, recorded interview, 5 October 1995.

112 Mansbridge, 21 August 2006.

113 Allen Guy, recorded interview, 23 February 2004.

114 Perrow, 30 November 1995.

115 Richard Guy, recorded interview, 5 April 2005.

116 Allen Guy, 23 February 2004.

117 Hewat, *Banking on the Bendigo,* pp. 68–69. Edith Lunn, recorded interview, 15 March 2004.

118 Bill Beischer, recorded interview, 13 October 2006.

119 Thomas, 5 October 1995.

120 ibid.

121 SBS, *Monthly Minutes 1959–1962,* 31 July 1962.

122 Perrow, 30 November 1995.

123 BBS, *Minute Book 1925–1940,* 17 March 1933, pp. 432–3.

124 'Sandhurst Building Society's Good Year: Home-Building Popular', unattributed newspaper insert, SBS, *Minute Book 1939–1945,* p. 64.

125 SBS, *Monthly Minutes 1959–1962,* 9 January 1959.

126 Allen Guy, 23 February 2004.

127 '1949', typescript insert, StarBS, *Minute Book: General and Special General Meetings, 1901–1956,* 12 October 1949, pp. 119–120.

128 Manager's Report, 2 March 1971, in SBS, *Minutes 1969–1971.*

129 SBS, *Minutes 1980–1982,* 29 July 1981. The society did produce a short *1981 Centenary Annual Report.*

130 'Bendigo Mutual Permanent Land and Building Society. Annual Report, Statement of Accounts and Balance Sheet, 1972', in BBS, *Balance Sheets 1950–1979.*

131 *Bendigo Advertiser*, 18 March 1952, 'Bendigo Best-Off for Homer Finance', in BBS, *Newspaper Cuttings 1948–1967.* Lunn, 15 March 2004.

132 BBS, *Annual Report 1982.*

133 'Bendigo Mutual Permanent Land and Building Society. Bull Street, Bendigo. Seventy-Fourth Annual Balance. October 17th 1939', in BBS, *Balance Sheets 1925–1949.* BBS, *Annual Minute Book 1858–1942,* 24 November 1938.

134 *Bendigo Advertiser*, 25 November 1949; ibid., 18 March 1952, 'Bendigo Best-Off For Homer Finance', in BBS, *Newspaper Cuttings 1948–1967.*

135 'Bendigo Mutual Permanent Land & Building Society. Bull Street, Bendigo. Sixty-Ninth Annual Balance. October 17th, 1934', in BBS, *Balance Sheets 1925–1949.*

136 'The Sandhurst Mutual Permanent Investment and Building Society. The Sixty-Second Annual Report', insert, SBS, *Minute Book 1939–1945,* 13 December 1943.

137 Thomas, 5 October 1995.

138 See 'Manager's Report', 6 November 1969, in SBS, *Minutes 1967–1969.*

139 Thomas, 5 October 1995.

140 SBS, *Minutes 1971–1975,* 5 February 1974.

141 BBS, *Annual Minute Book 1858–1942,* 26 November 1942.

142 Thomas, 5 October 1995.

143 BBS, *Monthly Minutes 1953–1956,* 18 June 1956.

144 BBS, *Annual Report & Balance Sheet. 100 Years.*

145 Richard Guy, 5 April 2005.

146 Perrow, 30 November 1995.

147 Melbourne *Argus*, 27 July 1951, 'Will We Ever Be Able To Build A Home?'; *Age*, 6 August 1962, 'Today's housing problem', in BBS, *Newspaper Cuttings 1948–1967.*

148 Bendigo Mutual Permanent Land and Building Society, 'Annual Report, Statement of Accounts and Balance Sheet, 1973', in BBS, *Balance Sheets 1950–1979.*

149 *Sun*, 22 July 1955, 'Finance to Build', in BBS, *Newspaper Cuttings 1948–1967. Bendigo Advertiser*, 7 July 1981, in BBS, *Newspaper Cuttings 1978–1985.*

150 SBS, *Monthly Minutes 1954–1957,* 10 April 1956, 30 April 1956. SBS, *Monthly Minutes 1959–1962,* 16 March 1961.

151 *Bendigo Advertiser*, 4 December 1953, in BBS, *Newspaper Cuttings 1948–1967.*

152 'Satisfactory Year. Sandhurst Building Society', unattributed insert, Sandhurst Mutual Permanent Investment and Building Society, 'The 49th Annual Meeting of Members', in SBS, *Minute Book 1923–1933,* 15 December 1930, p. 302.

153 Bendigo Mutual Permanent Land and Building Society, 'Sixty-Fifth Annual Balance. October 17th, 1930'; 'Sixty-Sixth Annual Balance. October 17th, 1931', in BBS, *Balance Sheets 1925–1949.*

154 Sandhurst Mutual Permanent Investment and Building Society, 'The 55th Annual Meeting of Members', insert, SBS *Minute Book 1933–1939,* 14 December 1936, p. 292.

155 *Bendigo Independent*, 'Sandhurst Building Society has Highly Successful Year', undated insert, ibid., 12 December 1938, p. 454.

156 SBS, *Monthly Minutes 1954–1957,* 28 May 1957.

157 BBS, *Minute Book 1925–1940,* 7 December 1936, p. 674. Bendigo Mutual Permanent Land and Building Society, 'Seventy-Fourth Annual Balance. October 17th 1939', in BBS, *Balance Sheets 1925–1949.*

158 SBS, *Monthly Minutes 1959–1962,* 22 May 1962.

159 Bendigo Mutual Permanent Land and Building Society, 'Bendigo Building Society: Annual Report Statement of Accounts and Balance Sheet 1974', in BBS, *Balance Sheets 1950–1979.*

160 See Rob Linn, *For the Benefit of the People: A History of Hindmarsh Adelaide Building Society.* Adelaide: Hindmarsh Adelaide Group, 1989.

161 *Age*, 26 July 1980, in BBS, *Newspaper Cuttings 1978–1985.*

162 *Age*, 12 September 1980, ibid.

163 Allen Guy, 23 February 2004.

164 Thomas, 5 October 1995.

165 ibid.

166 ibid.; also Perrow, 30 November 1995.

167 Thomas, 5 October 1995.

168 Richard Guy, 5 April 2005.

169 *Bendigo Advertiser*, 20 June 1981, in BBS, *Newspaper Cuttings 1978–1985.*

170 SBS, *Minutes* 1980–1982, 7 January 1982.

171 *Bendigo Advertiser*, 18 December 1982, in BBS, *Newspaper Cuttings 1978–1985.*

172 Thomas, 5 October 1995.

173 Bendigo Sandhurst Building Society, 1983 *Annual Report.*

174 Thomas, 5 October 1995.

175 Perrow, 30 November 1995; Thomas, 5 October 1995.

176 Mansbridge, 21 August 2006.

177 ibid.

178 ibid.

179 BBS, *Annual Report* 1991.

Chapter three Settlers

1 SBS, *Minute Book 1881–1897*, 21 January 1896.

2 SBS, *Minute Book 1897–1908*, 23 May 1899, p. 63. ibid., 15 August 1899, p. 70.

3 ibid., 2 October 1902, p. 176.

4 ibid., 21 March 1905, p. 260.

5 SBS, *Minute Book 1881–1897*, 10 November 1890.

6 *Bendigo Advertiser*, 'Gratifying Position. Sandhurst Building Society. The Annual Meeting', newspaper cutting pasted to 1928 annual report, in SBS, *Minute Book 1923–1933*, 17 December 1928, p. 206.

7 *Bendigo Advertiser*, 27 March 1886, 'Operations of Building Societies. The Bendigo Mutual Permanent Land & Building Society', in BBS, *Newspaper Cuttings 1894–1921*, p.151.

8 Bendigo Permanent Land, Building and Investment Society, Directors Monthly Meetings, 12 December 1884, in BBS, *Directors Monthly Meetings 1860–1885*, p. 517.

9 ibid., 25 August 1883, p. 470.

10 SBS, *Minute Book 1881–1897*, 3 October 1882.

11 ibid., 13 September 1894.

12 Bendigo Mutual Permanent Land and Building Society, 'Diamond Jubilee 1865–1925. Sixtieth Annual Balance. October 17th, 1925', in BBS, *Balance Sheets 1925–1949*.

13 Bendigo Mutual Permanent Land and Building Society, 'Three Quarter Century 1865–1940: Seventy-Fifth Annual Balance Sheet, 17 October 1940', in BBS, *Balance Sheets 1925–1949*.

14 *Bendigo Advertiser*, 27 March 1886, 'Operations of Building Societies. The Bendigo Mutual Permanent Land & Building Society', in BBS, *Newspaper Cuttings 1894–1921*, p.151.

15 BBS, *Annual Minute Book, 1858–1942*, 26 November 1897, 24 November 1899.

16 *Bendigo Advertiser*, 25 November 1899, 'Bendigo Mutual Permanent Land and Building Society', in BBS, *Newspaper Cuttings 1894–1921*, p. 154.

17 BBS, *Annual Minute Book, 1858–1942*, 25 November 1904, 27 November 1914. 'The Sandhurst Mutual Permanent Investment and Building Society. 34th Yearly Balance, October 31st, 1915', p. 5, in SBS, *Minute Book 1908–1923*.

18 BBS, *Secretary's Monthly Reports 1880–1889*, 17 May 1883.

19 *Daily Telegraph*, 28 April 1886, 'Operations of Building Societies. No. XIII: Sandhurst Mutual Permanent', cutting pasted to inside back cover of SBS, *Minute Book 1881–1897*.

20 SBS, *Minute Book 1897–1908*, 30 May 1901, p. 126.

21 *Daily Telegraph*, 28 April 1886, 'Operations of Building Societies', in SBS, *Minute Book 1881–1897*.

22 Weston Bate, 'The Urban Sprinkle: Country Towns and Australian Regional History'. *Australian Economic History Review*, vol. 19, no. 2, September 1970, pp. 204–17.

23 SBS, *Minute Book 1881–1897,* 8 July 1890.
24 ibid., 22 September 1890.
25 ibid.
26 ibid., 10 November 1890.
27 ibid., 5 February 1891.
28 ibid., 19 December 1895.
29 SBS, *Minute Book 1897–1908,* 8 June 1897, p. 4.
30 SBS, *Minute Book 1908–1923,* 31 May 1909, p. 35.
31 BBS, *Secretary's Monthly Reports 1880–1889,* 10 May 1882.
32 SBS, *Minute Book 1881–1897,* 23 May 1895. SBS, *Minute Book 1897–1908,* 17 July 1900, p. 94.
33 Bendigo Permanent Land, Building and Investment Society, Directors Monthly Meetings, 13 April 1883, in BBS, *Directors Monthly Meetings 1860–1885,* p. 424.
34 SBS, *Minute Book 1897–1908,* 11 November 1903, p. 212.
35 SBS, *Minute Book 1881–1897,* 5 August 1890.
36 SBS, *Minute Book 1908–1923,* 26 October 1915, p. 260.
37 SBS, *Minute Book 1897–1908,* 26 March 1901, p. 120.
38 ibid., 26 September 1907, p. 345, 21 November 1907, p. 350.
39 'The Sandhurst Mutual Permanent Investment and Building Society. 28th Yearly Balance, 31st October, 1909', p. 5, in SBS, *Minute Book 1908–1923,* 20 December 1909.
40 ibid., 23 February 1911, p. 102.
41 'The Sandhurst Mutual Permanent Investment and Building Society. 32nd Yearly Balance, 31st October, 1913', p. 5, ibid., 15 December 1913.
42 *Bendigo Advertiser,* 28 November 1914, 'Bendigo Building Society', in BBS, *Newspaper Cuttings 1894–1921,* p. 14. 'Successful Building Society' (ms insert: *Advertiser, Independent,* 14 November 1916), ibid., p. 16.
43 'Report of Directors', Bendigo Mutual Permanent Land and Building Society, Bull Street. 54th Annual Balance, October 17th, 1919, p. 5, in BBS, *Balance Sheets 1886–1924.*
44 'Report of Directors', Bendigo Mutual Permanent Land and Building Society. Bull Street, Bendigo. Fifty Ninth Annual Balance. October 17th, 1924, p. 2, ibid. Bendigo Mutual Permanent Land and Building Society, *Directors' Minute Book 1925–1940,* 4 May 1928, p. 174.
45 John Andrew Balsillie, recorded interview, 14 December 2004.
46 'Report of Directors', Bendigo Mutual Permanent Land and Building Society. Bull Street, Bendigo. Fifty-Sixth Annual Balance. October 17th, 1921, p. 3, in BBS, *Balance Sheets 1886–1924.*
47 Bendigo Mutual Permanent Land and Building Society. Bull Street, Bendigo. Diamond Jubilee 1865–1925. Sixtieth Annual Balance. October 17th, 1925, in BBS, *Balance Sheets 1925–1949.*
48 Unattributed newspaper cutting, 'Sandhurst Building Society. Another Very Good Year', insert in SBS, *Minute Book 1923–1933,* 15 December 1924.

49 Unattributed newspaper cutting, 'Sandhurst Building Society. Enjoys Successful Year', insert, ibid., 13 December 1926, p. 116.

50 ibid.

51 Unattributed newspaper cutting, 'Very Good Year. Sandhurst Building Society', insert, ibid., 20 December 1923.

52 SBS, *Minute Book 1908–1923,* 2 July 1920, p. 461.

53 SBS, *Minute Book 1923–1933,* 23 December 1926, p. 119.

54 Unattributed newspaper cutting, 'Sandhurst Building Society. Another Very Good Year', ibid., 15 December 1924.

55 ibid., 5 December 1927, p. 158; 27 February 1928, p. 170.

56 SBS, *Minute Book 1933–1939,* 3 March 1936, p. 222.

57 Unattributed newspaper cutting, 'Sandhurst Building. Expansion of Business', insert, ibid., 14 December 1936, p. 292.

58 Unattributed newspaper cutting, 'Sandhurst Building Society Reports Steady Progress', insert, ibid., 13 December 1937, p. 366.

59 Unattributed newspaper cutting, 'Sandhurst Building Society's Good Year: Home-Building Popular', insert in SBS, *Minute Book 1939–1945,* 11 December 1939, p. 64.

60 *Bendigo Advertiser*, 'Gratifying Position. Sandhurst Building Society. The Annual Meeting', cutting pasted to annual report in SBS, *Minute Book 1923–1933,* 17 December 1928, p. 206.

61 SBS, *Minute Book 1908–1923,* 7 March 1922, p. 521.

62 BBS, *Minute Book 1925–1940,* 18 November 1929, p. 264.

63 Unsourced newspaper cutting, 'Building Societies', loose insert within annual report, in SBS, *Minute Book 1923–1933,* 13 December 1932, p. 448.

64 Geoffrey Blainey, *This Land is all Horizons: Australian Fears and Visions.* Sydney: ABC Books, 2001, p. 38.

65 *Bendigo Advertiser*, 25 November 1949, in BBS, *Newspaper Cuttings 1948–1967.*

66 BBS, *Minute Book 1953–1956,* 7 September 1953.

67 E. Brian Thomas, recorded interview, 5 October 1995.

68 SBS, *Monthly Minutes 1959–1962,* 28 March 1961.

69 John Perrow, recorded interview, 30 November 1995 (tape 2).

70 *Donald Birchip Times,* 15 January 1985, newspaper cutting in folder marked 'Advertising'. The newspaper was later renamed *Donald Buloke Times.*

71 Bendigo Bank, *Annual Report 1996.*

72 Bendigo Bank, *Annual Report 1998.*

73 Richard Guy, recorded interview, 5 April 2005.

74 Bendigo Bank, *Annual Report 1998.*

75 Minutes of Directors Meetings July 1998–June 1999, 24 August 1998 (Bendigo Bank Boardroom).

76 *Financial Review*, 28 August 1998, 'Bendigo to go even more rural'; *Weekly Times*, 2 September 1998, 'Banking boost', both in Owen Davies' newspaper cuttings, 1997–1998 folder, Bendigo Bank.

77 *Business Review Weekly*, 1 April 1999, 'Rob Hunt', in Community Bank File 5, Bendigo Bank archived files, Box 163.

78 *Adelaide Advertiser*, 28 August 1998, 'Elders leaps into banking', in Owen Davies' newspaper cuttings, 1997–1998.

79 *Bendigo Advertiser*, 29 August 1998, 'An idea to bank on', ibid.

80 Rob Hunt, recorded interview, 24 January 2006.

81 ibid.

82 Robert Johanson, recorded interview, 13 October 2006.

83 Ian Mansbridge, recorded interview, 21 August 2006.

84 Johanson, 13 October 2006.

85 Hunt, 24 January 2006.

86 Max Ormsby, recorded interview, 21 July 2006.

87 Hunt, 24 January 2006.

88 Rob Hunt to Russell Jenkins, 6 June 1997, attached reply to memo from Russell Jenkins to Rob Hunt, 5 June 97, in Community Bank File 1, Bendigo Bank archived files, Box 157.

89 Bill Beischer, recorded interview, 13 October 2006.

90 Mansbridge, 21 August 2006.

91 ibid. Emphasis in the original.

92 Elders Rural Bank, *Annual Report 2000.*

93 Minutes of Directors Meetings July 1998–June 1999, 24 May 1999. Hunt, 24 January 2006.

94 Beischer, 13 October 2006.

95 ibid.

96 *Minutes of Directors Meetings July 2000–June 2001,* 23 April 2001.

97 *Minutes of Directors Meetings, July 2002–June 2003,* 26 August 2002.

98 Johanson, 13 October 2006.

99 Ormsby, 21 July 2006.

100 Hunt, 24 January 2006.

101 Mansbridge, 21 August 2006.

102 Jean Wright to Rob Hunt, 28 August 1998, in Community Bank File 3, Bendigo Bank archived files, Box 157.

103 Russell Jenkins to Jean Wright, 14 September 1998, ibid.

104 Hunt, 24 January 2006.

105 Attachment to Russell Jenkins to Jean Wright, 28 June 2000, 'FW: elders rural bank', in Community Bank File, Box 156.

106 Simon Cornwell to Russell Jenkins, 28 June 2000, 'RE: Elders venture', ibid.

107 Laurie Win to to Simon Cornwell, 28 June 2000, 'Elders Rural Bank Ltd', ibid.

108 Rob Hunt, 29 June 2000, 'Statement Re Elders', ibid.

109 Rob Fairweather to Rob Hunt, 12 July 2000, ibid.

110 Rob Hunt to Rob Fairweather, 24 August 2000; Rob Fairweather to Rob Hunt, 28 August 2000, ibid.

111 Beischer, 13 October 2006.

112 Hunt, 24 January 2006.

Chapter four Communities

1 *Herald Sun*, 8 March 2000, 'Interest Grows in People's Banking', Community Bank File 8, Bendigo Bank archived files, Box 163. See also *Australian*, 2 September 1998, 'Bendigo Becomes People's Bank', Owen Davies' newspaper cuttings, 1997–1998, Bendigo Bank.

2 Bendigo Bank, 'Annual Report 1996'. See Bendigo Bank, *Minutes of Annual General Meetings*, 26 October 1998.

3 *Age*, 28 March 1998, 'Rural Towns Begin a Banking Revolution', Community Bank File 2, Box 157.

4 *Herald Sun*, 5 July 1998, 'Banks Deposit New Hope', in Davies, 1997–1998.

5 *Age*, 28 March 1998, 'Rural Towns Begin a Banking Revolution', Community Bank File 2, Box 157. See also *Geelong Advertiser*, 21 March 1998, 'Tiny Wheat-belt Communities Pioneer Scheme to Keep their Bank Doors Open', in Owen Davies' newspaper cuttings, 1997–1998, Bendigo Bank.

6 *Age*, 12 April 1999, 'Locals Bank on Community Spirit', Community Bank File 5, Box 163.

7 ibid.

8 *Age*, 28 March 1998, 'Rural Towns Begin a Banking Revolution', Community Bank File 2, Box 157.

9 Rob Hunt to Cheryl Rix, 12 July 1999, Community Bank File 5, Box 163.

10 Attachment 6, 'Bendigo Bank: Concept Outline' in Owen Davies to Rob Hunt, 30 September 1997, 'Re: Community Bank', Community Bank File 1, Box 157.

11 *Herald Sun*, 5 July 1998, 'Banks Deposit New Hope', in Owen Davies' newspaper cuttings, 1997–1998, Bendigo Bank.

12 Rob Hunt, 'Rupanyup/Minyip Community Bank Notes—Opening 26 June 1998', Community Bank File 3, Box 157.

13 *Australian Financial Review*, 3 November 1997, '"Community Bank" Plan'; *Ag-Journal*, November 1997, 'Bendigo Bank to Pilot Community Bank Concept', both in Owen Davies' newspaper cuttings, 1997–1998, Bendigo Bank.

14 Rob Hunt to Russell Jenkins, Bevan O'Keeffe, and Malcolm Campbell, 26 November 1997, 'ABA and Community Bank', Community Bank File 1, Box 157. Russell Jenkins, recorded interview, 16 December 2004.

15 *Farm Weekly*, 21 October 1999, 'Great Day for Kulin', in Max Trenorden, Community Bank papers. Attachment, 'Community Bank: A Regional Banking Initiative from Australia's Only Regionally-based Bank,' in Rob Hunt to C. Paterson, House of Representatives Standing Committee on Financial Institutions and Public Administration, 6 January 1998,

in Community Bank File 1, Box 157. Bendigo Bank Media Release: 'Bendigo looking to pilot Community Bank concept', 2 November 1997, ibid.

16 Rob Hunt to Les Phelps, 22 March 1999, Community Bank File 4, Box 157.

17 '3LO Radio Interview—Thursday 4 June 1998', Community Bank File 3, Box 157.

18 Rob Hunt to Russell Jenkins, 4 January 1999, 'Community Banks in the United States', Community Bank File 4, Box 157.

19 'Sustainable Communities', presentation by Rob Hunt, La Trobe University, 4 November 1998, ibid.

20 *Age*, 4 November 1998, 'For Decades a Solid Citizen', Community Bank File 3, Box 157.

21 *Herald Sun*, 8 March 2000, 'Interest Grows in People's Banking', Community Bank File 8, Box 163.

22 ibid.

23 Jean Wright to Rob Hunt, 8 February 2000, 'Community Bank—some ideas', Community Bank File, Box 156, emphasis in the original.

24 Rob Hunt, recorded interview, 5 May 2005.

25 Rob Hunt, 'Community Bank Message at This Point in Time', 30 October 1998, Community Bank File 4, Box 157.

26 Rob Hunt to C. Paterson, 6 January 1998, in Community Bank File 1, Box 157. Rob Hunt to Jeff Kennett, 6 January 1998, ibid.

27 Bendigo Bank, *Annual Report 1998. Age*, 4 November 1998, 'For Decades a Solid Citizen', Community Bank File 3, Box 157.

28 Rob Hunt, 'Community Bank Message at This Point in Time', 30 October 1998, Community Bank File 4, Box 157.

29 'Community Bank', 25 November 1998, ibid.

30 Rob Hunt to C. Paterson, 6 January 1998, in Community Bank File 1, Box 157.

31 Rob Hunt, 'Community Bank Message at This Point in Time', 30 October 1998, Community Bank File 4, Box 157. 'Community Bank', 25 November 1998, ibid. Attachment 'Community Bank: A Regional Banking Initiative from Australia's Only Regionally-based Bank', in Rob Hunt to C. Paterson, 6 January 1998, Community Bank File 1, Box 157.

32 'Sustainable Communities', presentation by Rob Hunt, La Trobe University, 4 November 1998, Community Bank File 4, Box 157.

33 *Wimmera Mail Times*, 3 October 1997, 'Bendigo Bank to Move In', in Owen Davies' newspaper cuttings, 1997–1998, Bendigo Bank.

34 Hunt, 5 May 2005.

35 'Sustainable Communities', presentation by Rob Hunt, La Trobe University, 4 November 1998, Community Bank File 4, Box 157.

36 Rob Hunt to Russell Jenkins and Simon Cornwell, 15 June 1999, 'Notes From Meeting', Community Bank File 1, Box 163.

37 Rob Hunt, 'Community Bank Message at This Point in Time', 30 October 1998, Community Bank File 4, Box 157. Rob Hunt, 'Rural and Regional Strategy: Commentary on Leadership Strategies', 3 September 1998, ibid.

38 *Age*, 4 November 1998, 'For Decades a Solid Citizen', Community Bank File 3, Box 157.

39 Rob Hunt, 'Community Bank Message at This Point in Time', 30 October 1998, Community Bank File 4, Box 157.

40 'Sustainable Communities', presentation by Rob Hunt, La Trobe University, 4 November 1998, ibid.

41 'Rupanyup. 3.00 p.m. Monday 9/2/98', Community Bank File 2, Box 157. Bendigo Bank, *Annual Report 1998*.

42 Hunt, 5 May 2005.

43 Bendigo Bank Executive Committee Meeting: 3 December 1996, 'New Project: Wealth Creation', Community Bank File 1, Box 157.

44 Hand written memo by Russell Jenkins to Rob Hunt, 5 June 1997, ibid.

45 Rob Hunt, 'Banking in the Bush', speech notes for Wimmera 2020 dinner, ibid.

46 Owen Davies, recorded interview, 5 May 2005; also John Millington, recorded interview, 20 August 2005.

47 Rob Hunt, 'Banking in the Bush', emphasis in the original.

48 Owen Davies to Rob Hunt, 30 September 1997, 'Community Bank', Community Bank File 1, Box 157.

49 Davies, 5 May 2005.

50 *Weekly Times*, 25 February 1998, 'Nhill to Bank on its Future', in Owen Davies' newspaper cuttings, 1997–1998, Bendigo Bank.

51 Bendigo Bank Media Release: 'Country towns losing control of their destinies, warns Hunt', 5 October 1997, Community Bank File 1, Box 157.

52 Owen Davies to Rob Hunt, 7 October 1997, 'Community Bank Media', ibid. *Wimmera Mail Times*, 3 October 1997, 'Bendigo Bank to Move In'; *Bendigo Advertiser*, 6 October 1997, 'New Rural Bank', both in Davies, 1997–1998.

53 Bendigo Bank Media Release: 'Bendigo looking to pilot Community Bank concept', 2 November 1997, attachment in Rob Hunt to Pat Murnane, 5 January 1998, Community Bank File 1, Box 157.

54 For example, Premier Kennett was sent one, along with a detailed supporting letter; see Rob Hunt to Jeff Kennett, 6 January 1998, ibid.

55 Briefing paper by Owen Davies for Rob Hunt, 18 November 1997, ibid.

56 *Herald Sun*, 8 March 2000, 'Interest Grows in People's Banking', Community Bank File 8, Box 163. *Bendigo Advertiser*, 11 August 1998, 'Bank Profit Rises', in Davies, 1997–1998.

57 Greg Gillett to Rob Hunt, 12 December 1997, 'Community Bank', Community Bank File 1, Box 157.

58 *Australian*, 15 December 1997, 'Westpac Banks on Newsagents in the Bush', in Davies, 1997–1998.

59 *Australian Financial Review*, 18 March 1998, 'Colonial goes Bush with Franchises', Community Bank File 2, Box 157. Andrew Watts to Jean Wright, 20 September 1999, Community Bank File 6, Box 163.

60 Mark Genovese to Rob Hunt, 26 June 1998, Community Bank File 3, Box 157.

61 *Australian Financial Review*, 5 November 1997, 'Credit Unions Wary of Bendigo Branch Franchise Plan', in Owen Davies' newspaper cuttings, 1997–1998, Bendigo Bank. Mark Genovese to Rob Hunt, 26 June 1998, Community Bank File 3, Box 157. Owen Davies to Rob Hunt, 4 November 1997, 'Community Bank Media', Community Bank File 1, Box 157.

62 'Community Bank . . . "Our bank"', attachment in Rob Hunt to Jeff Kennett, 6 January 1998, ibid.

63 Robert Musgrove, 'Community Banking Program', information paper for Bendigo Bank Board Meeting, 28 June 1999, Community Bank File 5, Box 163.

64 Bendigo Bank, *Annual Report 1996.*

65 'Franchising: Discussion Session, held 14 October 1997', Community Bank File 1, Box 157.

66 Russell Jenkins and Robert Musgrove to All Staff, 11 May 1998, 'Community Bank', Community Bank File 2, Box 157. The standing committee's investigation was formally titled the Commonwealth Inquiry into Alternative Means of Providing Banking and Like Services in Regional Australia.

67 'Media News: Money too far away—no longer?', press release by House of Representatives Standing Committee on Economics, Finance and Public Administration, 22 March 1999, Community Bank File 4, Box 157.

68 Phil King to Jean Wright, 12 September 1997, 'Proposed Meeting with Hindmarsh Shire Council', Community Bank File 1, Box 157. John Millington, 20 August 2005.

69 ibid.

70 'Country Banking', draft letter from Rob Hunt to Les Austin (Assistant Governor, Reserve Bank of Australia), 23 October 1997, attachment in Rob Hunt to David Lurie and Sue Gatford, 24 October 1997, Community Bank File 1, Box 157. Annotation by Rob Hunt to draft media release, 'Country towns losing control of their destinies, warns Hunt', 5 October 1997, ibid.

71 Malcolm Anderson, recorded interview, 20 August 2005.

72 Jean Wright to Rob Hunt, 11 September 1997 (10.00 a.m.), Community Bank File 1, Box 157.

73 Jean Wright to Rob Hunt, 23 September 1997 (12.10 p.m.), ibid.

74 Jean Wright to Rob Hunt, 22 September 1997, ibid. Emphasis in original.

75 David Matthews, recorded interview, 19 April 2005.

76 'Franchising: Discussion Session, held 14 October 1997', Community Bank File 1, Box 157. Undated and unattributed memo. 'Community Bank Partnerships', ibid.

77 Owen Davies to All Staff, 31 October 1997, 'Community Bank', ibid.

78 'Community Banking: Need to Inform Staff and Management', no date [early November 1997], ibid.

79 Sue Gatford to Bevan O'Keeffe, 16 October 1997, 'Community Banking—Reserve Bank of Australia Approval', ibid.

80 Owen Davies to Glen Bartholomew, 1 June 1997, Community Bank File 2, Box 157.

81 'Country Banking', draft letter from Rob Hunt to Les Austin, 23 October 1997, attachment in Rob Hunt to David Lurie and Sue Gatford, 24 October 1997, Community Bank File 1, Box 157.

82 Russell Jenkins, 'Community Bank', information paper for Bendigo Bank Board, 27 July 1998, Community Bank File 3, Box 157.

83 Circular letter by Hindmarsh Shire Mayor Darryl Argall, 24 October 1997, Community Bank File 1, Box 157.

84 Matthews, 19 April 2005; Stewart Petering, recorded interview, 16 September 2005.

85 ibid.

86 Memo by Jean Wright, 20 October 1997, Community Bank File 1, Box 157.

87 Jean Wright to Rob Hunt, 31 October 1997, ibid.

88 *Herald Sun*, 2 November 1997, 'Country Towns Bank on Future', ibid. *Bendigo Advertiser*, 1 November 1997 'Bendigo's Bold Plan Revealed', in Davies, 1997–1998. *Wimmera Mail Times*, 3 November 1997, 'Banking Trial for Nhill', Community Bank File 1, Box 157.

89 *Age*, 12 April 1999, 'Locals Bank on Community Spirit', Community Bank File 5, Box 163.

90 Anderson and Millington, 20 August 2005.

91 ibid.

92 Millington, 20 August 2005.

93 Rob Hunt to David Colbert, 17 December 1997, Community Bank File 1, Box 157. *Nhill Free Press*, 16 December 1997, 'Stage One of Community Banking in Nhill Gets Public Support at Meeting', in Malcolm Anderson, personal papers.

94 Russell Jenkins to Rob Hunt and Greg Gillet, 22 December 1997, 'Franchising Update'; Robert Musgrove to Russell Jenkins, 9 January 1998, 'Update on Rupanyup/Minyip Projects', both in Community Bank File 1, Box 157.

95 Millington, 20 August 2005.

96 Russell Jenkins to Greg Gillett and Rob Hunt, 15 January 1998, Community Bank File 1, Box 157.

97 Millington, 20 August 2005.

98 Anderson, 20 August 2005.

99 Millington, 20 August 2005.

100 ibid. The priest would later become chairman of Dimboola's Community Bank.

101 Russell Jenkins to Rob Hunt, 30 January 1998, 'Nhill, Rupanyup and Minyip Visit', Community Bank File 1, Box 157. *Wimmera Mail Times*, 23 January 1998, 'How Community Banking Works', in Anderson, personal papers. *Weekly Times*, 25 February 1998, 'Nhill to Bank on its Future', in Davies, 1997–1998.

102 *Nhill Free Press*, 10 February 1998, 'Community Bank a Step Closer for Nhill', Community Bank File 2, Box 157. *Nhill Free Press*, 15 April 1998, 'Community Bank Discussions Continue', in Anderson, personal papers.

103 Anderson, 20 August 2005.

104 Russell Jenkins to Rob Hunt, 19 August 1998, 'Nhill', Community Bank File 3, Box 157.

105 Managing Director's Office, 'Community Bank', 10 March 2000, Community Bank File 8, Box 163. Malcolm Anderson, circular to 'Nhill Community Bank Supporters', no date, in Anderson, personal papers.

106 Anderson and Millington, 20 August 2005.

107 Millington, 20 August 2005.

108 *Wimmera Mail Times*, 5 March 1998, 'Bank to Cut Jobs'; *Nhill Free Press*, 24 March 1998, 'Community Bank Survey Data being Compiled', in Anderson, personal papers.

109 *Weekend Australian*, 21–22 March 1998, 'Bushwhacked Banks Redraw Rural Battle Lines', in Owen Davies' newspaper cuttings, 1997–1998, Bendigo Bank.

110 Unattributed newspaper cutting, 30 April 1998, 'More Bush Bank Closures Flagged', ibid. *Australian*, 29 December 1998 'Banking's Bull Run, Four Pillars Survive.'

111 '3LO Radio Interview—Thursday 4 June 1998', Community Bank File 3, Box 157. Matthews, 19 April 2005.

112 Jenkins, 16 December 2004. Davies, 5 May 2005.

113 Russell Jenkins, recorded interview, 17 March 2005.

114 Petering, 16 September 2005.

115 *Wimmera Mail Times*, 26 June 1998, 'A First Step to Financial Independence'; *Herald Sun*, 5 July 1998, 'The Bush Fights Back', in Owen Davies' newspaper cuttings, 1997–1998, Bendigo Bank.

116 Hunt, 5 May 2005.

117 Owen Davies to Rob Hunt, 17 November 1997, 'Community Bank Media Coverage/Response', Community Bank File 1, Box 157.

118 *Australian*, 2 September 1998, 'Bendigo Becomes People's Bank', in Owen Davies' newspaper cuttings, 1997–1998, Bendigo Bank.

119 *Age*, 12 April 1999, 'Locals Bank on Community Spirit', Community Bank File 5, Box 163.

120 *Age*, 8 November 1999, 'Banks to Make a Rural Return', Community Bank File 6, Box 163.

121 *Age*, 20 December 1998, editorial leader, ibid.

122 *Bendigo Advertiser*, no date, 'Country Communities in Rush to Enlist in Bendigo's Venture Plan', in Owen Davies' newspaper cuttings, 1997–1998, Bendigo Bank. *Herald Sun*, 18 October 1998, 'Upwey's Bank is Up and Running', Community Bank File 3, Box 157.

123 Jenkins, 17 March 2005.

124 Owen Davies to Helen McCombie,13 April 1999, 'Community Bank Story', Community Bank File 5, Box 163.

125 *Gippsland Farmer*, January 1999, 'Sth Gippsland Town Decides to Stand and Fight', Community Bank File 4, Box 157.

126 Rob Hunt to Helene Bender, 5 January 1998, attachment in Rob Hunt to Pat Murnane, 5 January 1998, 'Banking Facilities in Newtown', Community Bank File 1, Box 157.

127 Rob Hunt to Craig Langdon MP, 29 April 1998, Community Bank File 2, Box 157.

128 Robert Musgrove, 'Community Banking Program', information paper for Bendigo Bank Board Meeting, 26 April 1999, Community Bank File 5, Box 163.

129 Jenkins, 17 March 2005.

130 Max Davidson to Rob Hunt, 30 June 1998, Community Bank File 3, Box 157.

131 *Border Mail*, 10 July 1998, 'Town Banks on its Own Strength', in Owen Davies' newspaper cuttings, 1997–1998, Bendigo Bank Russell Jenkins to Robert Musgrove, 21 July 1998, 'Henty', Community Bank File 3, Box 157.

132 ibid. *Border Mail*, 28 July 1998, 'Help Arrives Late', ibid.

133 Unattributed news item, 28 November 1998, 'We Bought the Bank!', ibid.

134 *Sunraysia Daily*, 19 March 1999, 'Well Done, Wenty!, Community Bank File 4, Box 157.

135 Russell Jenkins to Rob Hunt, 3 August 1998, 'Community Bank Update', Community Bank File 3, Box 157.

136 Owen Davies to Rob Hunt, 17 March 1999, Community Bank File 4, Box 157.

137 Robert Musgrove, 'Community Banking Program', information paper for Bendigo Bank Board Meeting, 26 April 1999, Community Bank File 5, Box 163.

138 Graeme Campbell Scott Elkington, 1 April 1998, Community Bank File 2, Box 157.

139 Russell Jenkins, 'Community Bank Update', information paper for Bendigo Bank Board Meeting, 19 November 1998. Max Trenorden, recorded interview, 8 December 2005.

140 ibid. Greg Hadlow, recorded interview, 8 December 2005.

141 Regional Financial Services Taskforce, *Report concerning the Withdrawal of Banks from Country Towns*, Government of Western Australia, Ministry of Fair Trading, 1998, p. 6, in Trenorden, Community Bank papers. Trenorden, 8 December 2005.

142 Max Trenorden, undated typescript (2001), in Trenorden, Community Bank papers.

143 Trenorden, 8 December 2005.

144 ibid.

145 Max Trenorden, undated typescript (2001), in Trenorden, Community Bank papers. Trenorden resigned the Nationals leadership in 2005.

146 Nationals Western Australia Media Statement, 'Nationals Encourage Community Banking Move', 26 November 1998, ibid.

147 Russell Jenkins to Rob Hunt and Greg Gillett, 'Support Requirements – Community Bank Development', handwritten memo, undated and marked 'private and confidential', for the November 1999 Bendigo Bank Board Meeting, Community Bank File 3, Box 157.

148 Trenorden, 8 December 2005.

149 ibid.

150 *Western Australian Business News*, 18 February–3 March 1999, 'Regional Banking Arrives', ibid.

151 Hadlow, 8 December 2005. Unattributed newspaper cutting (c. 23 February 1999), 'Concept Receives Warm Welcome', Community Bank File 4, Box 157.

152 Jenkins, 17 March 2005. Trenorden, 8 December 2005.

153 'Western Australia Sites', 7 pp. typescript dated by hand June 1999, Community Bank File 5, Box 163.

154 Hadlow, 8 December 2005.

155 Clem Kerp, recorded interview, 9 December 2005.

156 *Great Southern Herald*, 5 May 1999, 'Strong Support for Community Bank', Community Bank File 5, Box 163, which also holds a draft of the Matthews advertisement, dated 20 April 1999. Another draft, dated 9 April 1999, is in Trenorden, Community Bank papers.

157 Russell Jenkins to Jean Wright, 2 June 1999, 'FW: WA Surveys', Community Bank File 5, Box 163.

158 *Farm Weekly*, 21 October 1999, 'Great Day for Kulin', in Trenorden, Community Bank papers.

159 Simon Cornwell to Jean Wright, 15 August 1999, 'WA Community Banking', Community Bank File 6, Box 163.

160 ibid.

161 *Farm Weekly*, 21 October 1999, 'Great Day for Kulin'; Max Trenorden, typed speech notes, both in Trenorden, Community Bank papers.

162 Kerp, 9 December 2005.

163 Max Trenorden, typed speech notes, in Trenorden, Community Bank papers.

164 Russel Jenkins to John Anderson, 2 December 1999, Community Bank File 7, Box 163.

165 *West Australian*, 5 January 2000, 'Banks in WA Withdrawal', in Trenorden, Community Bank papers.

166 *Age*, 4 February 1999, 'Bendigo Bank Sets Sights on WA Bush', Community Bank File 4, Box 157.

167 Owen Davies to Rob Hunt, 15 January 1999, ibid. Owen Davies to Rob Hunt, 17 January 2000, 'Community Bank Media', Community Bank File 7, Box 163.

168 Russell Jenkins to Greg Gillett, 2 December 1999, 'Griffith', ibid. Jean Wright to Rob Hunt, 28 August 1998, Community Bank File 4, Box 157.

169 Russell Jenkins to Jean Wright, 18 January 2000, 'Elwood Board', Community Bank File 7, Box 163.

170 Rob Hunt to Senator Ian Macdonald, 1 April 1999, Community Bank File 5, Box 163.

171 Greg Gillett to Wilson Tuckey, 6 December 1999, Community Bank File 7, Box 163.

172 Russell Jenkins to Rob Hunt, 11 June 1998, 'Community Bank Development', Community Bank File 3, Box 157.

173 Rob Hunt to Russell Jenkins, 30 October 1998, 'Community Bank Sites', ibid.

174 Russell Jenkins to Robert Musgrove, 21 May 1999, 'Community Bank Board Meetings', Community Bank File 5, Box 163.

175 Rob Hunt to Cheryl Rix, 12 July 1999, ibid. 'Filenote: Community Bank', 1 December 1999, Community Bank File 7, Box 163.

176 Rob Hunt to Russell Jenkins, 4 January 1999, 'Community Bank', Community Bank File 4, Box 157.

177 Jenkins, 17 March 2005.

178 Anderson papers. *Background Briefing*, 'The Unbanking of Australia', ABC Radio National, 22 October 2000, transcript in Anderson, personal papers.

179 Jenkins, 16 December 2004.

180 Albany 6AL Radio News, reported in Newslines facsimile to Owen Davies, 11 April 2000, Community Bank File 8, Box 163.

181 *Border Mail*, 26 February 2001, 'Henty: the Town that Fought Back', Community Bank File, Box 156.

182 Rob Hunt to Greg Gillett and Owen Davies, 14 November 2000, ibid.

183 Jean Wright to Rob Hunt, 8 February 2000, 'Community Bank—Some Ideas', ibid.

184 Rob Hunt to All Staff, 17 March 2000, 'Community Bank Expansion', Community Bank File 8, Box 163.

185 Rob Hunt to Russell Jenkins and Peter English, 11 August 2000, 'Notes Re. Community Bank Board Meetings', Community Bank File, Box 156.

186 Hadlow, 8 December 2005.

187 Email message to Max Trenorden, 9 May 2005, in Trenorden, Community Bank papers.

188 Handwritten note, attached to memo from Rob Hunt to Russell Jenkins, 24 February 2000, 'Community Bank Chair Conference', Community Bank File 8, Box 163.

189 Russell Jenkins to Rob Hunt and Greg Gillett, 28 June 2000, 'Elders', Community Bank File, Box 156.

190 Simon Cornwell to Russell Jenkins, 28 June 2000, 'RE: Elders Venture', ibid.

191 Russell Jenkins to Jean Wright, 30 June 2000, 'This Morning's Discussion', ibid.

192 Hunt, 24 January 2006. Russell Jenkins to Rob Hunt, 1 March 2001, 'WA Lending'; Russell Jenkins to Peter English and Robert Musgrove, 10 April 2001, both in Community Bank File, Box 156.

193 Rob Hunt to Russell Jenkins and Peter English, 11 August 2000, 'Notes Re. Community Bank Board Meetings', Community Bank File, Box 156. Jean Wright to Jason McGovern, 18 April 2000, 'Community Bank Stage 2 - Letter to Communities', Community Bank File 8, Box 163.

194 Hunt, 5 May 2005.

195 Bendigo Bank, *Helping to Create Sustainable Communities: Bendigo Bank's Community Initiatives*, April 2000.

196 Rob Hunt to Russell Jenkins and Owen Davies, 17 July 2000, 'Community Bank', Community Bank File, Box 156.

197 ibid. Rob Hunt to Rob Fairweather, 17 July 2000, ibid.

198 Rob Hunt, speaking at the Ninth Annual Community Bank National Conference, September 2007, *Bendigo Bank DVD.*

199 Hunt, 5 May 2005.

200 Rob Hunt to Bendigo Bank Executive, 23 January 2006.

201 Owen Davies, speaking at Community Bank National Conference, 1 September 2005.

202 Rob Hunt, printed copy of a Powerpoint presentation, attached to 'Community Bank Message at This Point in Time', 30 October 1998, Community Bank File 4, Box 157.

203 Andrew Watts to Jean Wright, 11 May 1998, 'Community Bank', Community Bank File 2, Box 157.

204 Trenorden, 8 December 2005.

205 Rob Hunt to Jim Starbuck, 20 October 1999, Community Bank File 6, Box 157.

206 Rob Hunt, notes from a conversation with the author, 26 May 2004.

Conclusion

1 *Sydney Morning Herald*, 13 February 2007, 'The Likeable Bank Earns a Bit More Kudos'.

2 Hunt, 5 May 2005.

3 ibid.

4 Jenkins, 16 December 2004.

5 Hunt, 5 May 2005.

6 Johanson, 13 October 2006.

7 Rob Hunt, 'Creative Capital, Creative Strategies, Community-based Wealth Creation', Alfred Deakin Innovation Lectures, 6 May 2005, p. 1.

8 ibid.

9 Stiglitz, *Making Globalization Work*, p. 52.

10 Jenkins, 16 December 2004.

11 Hunt, 5 May 2005.

12 Johanson, 13 October 2006.

13 Matthews, 19 April 2005.

14 Hunt, 5 May 2005. Hunt, 'Creative Capital, Creative Strategies', pp. 8–9.

15 Hunt, 5 May 2005.

16 Rob Hunt at Bendigo Bank executive meeting, Melbourne Docklands, 4 July 2008.

Index

C

D

E

F

G

H

I

J

K

L

M

N

O

P

Q

R

S

T

U

V

W

Y

Wakefield Press is an independent publishing and distribution company based in Adelaide, South Australia. We love good stories and publish beautiful books. To see our full range of titles, please visit our website at www.wakefieldpress.com.au.